The

CURIOUS FATES

of

FAMOUS CORPSES

REST

IN

PIECES

BESS LOVEJOY

SIMON & SCHUSTER

New York   London   Toronto   Sydney   New Delhi

Simon & Schuster
1230 Avenue of the Americas
New York, NY 10020

First Simon & Schuster hardcover edition March 2013

SIMON & SCHUSTER and colophon are
registered trademarks of Simon & Schuster, Inc.

For information about special discounts for bulk purchases,
please contact Simon & Schuster Special Sales at
1-866-506-1949 or business@simonandschuster.com.

The Simon & Schuster Speakers Bureau can bring authors to
your live event. For more information or to book an event,
contact the Simon & Schuster Speakers Bureau at
1-866-248-3049 or visit our website at www.simonspeakers.com.

Designed by Jason Heuer
Illustrations by Mark Stutzman

Manufactured in the United States of America

1   3   5   7   9   10   8   6   4   2

Library of Congress Cataloging-in-Publication Data
Lovejoy, Bess.
Rest in pieces : the curious fates of famous corpses / Bess Lovejoy.
p. cm.
Includes bibliographical references and index.
1. Dead—Miscellanea. 2. Celebrities—Biography—Miscellanea.
3. Celebrities—Death—Miscellanea. I. Title.
CT105.L68 2013
306.9—dc23
2012034706

ISBN 978-1-4516-5498-1
ISBN 978-1-4516-5501-8 (ebook)

To Jack, who kept me alive while writing this book, and to my parents, without whom I wouldn't be here in the first place.

CONTENTS

REST
IN
PIECES

INTRODUCTION

A corpse is always a problem—both for the living and for the dead. The problems are both conceptual and practical: a dead body hovers uneasily between the animate and the inanimate, the past and the future. Even ordinary deaths often lead to questions about who has control over the memory and estate of the deceased. Famous corpses are more complicated still: not just family and friends but the church, state, admirers, and enemies often lay claim to the famous dead.

As a result, some of the most notable lives in history have had surprising postscripts. Famous corpses have been bought and sold, studied, collected, stolen, and dissected. They've been used to found churches, cities, and even empires. Pieces of them have languished in libraries and museums, in coolers and filing cabinets, and in suitcases underneath beds. These stories often have something to say about what the dead meant to the living: it's no coincidence that Descartes lost his skull, Einstein his brain, or Rasputin his penis (supposedly).

This is a book about how the living have tried to solve the problems of the dead—or gotten them into even deeper trouble—by using their bodies in different ways. Many of those uses have been political, religious, or scientific. Alexander the Great's bones established the Ptolemaic dynasty, the last in ancient Egypt, while the allegedly miraculous powers of relics from saints such as Thomas Becket made their bodies the hot commodities of the Middle Ages. The nineteenth-century pseudoscience of phrenology led to a rash of skull-stealing across Europe, which is how Haydn (to name but one example) lost his head. Criminals, too, have used corpses for their own ends, from the counterfeiters who tried to steal Abraham Lincoln's coffin to the modern-day body snatchers who sold the bones of broadcaster Alistair Cooke.

The living have also used the dead simply for the consolation of memory. Bodies can become mementos, as when Mary Shelley kept Percy Shelley's heart, or when Greek independence fighters asked for Lord Byron's lungs. And famous corpses sometimes become museum pieces symbolic of genius or notoriety, which is what happened to the skulls of Mozart and the Australian outlaw Ned Kelly.

But the living don't always override the wishes of the deceased. The philosopher Jeremy Bentham left explicit instructions about turning his body into a statue—stripped, stuffed, and mounted in a cabinet like an exotic bird. Musician Gram Parsons left an even weirder request—to have his body burned in the Mojave Desert—but that, too, was fulfilled, much to the chagrin of his family. Both Timothy Leary and Hunter S. Thompson also went out the way they wanted: with a bang, and major parties.

Strange as these stories are, this book intends to deliver more than a rich supply of inappropriate cocktail chatter. Although I don't believe in heaven or hell, it's hard to deny that how you live often has something to do with what happens after you die. The postmortem journeys of controversial corpses (like that of Argentina's first lady Eva Perón) often look like a game of hot potato, while those of widely revered geniuses, like Beethoven, are stories of carefully guarded treasure. These tales can tell us something about their subjects, and the times and places in which they lived. What does it say about Voltaire's France that he was terrified of his bones ending up in the trash? What does it say about

Restoration England that Oliver Cromwell was posthumously hanged? What does it say about America that Lee Harvey Oswald was exhumed to make sure he wasn't a Russian spy?

The stories in this book also sketch the evolution of our attitudes toward death and mourning. Not so long ago, death was both more familiar and more sacred, and it wasn't so strange to keep a famous skull around, or to wear a ring showing off some strands of a dead friend's hair. These attitudes have faded, but their shadows remain. Putting the pieces back together might help us understand famous figures—and our own ancestors—a bit better.

I've collected these strange stories with that goal in mind. But humans have been dying as long as we've been living, so a book like this could easily run to several volumes if I didn't set some boundaries. For one thing, everyone in these pages was famous before becoming a corpse. This is not just a book about all the weird things that can happen to any dead body, fun as that might be.

Secondly, while there are plenty of tall tales about famous bodies (my favorite being that Walt Disney's frozen corpse is buried beneath the Pirates of the Caribbean ride at Disneyland), I've included only stories that could be documented. However, the history of the deceased is often murky territory, so where sources conflict, I've presented multiple variants of a story, or chosen to trust the most-respected source. For those who want to take their own stab at unraveling the mysteries, there's an extensive bibliography at the back of the book.

Because the stories in this book reflect the culture of their time, you'll notice a lot of dead white men. The corpses of women and people of color have also suffered many misadventures, but because most of their owners weren't famous, they often didn't fit the framework of this book—not that this is a project anyone would clamor to be included in.

But while death troubles us, it also intrigues us. Death is the ultimate mystery, and contemplating it does us good. Kierkegaard said, "The thought of death is a good dancing partner." The more you dance, the less you fear. This book is a form of exposure therapy, looking directly at the thing many of us most want to avoid. Spending time with famous dead bodies has made me worry a little less about the Grim Reaper. I hope that this book will do the same for you.

SAINTS

AND

SINNERS

In the divided body, the grace survives undivided . . .
—THEODORET OF CYRUS (*CA.* 393—*CA.* 458)

For much of Western history, one institution has had more control than any other over the care of the dead: the Catholic Church. The Church has long been responsible for how Christian dead were handled, where they were buried, and even how they were mourned. Some of the deceased benefited from this arrangement: for saints, even the most mundane bits of bones, skin, and hair could be transformed into relics, objects imbued with divine presence and miraculous powers. But for those who criticized the church, death could be an obstacle course. Voltaire's corpse had to be smuggled into the countryside (dressed as if he were still alive) just to get a decent grave, while the controversy surrounding the playwright Molière's burial led to a case of mistaken identity in one of the world's most famous cemeteries—a case that persists today.

SAINT NICHOLAS

LIVED FIRST HALF OF FOURTH CENTURY AD
BORN: PATARA, LYCIA
DIED: MYRA, LYCIA

Don't tell the kids, but Santa Claus has been dead for more than sixteen hundred years. No, his body is not at the North Pole, and he's not buried with Mrs. Claus. In fact, his remains are thousands of miles away, on Italy's sunny Adriatic coast. And while Santa might be enjoying his Mediterranean vacation, he's probably not too happy about what happened to his remains. They were stolen in the eleventh century, and people have been fighting over them ever since.

Of course, the Santa Claus of folklore doesn't have a skeleton. But his inspiration, Saint Nicholas, does. That's about all we can say for sure about Nicholas: he was a bishop who lived and died in what is now Turkey in the first half of the fourth century. Legend tells us that he was born into a rich family and delighted in giving gifts. Once, he threw three bags of gold into the window of a poor family's house, saving the three daughters who lived there from a life of prostitution. Another time, he raised three children from the dead after a butcher carved them up and stored them in a vat of brine. He also protected sailors, who were said to cry out his name in rough seas, then watch the waves mysteriously smooth.

The sailors spread Nicholas's cult around the world. Within a century of his death, the bishop was worshipped as a saint, lending his name to hundreds of ports, islands, and inlets, and thousands of baby boys. He became one of the best-loved saints in all of Christendom, adopted by both the Eastern and Western traditions. Christmas probably owes something to his December 6 feast day, while Santa Claus's red outfit may come from his red bishop's robes. "Santa Claus" is derived from "Sinterklaas," which was how Dutch immigrants to New Amsterdam pronounced his name.

As one of the most popular saints in the Christian world, Nicholas had a particularly powerful corpse. The bodies of saints and martyrs had been important to Christianity since its beginning: the earliest churches were built on the tombs of saints. It was thought that the bodily bits of saints functioned like spiritual walkie-talkies: you could communicate with higher powers through them, and they, in turn, could manifest holy forces on Earth. They could heal you, protect you, and even perform miracles.

Sometimes, the miracles concerned the saints' own bodies. Their corpses would refuse to decay, exude an inexplicable ooze, or start to drip blood that mysteriously solidified and then reliquefied. So it was with Nicholas: at some point after his death, his bones began to secrete a liquid called manna or myrrh, which was said to smell like roses and possess potent healing powers.

The appearance of the manna was taken as a sign that Nicholas's corpse was especially holy, and pilgrims began flocking by the thousands to his tomb in the port city of Myra (now called Demre). By the eleventh century, other cities started getting jealous. At the time, cities and churches often competed for relics, which brought power and prestige to their hometowns the way a successful sports team might today. Originally, the relics trade had been nourished by the catacombs in Rome, but when demand outstripped supply, merchants—and even monks—weren't above sneaking down into the crypts of churches to steal some holy bones. Such thefts weren't seen as a sin; the sanctity of the remains trumped any ethical concerns. The relics were also thought to have their own personalities—if they didn't want to be stolen, they wouldn't allow it. Like King Arthur's sword in the stone, they could only be removed by the right person.

That was how Myra lost Saint Nicholas. The culprits were a group of merchants and sailors from the town of Bari, located on the heel of Italy's boot. Like other relic thefts, this one came at a time of crisis for the town where the thieves lived, which in this case had recently been invaded by a horde of rapacious Normans. The conquerors wanted to compete with the Venetians, their trading rivals to the north, who were known for stealing the bones of Saint Mark (disguised in a basket of pork) from Alexandria in 827. And when the Normans heard that Myra had recently fallen to the Turks, leaving Nicholas's tomb vulnerable, they decided to try stealing a saint for themselves.

According to an account written shortly after the theft by a Barian clerk, three ships sailed from Bari into Myra's harbor in the spring of 1087. Forty-seven well-armed Barians disembarked and strode into the church of Saint Nicholas, where they asked to see the saint's tomb. The monks, who weren't idiots, got suspicious and asked why they wanted to know. The Barians then dropped any pretense of politeness, tied the monks up, and smashed their way into Nicholas's sarcophagus. They found his skeleton submerged in its manna and smelled a heavenly perfume wafting up from the bones, which "licked at the venerable priests as if in insatiable embrace."

And so Nicholas of Myra became Nicholas of Bari. The relics *made* the town, and the men who stole them. The thieves became famous in the area, and for centuries their descendants received a percentage of the offerings given on the saint's feast day. The townspeople built a new basilica to hold the remains, which drew thousands of pilgrims throughout the Middle Ages. Even today, Bari remains a major pilgrimage site in southern Italy, visited by both Roman Catholics and Orthodox Christians. Every May an elaborate festival, the Feast of the Translation, celebrates the arrival of Nicholas's relics. As one of the highlights, the rector of the basilica bends over Nicholas's sarcophagus and draws off some of the manna in a crystal vial. The fluid is mixed with holy water and poured into decorated bottles sold in Bari's shops; it is thought to be a curative drink.

But Bari is not the only place that boasts of the bones of Saint Nicholas. If you ask the Venetians, they will say their own sailors visited Myra during the First Crusade and stole Nicholas's remains, which have been in Venice ever since. For centuries, both Bari and Venice have claimed the saint's skeleton.

In the twentieth century, scientists waded into the dispute. During renovations to the basilica of Bari in 1953, church officials allowed University of Bari anatomy professor Luigi Martino to examine the remains—the first time the tomb had been opened in more than eight hundred years. Martino found the bones wet, fragile, and fragmented, with many of them missing. He concluded that they had belonged to a man who died in his seventies, although because Martino was given only a short time with the bones, he could say little more.

Four decades later, Martino and other scientists also studied the Venetian bones. They concluded that those relics and the ones in Bari had come from the same skeleton, and theorized that the Venetian sailors had stolen what was left in Myra after the Barians had done all their smashing.

As for Demre, all they have is an empty tomb. And they want their bones back. In 2009, the Turkish government said it was considering a formal request to Rome for the return of Nicholas's remains. Though the bones have little religious significance in a nation that's 99 percent Muslim, there's still a sense in Turkey that the centuries-old theft was a cultural violation. Its restitution would certainly be an economic benefit: according to local officials, tourists in Demre frequently complain about the barren tomb, and they weren't satisfied by the giant plastic sculpture of Santa Claus that once stood outside Nicholas's church. Even though Santa has become an international cultural icon, his myth is still rooted in a set of bones far from home.

BLESSED BITS

Saint Anthony of Padua (1195–1231) was a Portuguese Franciscan renowned for his oratorical skills. A few decades after his death, his Franciscan brothers opened his tomb, where they found only dust and bones—except for his tongue, which appeared perfectly preserved. The friars took this as a tribute to the saint's eloquence, and today the tongue is displayed in a crystal urn at the Basilica of Saint Anthony in Padua, Italy. At least one visitor describes it as looking like a shriveled strawberry.

The Hazratbal Shrine in Kashmir, India, is said to contain a hair plucked from the beard of the Prophet Muhammad. In 1963 the holy whisker was stolen, but after mass protests across the region, it was returned the following year. The *Moi-e-Muqaddas* (sacred hair), as it is known, goes on display ten times each year.

According to legend, several of the Buddha's teeth

were plucked out of his ashes after his cremation some-time around the sixth century BCE. The most famous of these (his left canine), is supposed to have been smuggled into Sri Lanka in the hair of a princess after centuries of wars over its possession, which was said to confer the right to rule the land. Today, the tooth is on display at the Temple of the Holy Tooth in Kandy, Sri Lanka, where it is venerated by hundreds of pilgrims each day, and during a ten-night Sacred Tooth Festival each summer.

BORN: *CA.* 1118,
LONDON, ENGLAND
DIED: DECEMBER 29, 1170 (*CA.* AGE 52),
CANTERBURY, ENGLAND

Thomas Becket knew what was coming. As the archbishop of Canterbury Cathedral walked from his chambers toward the choir that December evening in 1170, he knew he would soon have visitors. Not the townspeople gathering outside for evensong in the nave, but four heavily armed assassins under orders from King Henry II.

Becket locked no doors as he walked. When the king's knights found him, he looked at their gleaming swords and announced, according to one eyewitness, "I accept death in the name of the Lord." When the blows came, Becket did not defend himself; he simply wiped away his blood with his sleeve. By the fourth strike, the crown of his head had been severed. One of the knights, Hugh of Horsea, dug his sword into the wound and scattered some of Becket's brains onto the stone floor.

"Let us go, knights," he said. "This fellow will not rise again."

Not in body, anyway. But if the king truly hoped to be rid of Becket, who had grown irritatingly insistent on the church's independence from the crown, his martyrdom ensured the opposite result. In death, Becket's power was far stronger than it had been in life.

The miracles began almost immediately. That night, with Becket's head wrapped in cloth and his body lying on the altar, wailing townspeople crowded into the cathedral to dip their fingers and clothes in his blood. A blind woman who applied a bloody rag to her eyes said she had regained her sight. A sick woman who drank some of Becket's blood mixed with water declared herself healed. Becket became capable of things he had never done while he was still breathing.

The next morning, the monks buried Becket's body in a marble coffin at the eastern edge of the cathedral's crypt. But as tales of his brutal murder and the miracles that followed spread throughout the countryside, pilgrims began descending on Canterbury. Along with the sick or wounded hoping for a miracle, dignitaries came bearing gifts: Louis VII brought a huge ruby called the Régale, a cup crafted of pure gold, and an annual wine stipend of about sixteen hundred gallons (lucky monks). Eventually, Canterbury became the most important pilgrimage site in all of England.

But a dank crypt is no place to worship a famous saint, and so in 1220 the monks transferred Becket's remains into an elaborate main-floor shrine. His bones were nestled inside a gilded casket topped by a canopy barnacled with sapphires, diamonds, emeralds, and rubies, including the Régale. According to the scholar Erasmus, who visited in 1512, "every part glistened, shone and sparkled with rare and very large jewels, some of them exceeding the size of a goose's egg." When pilgrims approached, the canopy would rise up via a series of pulleys, tinkling with silver bells. A clerk would approach with a wand, pointing out all the jewels and naming each of their very generous donors.

Or at least they did before the Reformation. In 1538, a few years after Henry VIII split from Rome to marry Anne Boleyn, he also outlawed the worship of relics. Though no Protestant himself, Henry VIII encouraged the Reformation cause as a way to maintain his independence from Rome. And the Protestants loathed relics: John Calvin called them an "execrable sacrilege," while Martin Luther attacked them in his Ninety-five Theses. Shrines were demolished, statues smashed, relics hauled away and thrown into the trash.

The king's commissioners arrived at Canterbury Cathedral in September 1538. Most likely, they stripped all the gold and jewels from the shrine and carried them to the Tower of London. (The Régale ended up on a royal thumb ring.) As for Becket's bones, the pope reported that they were "burnt and the ashes scattered to the wind." That account became accepted as fact on the Continent, but royal statements from England suggested the bones had not been burned; they had merely been hidden so that they could no longer be worshipped.

Today, only a white candle on the cathedral floor marks the spot where the shrine once stood. But Canterbury Cathedral still holds many secrets. In 1888, a team excavating in search of an earlier Norman church made a discovery that has fascinated historians ever since. When workers broke through the stone floor of the eastern crypt, they found a long, thin stone coffin with a jumble of bones inside. Could these have belonged to Becket? The location was tantalizing: the coffin was unearthed right next to the spot where Becket's corpse had rested before being moved to the main-floor shrine.

To find out whether the monks had saved Becket's remains after all, cathedral officials turned the bones over to a local surgeon named W. Pugin Thornton. Thornton said that the bones were very old, though he could not say how old, and declared that they belonged to a male of roughly Becket's age and height. He also said that the skull exhibited fractures indicating blows from a weapon—particularly on the left side, where the straight border of a gaping crack seemed consistent with a wound "caused by a heavy cutting instrument such as a two-handed sword."

The bones stayed aboveground for only sixteen days, long enough that a boy with failing sight was taken to see them in the hopes that he would be healed. The boy's father believed the bones to be Becket's, but not everyone was convinced. Much of the dispute centered on the crown of the skull, which was intact despite the wounds on its side. For skeptics, the uninjured crown was critical: if, as was emphasized in medieval writings, the top of Becket's skull had been severed during his murder, how could this skull have belonged to the saint?

While skeptics remained, over the years the consensus evolved. Thornton declared himself convinced that the bones had belonged to the saint, and a 1920 report—commissioned by the archbishop of Canterbury and gathering together all available evidence—agreed with the believers. By 1949 the public was convinced the body was Becket's, and the church decided to erect a monument to mark the spot where the skeleton had been found. But first they decided to open the grave one last time to examine the bones, and it's a good thing they did.

This time, the remains were given to anatomy professor Alexander Cave of St. Bartholomew's Hospital, who showed just how far science had progressed since Thornton's day. After two years of analysis, Cave revealed that the bones were warped as though they had been buried in soil for a long time, and displayed spade cuts that indicated a hasty exhumation. Neither of these revelations was consistent with the known treatment of Becket's remains, but the most damning evidence came from the skull. By reexamining the shape of the fractures and noting the lack of damage to the bony tissue beneath, Cave concluded that nothing on the skull indicated it had suffered trauma before death. All of the skull's cracks had been made through the process of natural decay and the pressure of earth on bone. Cave concluded that unless the accounts of Hugh of Horsea's sword poking its way inside Becket's skull were incorrect, there was no way the bones discovered in 1888 could have belonged to the saint.

Yet others insist Becket is still in the cathedral—somewhere. In 1997, an English biochemist and scholar named Cecil Humphery-Smith told the *Times* of London that his godfather, Canterbury canon Julian Bickersteth, had witnessed the exhumation of a body near the cathedral's Chapels of St. Mary Magdalene and St. Nicholas in 1943. According to Humphery-Smith, the bones Bickersteth saw were of a tall man—Becket was known for his stature—and did not include the right hand, which some say was severed after Becket's death. Humphery-Smith also claimed that fragments of Becket's episcopal vesture and seal ring had also been visible.

Those who believe Bickersteth saw something special point out that he and canon John Shirley paid to renovate the two chapels in the 1950s. In fact, Shirley's own ashes were later interred in St. Mary Magdalene's chapel, where he had paid for the installation of a red perpetual lamp. Believers say its bloody color symbolizes the presence of a martyr, and burns not for him, but for Becket.

VOLTAIRE

Born: November 21, 1694,
Paris, France
Died: May 30, 1778 (age 83),
Paris, France

"I am preparing myself philosophically enough for this great journey about which everyone speaks without knowledge of the facts. As one has not traveled before being born, one does not travel when one no longer exists."

Voltaire wrote those words in a letter in April 1773, five years before he passed away. A hypochondriac, the Enlightenment author and philosopher was obsessed with the "great journey" of death long before the Grim Reaper came knocking on his door. And while he did not believe in any kind of afterlife, he was often worried about what might become of his remains. He knew that his acerbic writings had scandalized the Catholic Church many times over, and he knew what happened to Christians who died outside the fold. He'd been at the bedside of the famous French actress Adrienne Lecouvreur when she died in 1730 without time to renounce her (morally suspect) profession; her body had been thrown onto waste land on the banks of the Seine, an event that Voltaire recorded in a maudlin poem and frequently declared would be his own fate.

But as much as he wanted a decent burial, Voltaire also wanted to do the minimum necessary to get one. A man who spent his entire life defending reason and freedom, he was unlikely to spend his last days bending over backward for the Church. When he fell ill for what would be the final time, on a trip to Paris, he prepared a simple and moving "confession": "I die worshipping God, loving my friends, not hating my enemies, and detesting superstition."

That was not enough for the Church, which may have recognized itself in the "superstition" bit. Shortly afterward, Voltaire received a letter from a local priest offering confessorial services. Voltaire agreed to let him visit, but when the cleric arrived, the most he got out of Voltaire was a statement that the author would die in the religion in which he was born and that he hoped God and the Church would forgive his offenses. Voltaire said nothing about his faith, and nothing about renouncing his (many) sins. He also found a sneaky way to refuse communion, telling the priest, "I would remind you that I am constantly spitting blood. We really must avoid getting the Almighty's blood mixed up with mine."

It was the best the Church would get. When the priest and the local curate came to his bedside a few hours before the end, Voltaire muttered, "Let me die in peace," and rolled over. It wasn't the response they were hoping for. The local curate had already been threatening to deny Voltaire a Christian burial, but the chief of police and the minister for law and order didn't want to take any chances about what might happen if the public's beloved Voltaire was consigned to the trash, so three days before his death, they struck a compromise with his family.

The deal was this: the night after Voltaire died, his corpse would be dressed as if he were still alive, propped up in his star-spangled carriage, and driven to his country estate at Ferney, near the Swiss border. Whatever happened to the body there was up to his family, but at least Voltaire would be long gone before the Parisian public learned of his demise and could ask what had become of his remains.

Voltaire's nephew, a lawyer and sometime-abbot named Alexandre Jean Mignot, had other ideas. Mignot doubted the authorities at Ferney would be any more interested in giving Voltaire a proper Christian burial than the authorities in Paris had been, and he also wondered how well his uncle's corpse would fare on the long trip. He decided to take Voltaire to his run-down monastery in the Champagne region instead. Mignot figured it would probably be okay that his monastery was surrounded by marshland and that the chapel resembled a barn; at least it wasn't the town dump.

With these preparations in place, Voltaire died, probably from prostate cancer. During the autopsy, an apothecary cut out his brain and carried it home in a jam jar, while Voltaire's friend the Marquis de Villette claimed his heart. The brain, which the apothecary's descendants offered to the nation several times (they were consistently refused), now rests in the administrator's office at the Comédie-Française. The heart eventually made its way to Voltaire's estate at Ferney, and is now kept at the Bibliothèque Nationale in Paris.

After the autopsy, Mignot strapped Voltaire's corpse inside the author's coach and drove him through the night to the monastery. The two monks who lived there were somewhat surprised when their abbot arrived and explained who, or rather what, was in the carriage, but they did not refuse Voltaire burial. On June 2, the most sparkling wit of the French Enlightenment was laid to rest beneath the chapel floor. A few parishioners who listened to the Mass said they distinctly remembered the sound of croaking frogs.

But the problems Voltaire's corpse presented were nothing compared to what the Church was about to suffer during the French Revolution, which was partly inspired by Voltaire's writings. Eleven years after his death, the feudal structure that had ruled France for centuries started to crumble, and the clergy lost many of their privileges. During this period, the Marquis de Villette renamed himself Citizen Villette and threw himself into defending both revolutionary ideals and Voltaire's memory.

Fearful about what might happen to the monastery where Voltaire rested—Church property was then being frequently seized and sold—Citizen Villette began agitating to bring his friend's remains back to Paris. He wrote articles and attended meetings, but that wasn't enough. In November 1790, during a performance of Voltaire's *Brutus* at the Comédie-Française, he jumped onstage and delivered a passionate speech in which he declared that Voltaire, the "foremost champion of the people," should be brought back to Paris, the city where he was born and died.

Villette wanted Voltaire's remains enshrined in the Church of Sainte-Geneviève, which was then under construction. Since it had not yet been consecrated and served no parish, the revolutionary government decided it was the perfect place to build a kind of national cathedral for French secular heroes, complete with a crypt for their remains. The building was called the Panthéon, in one of the revolution's many nods to ancient Rome, and the ceremonies to welcome the bones of the revolution's heroes were inspired by the celebrations that once greeted the arrival of saintly relics.

Voltaire's bones were the second set interred at the Panthéon, arriving shortly after those of the revolutionary politician Mirabeau. On July 11, 1791, a massive funeral procession honoring Voltaire took over Paris, as students, actors, musicians, and military men paraded through the streets holding paintings and statues of Voltaire, plus seventy volumes of his complete works. Voltaire's skeleton was carried along inside a porphyry sarcophagus, decorated by a sculpture of the author on his deathbed. At the end of the parade, his remains were placed inside the Panthéon's crypt.

Voltaire is still there, but in the nineteenth century, a rumor began spreading that royalist fanatics had stolen his bones and thrown them into a pit somewhere—just as Voltaire had always feared. The rumor also said that the remains of the philosopher Jean-Jacques Rousseau, buried nearby in the crypt, had suffered the same fate. In the years after the French Revolution, the Panthéon shifted from a secular temple to a church and then back again, depending on the whims of France's rulers and the climate of the time. The changes encouraged the idea that *something,* at least, had happened to Voltaire's tomb.

To put a stop to the rumors, officials opened the tombs in December 1897 and discovered the remains more or less intact. During their investigations, chemist and politician Marcellin Berthelot (himself later buried in the Panthéon) took Voltaire's skull from the coffin and posed with it. Everyone agreed that the skull still resembled Voltaire, with the skin drawn thin over the cheekbones, and the mouth giving a final smirk to the universe.

THE MUMMY OF ORLÉANS

Joan of Arc died on the same day of the year as Voltaire. After being burned at the stake in 1431, her executioners reburned her bones and dumped them into the Seine, just to make sure no one collected any relics. But that didn't stop the public from inventing them. In 1867, a jar bearing the inscription "Remains found under the stake of Joan of Arc, virgin of Orléans" was discovered in the attic of a Paris pharmacy. The relics were officially recognized by the Church and put on display in a museum belonging to the Archdiocese of Tours. However, a 2007 analysis by a French forensic scientist found that the blackened bones predated Joan's time: they were in fact a human rib and a cat femur, both from Egyptian mummies.

In the Middle Ages and beyond, mummies were a frequent ingredient in medicinal preparations, and it seems that some enterprising pharmacist decided to rebrand the tools of his trade as sacred remains. After all, his medicines could only cure the body; Joan's relics might heal the soul.

MOLIÈRE

BORN: JANUARY 15, 1622,
PARIS, FRANCE
DIED: FEBRUARY 17, 1673 (AGE 51),
PARIS, FRANCE

As an actor and playwright, Molière's job was to pretend. Real life got the better of him one February evening in Paris, however, when a coughing fit seized him during his performance as a hypochondriac in his own play *The Imaginary Invalid*. Eagle-eyed audience members might have noticed the strange coincidence: Molière, who had tuberculosis, was onstage playing the part of a man who only believed he was ill.

Molière died not long after stepping offstage that very night. Though his illness had been troubling him for some time, no one expected him to die quite so soon. There was no time for a priest to administer the last rites, or for Molière to renounce his profession. In those days, actors were not supposed to be buried in consecrated ground because of their lowly status, but most got around the rule by renouncing their livelihood just before they died. Molière didn't have the chance, and he died as he lived, a man of the stage.

The story of what happened next reads like one of the playwright's own farces. With nowhere sacred to bury her husband, Molière's widow, Armande, appealed first to the archbishop of Paris, and then King Louis XIV, who referred the matter back to the archbishop. Just when Armande must have been wondering if she would have to bury her husband by the side of the road, the king told the archbishop that he should figure out some way to settle the matter quickly and quietly. The archbishop offered a compromise: a night burial in the Cemetery of St. Joseph, with only two priests, no advertisement, and no ceremony. (Some sources say the body was also supposed to be buried at a depth of twelve feet, since the clergy had decreed that consecrated ground went down only about eight feet.)

Armande accepted the compromise, but promptly ignored it. At least four priests showed up at her husband's funeral, as well as waves of friends and fans carrying lighted torches. In fact, so many people came that the crowd grew rowdy, and Armande scattered coins to bribe the group into keeping quiet. But despite the number of people who attended, no one is exactly sure where Molière was buried. Some say he was given pride of place "at the foot of the cross," while others record that he was interred in a corner of the cemetery reserved for stillborns and suicides.

The grave's location didn't become an issue until more than a century later during the French Revolution, when Molière's corpse was transformed from a liability into an asset. The revolutionaries were looking for secular heroes, and Molière, who had frequently lampooned the Church and the bourgeoisie, fit the bill perfectly. In fact, when a neighborhood of Paris decided to name itself *La Section de Molière et de La*

Fontaine (after Molière and poet Jean de La Fontaine), the government decreed that it should have their remains as well as their names. Unfortunately, when the neighborhood's commissioners went to the Cemetery of St. Joseph, no one could tell them exactly where to dig. The men weren't too concerned; they unearthed two anonymous skeletons and called it a day—despite the fact that La Fontaine, at least, was buried in an entirely different cemetery.

Perhaps because of their lack of pedigree, the bones then spent seven years in the basement of St. Joseph's Church, and then only about a year in their eponymous neighborhood, where they languished in an attic. Afterward, they briefly joined the remains of Descartes (see pages 178–82) and other eminent Frenchmen in the *jardin élysée* (Garden of Elysium) in Paris's Museum of French Monuments, which flourished during the revolutionary period.

In 1817 the supposed bones of Molière went on to their next big act—as a publicity gimmick. Nicolas Frochot, a favorite of Napoleon's and the creator of the Père-Lachaise Cemetery, at first had a tough time convincing Parisians to bury their dead in his cemetery at the city's eastern edge. Like the promoters of today, he soon decided that the key to success was to find celebrities to demonstrate his product. He first got his hands on Henri III's queen, Louise de Lorraine, whose crypt had been used as a latrine during the revolution. When that didn't draw quite enough visitors (perhaps it was the smell?), Frochot bought the bodies of Molière, Fontaine, and the medieval lovers Héloïse and Abelard, burying them all in his new cemetery.

Frochot's strategy worked, and not long afterward bourgeois Parisians clamored to purchase a plot in Père-Lachaise. Burials soon numbered in the thousands, and today the cemetery claims close to a million permanent residents, plus twice as many (living) visitors each year. The association with celebrities has continued, and the cemetery is now home to some of the most famous graves in the world, including those of Chopin, Sarah Bernhardt, Oscar Wilde, and Jim Morrison. It doesn't seem to matter that the bones labeled "Molière" are only acting, while the real Molière, long since finished with his role on the world's stage, is probably somewhere in the Paris catacombs.

SCIENCE

AND

MEDICINE

We preserve our life with the death of others.
—LEONARDO DA VINCI (1452–1519)

The dead have long been used to heal the living. In ancient Rome, spectators drank the blood of slain gladiators to absorb their bravery and strength, while in the Middle Ages, corpses became ingredients in medicine (powdered skull was thought to cure headaches, while human fat was used to treat wounds). More recently, cadavers have been key to the study of anatomy, with unfortunate consequences for at least one famous corpse, that of the author Laurence Sterne. Today we use cadavers for organ transplants, but those too have their dark side, as the family of broadcaster Alistair Cooke found out. And while the quest to understand genius has evolved from the phrenology of Haydn's day to the neuroscience used to examine Einstein's brain, it often seems the answers haven't gotten much clearer.

LAURENCE STERNE

BORN: NOVEMBER 24, 1713,
CLONMEL, IRELAND
DIED: MARCH 18, 1768 (AGE 54),
LONDON, ENGLAND

It was a fitting fate for a man who nicknamed himself "Yorick."

Laurence Sterne was a rural parson who published mostly sermons until his forty-seventh year, when *The Life and Opinions of Tristram Shandy, Gentleman* made him an instant literary celebrity. The reading public loved the book's bawdy humor and wild experimentation, though the critic Samuel Johnson famously dismissed the work, saying "Nothing odd will do long." Modern critics have disagreed.

"Shandy" is Yorkshire slang for "crooked," and Sterne himself had a rather shandy afterlife. His death was ordinary enough: after suffering from tuberculosis for most of his life, he died of pleurisy (an inflammation of the lining around the lungs) in his lodgings on Old Bond Street, not far from where Oliver Cromwell's head would be exhibited a few decades later (see pages 221–25).

Like many modern stars, Sterne lived beyond his means. His celebrity lifestyle left him with debts that amounted to more than twice his assets, and as a result, his funeral was a simple one. He was buried at St. George's Church in Hanover Square four days after his demise, with only a handful of mourners in attendance. No funeral bells tolled, perhaps to save money—or perhaps to avoid announcing the burial to a more sinister quarter.

In the late eighteenth century, London was in terror of the "Resurrection Men," thieves who prowled cemeteries late at night in search of freshly dead bodies for medical schools. The rapidly expanding population of England during the Industrial Revolution had led to a growing need for doctors, but the number of corpses of executed criminals the crown provided could not keep up with the demand for cadavers to study. As a result, corpses became valuable commodities, and even though digging up graves was illegal, the Resurrection Men were protected by a chain of collusion that often extended from undertakers all the way to celebrated surgeons.

Laurence Sterne was their most famous victim. One night shortly after his burial, Resurrection Men dug up Sterne's corpse and sold it to an anatomy professor at Cambridge, Sterne's alma mater. The body snatchers likely didn't know or care who they'd dug up, but once the corpse found its way onto the dissection table in Cambridge, someone recognized Sterne—and promptly fainted. Sources for the tale, which include eighteenth-century newspaper accounts and diaries, disagree about whether the dissection continued, but the body is supposed to have eventually ended up back at St. George's, more or less in one piece.

Like so many cemeteries, St. George's Church did not stay a burial ground forever. It was closed to new burials in 1852, and in 1914 the land was turned into a private garden, with the tombstones arranged along the garden's perimeter. (Fortunately, Sterne's grave was in a western part of the cemetery that remained undisturbed.)

During World Wars I and II, much of the land was transformed into allotments for growing food, with four feet of topsoil added so that Londoners did not unearth bones alongside their carrots. In the 1920s, some parts of the former cemetery were used for archery, tennis, and netball grounds, and in 1964 (after an act of Parliament deconsecrated the ground) the land was sold to the Utopian Housing Society for £950,000.

In order to clear out the buried bones before building their condominiums, the society bought newspaper advertisements asking next of kin to claim the cemetery's remains. No one with Sterne's blood stepped forward, but one of his greatest twentieth-century admirers did.

Kenneth Monkman was a BBC radio journalist and devoted Sterne scholar who had recently taken on the task of rescuing the then-crumbling Shandy Hall, Sterne's former home in Coxwold, North Yorkshire. After hearing about the sale of St. George's, Monkman was determined to rescue Sterne's body. He managed to convince the Utopian Housing Society that any remains found in Sterne's grave should be turned over to the recently founded Laurence Sterne Trust for reburial in the church where Sterne had been parson. Of course, no one was exactly sure what would be found in the grave after all this time, and after the nasty business with the Resurrection Men. To confuse matters further, Sterne's headstone said the body lay "near" the grave, whatever that meant.

Early in the morning of June 4, 1969, Monkman and an official from the housing society gathered to watch the excavation of Sterne's plot at St. George's. It didn't take long before bones began appearing in the soil. Only one appeared relatively intact—a femur from a person said to be about Sterne's height. Five skulls were also found in the ground, and one displayed a rather intriguing disfigurement: the top had been sawn off. Such sawing was a common practice in anatomical dissections, and since it was rare for these purloined skeletons to be reinterred, the discovery got the party excited.

Monkman quickly went home to get one of his most prized possessions: a bust said to be the most accurate representation made of Sterne during his life. A surgeon was summoned, and after comparing the sawn-off skull with the bust, he found that the measurements of the two corresponded almost exactly. The other skulls in the ground were far too large to match the bust; it seems "Yorick" had an unusually tiny noggin.

The remains were reinterred at St. Michael's Church, Coxwold, the following Sunday. The *Times* of London noted that it was "200 years too late for flowers," but that donations could go to restoring Shandy Hall. Monkman devoted much of the rest of his life to renovating the hall, which is now a museum housing a collection of Sterne books, paintings, and memorabilia. When Monkman died in 1998, he was buried at the foot of Sterne's own grave.

BORN: JANUARY 29, 1688,
STOCKHOLM, SWEDEN
DIED: MARCH 29, 1772 (AGE 84),
LONDON, ENGLAND

Swedish genius Emanuel Swedenborg spent the first half of his life obsessed with science. He wrote pioneering treatises on physics, astronomy, engineering, chemistry, and physiology, displaying a remarkably intuitive grasp of the structure of the brain, atoms, and particles, and setting out ideas that took others decades—if not centuries—to confirm. He was also active in the Swedish mining industry, as well as in political and financial circles. He spoke nine languages, and to relax, taught himself skills like clock-making.

But in the middle of his fifties, everything changed.

Swedenborg began having disturbing, anxious dreams, which culminated in the onset of spiritual visions. During the Easter weekend of 1744, he experienced a vision of Jesus Christ, and the following year, the Lord himself began visiting Swedenborg. From then on, Swedenborg fell into trances that lasted for days, from which he would emerge to share the "inner" or "spiritual" meaning of Scriptures, as transmitted to him by God. Anticipating the New Age movement by more than two hundred years, Swedenborg proclaimed that God is love, and that everything springs from the same divine source. Though he never intended to found a new sect, his followers have come to be known as members of the "New Church," and today there are as many as thirty thousand of them worldwide. Johnny Appleseed, so beloved of American schoolteachers, was a Swedenborgian missionary.

Swedenborg finally joined his God for good at the age of eighty-four while on a visit to London. He'd left no instructions about the care of his remains, but friends decided that the most appropriate place to bury him was at the small Swedish church that his father, a Lutheran bishop, had founded in London's East End. The scientist-turned-seer was laid to rest inside a lead coffin in a vault beneath the church altar. There he was relatively safe from the Resurrection Men, but not from another scourge that would soon spread across the land—the phrenologists.

Phrenology was one of the sillier fads of the nineteenth century, right up there with wearing bustles and bleeding people with leeches for any ailment. Developed by Germans Franz Joseph Gall and Johann Spurzheim, phrenology was founded on the idea that mental activity changes the size and shape of the brain, which in turn changes the size and shape of the skull. According to phrenologists, various peaks and valleys of the skull were related to thirty-odd "organs," which governed things like love of family, knowledge, hope, or benevolence. Thus a bump near one ear might indicate destructiveness, while a bulge at the nape of the neck could be a clue to an overactive libido. This pseudoscience spawned hundreds of books, journals, private clubs, and public lectures, all of which promised better living through skull-fondling.

Phrenology might have been harmless enough were it not for the fact that some of its practitioners had well-developed organs for thievery—specifically, skull-stealing. In part, phrenologists liked to collect skulls because they could be used to demonstrate phrenological theories: the large eyes of a genius might "prove" one principle, for example, while the sloped forehead of a criminal might prove another. Joseph Haydn, Sir Thomas Browne, and even the Marquis de Sade were all posthumously separated from their skulls in the name of phrenology. And so was Swedenborg.

However, the first people inside Swedenborg's coffin weren't the phrenologists. According to a report published by printer and Swedenborgian Robert Hindmarsh in 1861, the culprit was a "foreign gentleman who held the absurd tenets of the sect of Rosicrucians" (an esoteric secret society obsessed with ancient occult symbols). According to Hindmarsh, one night this Rosicrucian attended a dinner party full of Swedenborgians, where he started making a lot of noise about how Swedenborg was not *really* dead, but had discovered the elixir of life and faked his demise. In the heat of the moment, the party decided that the only way to test this theory was to go to the church, cut open Swedenborg's coffin, and see if the great man was really inside.

Several members of the gathering left the group and went to the church, where they entered the vault and sawed open Swedenborg's coffin. Sure enough, there was his corpse, very much dead. Satisfied (if perhaps a bit disappointed), the group departed, although a few more curious Swedenborgians returned a few days later. Once they too had assured themselves of Swedenborg's mortality, the matter was dropped. But no one bothered to resolder Swedenborg's coffin, which made it easy pickings for the phrenologists.

In 1819, the pastor of the little church where Swedenborg was buried announced that Swedenborg's skull had been stolen some years before and only lately returned. According to the most recent analysis of the case, published by Swedish anthropologist Folke Henschen in 1960, the culprit was one Johan Didrik Holm. Holm was a wealthy Swedish naval captain known for turning his house into a phrenological cabinet of curiosities; among other treasures, his collection included the skull of poet Alexander Pope and that of French politician Casimir Perier. It's even said he tried to steal his own father's skull, although there's no word on how well that went.

And the story gets stranger. While *someone* returned a skull to pastor Johan Peter Wåhlin in 1819, Henschen doesn't believe it was Holm. In fact, multiple accounts suggest that another Swedish naval captain, Ludvig Granholm, confessed on his deathbed to stealing Swedenborg's skull, and returned it to Wåhlin. But there had long been whispers that the skull Granholm returned, which was subsequently reburied in Swedenborg's coffin, was the wrong one. And in fact there was another skull floating around London at the time with the name "E. S'Borg" drilled in tiny holes on one side.

The issue came to a head (so to speak) when the Swedish Church in London decided to move across town in 1908. When some Swedenborgians discovered the building was to be demolished, they decided the time was right to send their founder back to his native country. The British and Swedish governments agreed, and so Swedenborg was reburied in Uppsala Cathedral, where his mother and brother lay. Around the same time, however, a man named William Rutherford wrote to the Swedish legation in London about an antiquary, "generally a very veracious old gentleman," who had exhibited a skull said to be Swedenborg's in London's East End during the previous century. This was the skull with "E.

S'Borg" drilled in its side, and Rutherford was curious to know whether the old man had been telling the truth.

Eventually, Rutherford tracked down the skull and submitted a cast of it to Swedish scientists. But they dismissed it, in part because it showed a pronounced deformity: scaphocephaly, in which the parietal bones fuse to produce a long, narrow skull with an extended back. In pictures, the skull looks like something out of *Alien*. The scientists believed that it was extremely unlikely that such a deformity would not have been noted by Swedenborg's contemporaries, and even more improbable that such a deformed skull could ever have housed such a brilliant brain.

But in the 1950s, Henschen tracked down this other skull, and obtained permission to examine it alongside the remains in Swedenborg's coffin. He assembled two teams of more than a dozen scientists, one working in Sweden and the other at the British Museum. After conducting detailed reviews of the anatomical, chemical, and historical evidence, Henschen concluded that Rutherford had been right all along—the deformed skull was Swedenborg's. Among the most persuasive pieces of evidence was the fact that the skull Rutherford had owned matched perfectly with the impression left on the pillow that had long lain in Swedenborg's coffin.

But why had no historical source ever mentioned Swedenborg's oddly shaped head? Henschen suggested that Swedenborg had been able to conceal his misshapen skull with the long curly wig that was de rigueur for men of his era. Furthermore, the lack of portraits of Swedenborg in profile suggests that he made a conscious effort to hide his deformity. Henschen noted the example of the scholar Erasmus, who disguised his squashed-looking head with a tall padded hat, as well as the Athenian statesman and orator Pericles, whose peaked cranium earned him the nickname "onion head" and who was always depicted wearing a helmet. Despite what the phrenologists thought, we now know that even funny-looking heads can produce beautiful minds.

As for how the wrong skull got into the coffin, Henschen theorized that Holm had left an anonymous skull in Swedenborg's coffin at the time of his theft, and it was this *second* cranium that Granholm pocketed and returned on his deathbed. Henschen confirmed Holm's theft after being contacted by one of his descendants, who said that Holm had shown Swedenborg's skull to his niece in the 1840s. The matter had long been kept a family secret. According to Henschen, after Holm's death Swedenborg's real skull ended up with the "veracious" antiquary and later with Rutherford, while the fake skull lay with the rest of Swedenborg's skeleton in Uppsala.

In 1978, Swedenborg's true skull came up for auction. The winning bid, of $2,850, came from the Royal Swedish Academy of Sciences, who bought the skull in order to reunite it with the rest of Swedenborg's remains. But it's not clear what happened to the dummy skull, which raises the question, are there two skulls now lying in Swedenborg's grave?

THE MARKS OF THE MARQUIS

The remains of writer and libertine the Marquis de Sade were also plundered by phrenologists. Sade asked to be buried in the woods of his estate, where he wanted acorns scattered over him so that "the traces of my grave will vanish from the face of the earth as I like to think memory of me will be effaced from men's minds." His wishes were ignored, however, and he was buried in the cemetery of the insane asylum where he died in 1814. A few years later, his body was exhumed and his skull pocketed by his doctor, L. J. Ramon. A devout phrenologist, Ramon performed an analysis of Sade's skull, which showed "goodwill . . . no ferocity . . . no aggressive drives . . . no excess in erotic impulses." The skull was, Ramon concluded, "in every way similar to that of a father of the church." Along with the rest of Sade's remains, the skull was eventually lost, although one story says a cast of his cranium became a phrenological teaching tool used to demonstrate the characteristics of benevolence and religious faith.

JOSEPH HAYDN

BORN: MARCH 31, 1732,
ROHRAU, LOWER AUSTRIA
DIED: MAY 31, 1809 (AGE 77),
VIENNA, AUSTRIA

The composer Joseph Haydn had the bad luck to die during a war. Amid the chaos of Napoleon's invasion of Austria, the guns fired twenty-four hours a day, and one cannonball even landed right near Haydn's house, sending his servants into a panic. Even though he was far too old and ill to fight, Haydn rose from his sickbed every day to play his hymn to the Austrian emperor, his own private act of rebellion.

The timing of Haydn's death was even worse than he knew. If he had died just one year earlier or later, he would probably have been honored with a magnificent state funeral and buried in a lavish tomb. Instead, he was laid to rest in a simple grave at the Hundsturm cemetery in a suburb of Vienna, and the townspeople barely noticed his small funeral. Worse, the war made it possible for one of Haydn's own friends to steal his skull—a crime that would take one hundred fifty years to set right.

Haydn's friend Joseph Carl Rosenbaum was a man of two worlds. On the one hand, he was an accountant who spent his work life immersed in numbers and hard-nosed rationality. On the other, he was a devoted music lover who attended the theater almost every night and was married to Therese Gassmann, one of Vienna's most famous sopranos. Haydn had long been good friends with the couple and even played a hand in their court-ship, vouching for Rosenbaum after Gassmann's mother announced that an accountant was *not* what she wanted for a son-in-law.

While Therese was busy singing, Rosenbaum studied phrenology. The skull-reading "science" combined his twin passions of music and measurement, since musical ability was one of the many things that skull-readings were said to predict: the "organ of tune" took the form of a "projection above the external angle of the eye." Phrenologists had noticed particularly well-developed organs of tune in the portraits of Mozart, Beethoven, and even Haydn himself. It's hard not to wonder if Rosenbaum spent more than one dinner party secretly trying to check out his friend's skull.

When Haydn became ill, Rosenbaum decided he wanted his head. We don't know much about Rosen-baum's motives, but they were probably similar to those that led to an outbreak of skull-stealing across Europe at the time. The heads of geniuses like Haydn were prized objects for demonstrating the tenets of phrenology—and, of course, they also made fine desk ornaments.

To carry out his plan, Rosenbaum recruited his old pal (and fellow phrenologist) Johann Nepomuk Peter, governor of the Lower Austria provincial prison. Being the practical type that he was, Rosenbaum also decided to do a test run before Haydn's death. When Viennese actress Elizabeth Roose died in childbirth in October

1808, Rosenbaum and Peter bribed the gravedigger at the cemetery where she was interred to dig her up and decapitate her. They then brought her head to Peter's house, where they soaked it in quicklime in his garden. Soon the skull was clean and white—Rosenbaum's first phrenological trophy.

When Haydn died the following spring, he was buried in the same cemetery as Roose. His modest funeral was barely over when Rosenbaum approached the gravedigger with an offer he couldn't refuse. (He really couldn't: invading French soldiers had just stolen all of his possessions.) It took a few nights, but Rosenbaum and Peter finally got their prize. When Rosenbaum unwrapped the rags from his dead friend's face, he reacted in the only sensible way: he threw up.

After he recovered, he gave the head to his doctor, Leopold Eckhart, who had agreed to turn it over to employees at the Vienna General Hospital for cleaning. (Rosenbaum and Peter had decided the DIY quicklime recipe wasn't reliable, since Roose's head ended up dangerously brittle.) Once all traces of Haydn's skin and muscle had been removed, the stripped skull was returned to Rosenbaum, who built a beautiful black case for it, topped with a golden lyre. With the skull back in his possession, Rosenbaum went on with his middle-class life in the suburbs.

He might have thought he had gotten away with the crime, but the future had other plans. A decade later, in 1820, Prince Nicholas Esterházy, whose family had employed Haydn as musical director for most of the composer's lifetime, held a celebration for the visiting Duke of Cambridge. The evening's entertainment included a performance of Haydn's masterpiece *The Creation,* and the duke was so moved by the music that he told the prince how lucky he was to have been able to employ Haydn, and how fortunate it was that he now possessed his remains. The duke assumed that Esterházy had given Haydn a beautiful tomb—except he hadn't. The prince smiled and thanked his visitor, while secretly resolving to finally dig up Haydn's corpse and give him a proper burial.

The prince's plans were to bring Haydn's body to Eisenstadt, twenty miles northeast of Vienna, for burial in the Esterházy family crypt. But when workers unearthed Haydn's coffin, they noticed something strange: where Haydn's head should have been, they found only his curly wig.

The prince was furious, and ordered an immediate investigation. Rosenbaum and Peter had not been particularly discreet about their ownership of the skull, and the inquest soon pointed to them. But the police moved slowly, and the pair knew what was coming. They decided to blame the whole thing on Rosenbaum's doctor, Eckhart, who had recently died. They would admit that the skull had later come into their possession, but say they were now very, very sorry and willing to give up their ill-gotten gain.

At first the plot worked beautifully, even though the skull the duo handed over was a fake. But like so many criminals, Rosenbaum and Peter were overconfident. Anyone with medical training who looked at the substitute skull could tell it had belonged to a far younger man than Haydn had been at the time of his death. When the police eventually realized they'd been duped, they came back to search Rosenbaum's house, this time without any warning. Frantic, Rosenbaum hid Haydn's skull in a mattress, threw on some blankets, and told his wife to lie on top. When the police came into the room, they must have wondered why Frau Rosenbaum was lying in bed in the middle of the day, but they were far too polite to ask her to get up.

Frustrated, Prince Nicholas resorted to bribery, offering Rosenbaum a huge sum of money to hand over Haydn's head. Rosenbaum finally relented—or so it seemed. He actually handed over another fake skull, but this time, one that at least looked like it could have belonged to Haydn. The prince swallowed the ruse hook, line, and sinker, and reburied the dummy head with the rest of Haydn's body in the Esterházy family crypt.

Rosenbaum had gotten the last laugh, and managed to keep Haydn's real skull for the rest of his life. Some scholars think his stubbornness may have had to do with the fact that Prince Nicholas had once employed Rosenbaum, but sided with the future Mrs. Rosenbaum's mother in opposing his marriage. In other words, long ago the prince had tried to deny Rosenbaum something precious—and now Rosenbaum had succeeded in denying the prince.

It took more than a century for Haydn's real head to find its way back into his coffin. Upon his death in 1829, Rosenbaum willed the skull to his friend Peter, asking him to give it to the Society for the Friends of Music in Vienna upon his own death. The skull got there in the 1890s, when it was put on display on top of a piano. But the Esterházy family, once they realized they had been duped again, never gave up their claims to the composer's cranium. After years of negotiations, Haydn's skull finally joined the rest of his body in the Esterházy church in Eisenstadt in June 1954. Haydn's bones—all of them—now rest in a marble sarcophagus adorned with two plump cherubs. But there's a little more of him than there once was: Rosenbaum's decoy head was never removed from the tomb, which now has two skulls inside.

LUDWIG VAN BEETHOVEN

BORN: *CA.* DECEMBER 16, 1770,
BONN, GERMANY
DIED: MARCH 26, 1827 (AGE 56),
VIENNA, AUSTRIA

For a man who made such beautiful music, Beethoven's health was a mess. It wasn't just his hearing loss, though that was bad enough. From his stomach (which gave him agonizing pain) to his eyes (which were perennially infected), Beethoven's body was a source of constant torment to him. Not surprisingly, he was also prone to irritability and depression. After meeting him, Goethe called his personality "utterly untamed."

The most poignant record we have of Beethoven's thoughts about his health is known as the *Heiligenstadt*

Testament, after the town where Beethoven wrote it while coming to terms with his hearing loss. "Oh you men who think or say that I am malevolent, stubborn, or misanthropic," it begins, "how greatly do you wrong me. You do not know the secret cause which makes me seem that way to you."

The "secret cause" was Beethoven's deafness, which he often found difficult to discuss. Yet he longed to be absolved for his temper, which is why, later in the same document, he asked his brothers for a favor: "As soon as I am dead, if Dr. Schmid is still alive, ask him in my name to describe my malady . . . so that so far as it is possible at least the world may become reconciled to me after my death."

The world has long since forgiven Beethoven for his moods, but his request for an accurate diagnosis of his health problems has echoed down through the centuries. As it happens, a stolen part of his skull may prove key to understanding the ailments that plagued him.

Beethoven died after an extended illness that was diagnosed as pneumonia, but never entirely explained. Its most alarming symptom was a swollen midsection, from which liters of fluid were repeatedly drained. Beethoven's autopsy took place the day after his death, and while it did little to explain his maladies, it did report their effects in vivid detail. Johann Wagner, assistant pathologist at Vienna's Pathologic-Anatomical Museum, described Beethoven's body as emaciated and swollen, his liver leathery, his spleen black, his auditory nerves wrinkled, and his auricular arteries "larger in size than a crow's feather."

Wagner was usually noted for his speed and skill, but he must have been having an off day when he dissected Beethoven. During the autopsy, he sawed the bones of Beethoven's skull apart so roughly that they couldn't be fit neatly back together. In later photographs, Beethoven's skull has a ghoulish, misshapen look, with a wide crack encircling the crown.

That wasn't the only damage Wagner inflicted. At the

autopsy, the pathologist removed Beethoven's ear bones and never put them back. He was supposedly planning a study of the composer's hearing loss, but that never happened, and the bones—which might have been key to explaining Beethoven's deafness—have never resurfaced.

Wagner's hack job was discovered in 1863, when the composer's body was exhumed for reburial in a new vault designed to better preserve his remains. (Franz Schubert, who died the year after Beethoven and was buried nearby, was also exhumed for the same reason.) Although both skeletons were moved promptly to their new zinc coffins, the skulls were kept aboveground for nine days of measurements, cast-making, and photographs. The composers' bones were then returned to their respective coffins and reburied on October 22, 1863—or at least most of them were.

Several bone fragments from Beethoven's skull never made it back into the ground. The missing shards—at least three large chunks and a handful of smaller ones—weren't noticed until 1888, when poor Beethoven and Schubert were exhumed once more, this time as part of an effort to consolidate Vienna's many cemeteries into one central location. Again Beethoven's skull was examined by doctors, who were unable to uncover any significant medical findings, but did note that some of the bones were missing—and not just the ear bones Wagner took during the autopsy. At the time no one seems to have found this very surprising, since bones do have a way of disappearing below ground.

But at least one man in Vienna knew where they'd gone. Romeo Seligmann was an anthropologist, physician, author, and translator who became the first professor of the history of medicine at the University of Vienna. The brilliance of Seligmann's mind was matched by the warmth of his personality, a combination that earned him the nickname "Wonderful." It also earned him the attention of the beautiful Ottilie von Goethe, the great author's daughter-in-law, who was Seligmann's patient and—according to family lore—his lover.

Ottilie provided many of the gifts that decorated Seligmann's study, but the surfaces that weren't covered with her trinkets and mementos were decorated with skulls. Seligmann was a noted cranium collector whose cabinets grew heavy thanks in part to his brother Leopold, who brought him back specimens from the Austrian navy's round-the-world Novara Expedition. Seligmann's famous skull collection may have been one reason why he was asked to measure Beethoven's skull in 1863, and it may have been part of the reason why someone gave him the skull fragments to keep after the exhumation.

Not that anyone but Seligmann, the giver, and perhaps a few friends knew where they'd gone. Indeed, the precise location of the fragments remained murky until 1945, the year that Adalbert Seligmann (Romeo's son) died and the fragments were found among his effects. Scholars who have traced the history of the skull fragments—most notably William Meredith, director of the Ira F. Brilliant Center for Beethoven Studies at San Jose State University—think that the man responsible for taking them in the first place was someone who had been close to Beethoven: a physician named Gerhard von Breuning.

As a teenager, Breuning had been a friend of Beethoven's, visiting him so often the composer nicknamed him "trouser button" (because he stuck to Beethoven the way a button does to clothing). During the nine days the skulls were aboveground in 1863, Breuning was the only one allowed to be alone with them, ferrying them among the sculptors and scientists. At the same time, he had also been part of a contingent of scientists who argued that the skulls should stay among the living. "How important and interesting for science it would be if these skulls remained available for further, more thorough investigation," he argued in an 1866 essay.

Meredith also thinks that Breuning was probably the one responsible for placing the skulls back in the new coffins. Since the fragments were from the occipital and parietal regions at the back of the skull, their absence might not have been noticed by people viewing the coffin from the front, but they would have been obvious to any doctor examining the skull as a whole. This means that Breuning was at least aware of the theft.

The fragments probably stayed with Romeo until his death in Vienna in 1892, when they passed to his son Adalbert. It's not clear where Adalbert kept them during World War II, when many of his art pieces and items of Goethe memorabilia were seized and auctioned off by the Nazis. But somehow, the fragments stayed safe. In 1990, after passing among relatives, the fragments made their way to America. Paul Kaufmann, a Californian, took possession of them after dementia claimed Adalbert's grandnephew Tom Rosenthal.

Kaufmann had heard his uncle Tom mention a family connection to Beethoven, but he couldn't quite believe the light brown bones in the small metal box had come from the great composer. He figured that tracing their story could be a retirement project. But before that happened, he was contacted by Russell Martin, author of the book *Beethoven's Hair*. Martin said that scientists wanted to arrange DNA testing of the skull fragments, to compare them with a lock of the composer's wild mane.

It took several years to complete the tests, but in 2005, an analysis of one of the skull fragments showed a partial agreement with DNA patterns found in Beethoven's hair, which supported the idea that both hair and bone came from the same man. The tests also showed something that seemed like it might finally explain Beethoven's ill health: extremely high levels of lead. Those tests corroborated 1996 studies on other strands of Beethoven's hair, which showed lead levels forty-two times higher than control samples.

Lead poisoning can cause many of the symptoms the composer was known for: erratic behavior, gastrointestinal distress, vomiting, headaches, clumsiness. It can even contribute to hearing loss. Though the harmful effects of lead are now well understood, at the time Beethoven was alive, lead was commonly used in the glaze on household items, in pipes, and as an additive in cheap wine—which Beethoven loved to drink. For a time, scientists thought they had finally answered the plaintive call of the *Heiligenstadt Testament*.

The truth is not so straightforward. In 2010, tests performed on a larger fragment of the skull showed only average levels of lead. Scientists were not able to explain why the earlier tests, performed on a smaller portion of bone, had shown such high lead levels. (The hair sample results were easier to explain: hair only records a few months' worth of environmental exposure, and Beethoven likely spent his final days covered in lead-laced medicinal salves.)

The tests threw a significant wrench in the lead hypothesis, which had been all but accepted, at least in the media, as the key to Beethoven's suffering. However, there's no shortage of other theories that could explain his ailments, which have been posthumously diagnosed as everything from irritable bowel syndrome to lupus. As long as his skull fragments remain aboveground, there's a chance that one day they will help provide the answers the composer so desperately sought.

ALBERT EINSTEIN

BORN: MARCH 14, 1879,
ULM, GERMANY
DIED: APRIL 18, 1955 (AGE 76),
PRINCETON, NEW JERSEY

Einstein once said, "I have no special talents. I am only passionately curious." To hear him tell it, his discoveries arose simply because he wondered about the kinds of things children contemplate but adults ignore: What shape is space? How does gravity work? What would it be like to move at the speed of light? "A normal adult never stops to think about problems of space and time," he once said. "But my intellectual development was retarded, as a result of which I began to wonder about space and time only when I had already grown up."

This wasn't just false modesty. Einstein didn't think *anyone* deserved the kind of adulation he received, with fans clamoring to see him appear on hotel balconies, and advertisers asking him to endorse everything from hair serum to "Relativity Cigars." He objected to the whole "cult of individuals," as he put it, the idea that some people should be treated like gods because of their abilities. And as the years went on, he grew concerned about what might happen to him after he died. "I want to be cremated so people don't come to worship at my bones," he told his biographer Abraham Pais.

Einstein got his wish—mostly. The afternoon after he died of a ruptured abdominal aneurysm, his body was cremated in Trenton, New Jersey. In accordance with his instructions, no funeral was held, although his friend Otto Nathan, whom Einstein had named his executor, did utter a few words of Goethe at the crematorium. Then Nathan scattered Einstein's ashes at a secret location on the Delaware River. But not all of the great scientist went the way of the wind.

Earlier that morning, Einstein's body had been autopsied at the hospital where he died. The pathologist, Dr. Thomas Harvey, found blood frothing in Einstein's stomach, a telltale sign of a burst abdominal aneurysm. (He also found the aorta coated in cholesterol, testament to Einstein's love of fatty foods.) After his examination of the internal organs, Harvey moved on to the brain, and it was this final stage of the autopsy that would prove controversial. Using an electric saw, Harvey cut open Einstein's cranium a few inches below the scientist's cotton-white mane and pried open his skull with a chisel. After some careful snipping, he lifted out the century's most celebrated brain—and kept it.

In later years, the media would sometimes portray Harvey as a sticky-fingered thief. It's true that he did not seek permission from Einstein's family to remove the brain, but he didn't think that was necessary. At the time, hospitals frequently removed interesting or unusual organs from the dead for study, and to Harvey, the family's permission for an autopsy constituted permission to take the brain—plus whatever else the doctors wanted. (Einstein's ophthalmologist also removed the scientist's eyes, which are suspended in formaldehyde in a safety deposit box in New Jersey.)

The next day, news of Einstein's death was plastered on front pages throughout the world, and several articles mentioned the brain's removal. Soon enough, Harvey received a distraught phone call from Hans Albert, Einstein's oldest son, who declared that his father had not planned to leave his body to science. Harvey apologized for offending the family, but emphasized the scientific value of studying the brain of such a genius. He hoped, he said, to find out whether there was anything different about Einstein's brain—any anatomical sign of what made the scientist so great.

Eventually, Harvey managed to get permission from Hans Albert, and later Otto Nathan, to keep the brain, as long as it was used only for scientific study and the results of any examination published only in scientific journals.

But if anyone was expecting groundbreaking results from studies of Einstein's brain in the following months, they were sorely disappointed. Instead, the brain languished in obscurity for decades. Preserved in formaldehyde, encased in a plastic-like substance called celloidin, and sliced into more than a thousand pieces, the brain followed Harvey from job to job in New Jersey, Kansas, Missouri, and back to New Jersey, housed in a glass jar inside cardboard boxes, beneath beer coolers, and in closets underneath socks. No neuro-anatomist himself, Harvey knew he would need to rely on others to study the brain, but he was loath to hand it over to anyone he didn't know and trust. He feared another media frenzy, and more angry phone calls from Hans Albert.

Harvey also hoped that humanity's knowledge of the workings of the brain would advance, and saw his role partly as that of a caretaker. It turns out he was wise to wait. The few scientists Harvey did give samples to in the early years found nothing unusual. But in the late twentieth century, interest in neuroscience boomed. In the space of a century, we went from drawing funny phrenology maps on plaster skulls to performing brain scans that can "see" neural activity. And in the rush to study what lies between our ears, Einstein's gray matter wasn't left behind. Before the turn of the century, several major studies on his brain had been published.

In 1978, students of neuroscientist Marian Diamond at the University of California, Berkeley, tacked a news clipping about Einstein's brain on a lab wall. In those days Diamond was best known for her studies on how rat brains change in response to their environment: happy and well-fed rats, it turns out, have noticeably different brains from starved rats kept in cramped conditions. Around the time the clipping went up, Diamond had also become interested in glial cells, which protect and nourish the brain's neurons. Diamond reasoned— correctly, as it turned out—that a more active brain should contain more glial cells. After noticing the clipping, Diamond decided to try gathering support for her thesis by switching from studying rats to studying one of the century's smartest men: Albert Einstein.

Diamond spent three years convincing Harvey she could be trusted with samples of the brain. One spring morning in 1983, several chunks—floating in a mayonnaise jar—finally arrived at her university post office. After painstakingly counting the glial cells and neurons and comparing the numbers to those of a control group of brains from dead veterans, Diamond and her assistants discovered that Einstein did have more glial cells per neuron than expected. However, the difference was only statistically significant in one section of the left inferior parietal lobe, an area heavily involved in language, math, and processing visual stimuli and complex reasoning. There, Einstein had 73 percent more glial cells than the control group.

When they wrote up their results in a 1985 paper, Diamond and her coauthors concluded that Einstein's preponderance of glial cells might indeed reflect "enhanced use" of his brain tissue in this area. The results were interesting in part because Einstein had emphasized the importance of visualization in his mental process; he said he thought in pictures, not words. He claimed to experience an "associative play" of images, whether of the shape of space or a beam of light.

Diamond's research was followed by a 1996 study from Alabama neuroscientist Britt Anderson. Anderson had planned to study the architecture of Einstein's dendrites, the branched fibers that sprout from neurons and join with other neurons to form synapses. Unfortunately, Anderson discovered that the celloidin surrounding the samples of Einstein's brain blocked the stains that would make the dendrites visible. The only notable observation Anderson could make was that Einstein had a thinner cerebral cortex, more densely packed with neurons, than the control group. Anderson didn't jump to any big conclusions about what this might mean, in part because Einstein's cortex might have shrunk during its forty years of storage.

A third study, published in 1999, was the splashiest. This time, Ontario neuroscientist Sandra Witelson got access to something previous researchers didn't even know existed: photographs of Einstein's brain before it had been sliced. Ever the preservationist, Harvey had sketched and photographed the brain from multiple angles before cutting it apart. He'd even hired a local artist to paint its portrait (no word on whether it ever hung in his living room).

With the photographs in front of her, Witelson noticed a few things that seemed different about Einstein's brain. For one thing, his parietal lobes (in the upper back of the brain) were about 15 percent wider than normal. Even more interesting, his Sylvian fissure (a prominent groove that rises above the place where the legs of a pair of glasses rest) took an unusually short course, leaving him without a small depression known as the parietal operculum. Taken together, Witelson theorized that the architecture of Einstein's brain allowed for more efficient connections between neurons in areas involved in visual, spatial, and mathematical processing.

Diamond's and Witelson's studies made for great headlines, but they also faced a barrage of criticism. In both studies, the most obvious issue was that the sample size, in Einstein's case, was a group of one; neither project had other genius brains for comparison. To critics, the studies smacked of the phrenology that had come before them. Just because one brain shows an unusual feature, whether it's the "organ of tune" supposedly located on Haydn's temples or the bulging parietal lobes of Einstein, that doesn't mean that feature is what made the brain so amazing. The brain is by far the most complex organ in the human body, and varies greatly from person to person. Its workings are a mystery just as great as the problems of space and time that Einstein tried to solve.

In 1998, Harvey finally returned what remained of the brain to Princeton Hospital, handing over his assortment of boxes and jars to the pathologist who held his old position. Scientists can still study the brain samples, but it's unclear how much value they now hold. After decades of storage and multiple trips across the country, the importance of the brain probably lies most in its significance as a memento of a famous man.

In late 2011, on the day this story was being written, forty-six slides of Einstein's brain went on display at the Mütter Museum of the College of Physicians of Philadelphia—the first time the samples have ever been displayed to the public. As visitors contemplate the small gold-and-black splotches, which look like miniature stained glass windows, they may have a feeling that Einstein himself once praised: "The most beautiful and deepest experience a man can have," he said, "is the sense of the mysterious."

Accidents Happen

"If I worship one thing more than another it shall be the spread of my own body," Walt Whitman wrote in his "Song of Myself." The poet was fascinated by anatomy, physiology, and phrenology—he even had his phrenological reading reprinted in some editions of *Leaves of Grass*. But several of his physicians were more interested in brains than skulls, and belonged to a secretive society in which members willed their own gray matter to science for study. Whitman may or may not have been a member, but after his death in 1892, his doctors removed his brain for analysis. The organ was accidentally destroyed some time later; the official story is that a lab assistant dropped it, but some say Whitman's doctors bungled their experiments.

ALISTAIR COOKE

BORN: NOVEMBER 20, 1908,
SALFORD, LANCASHIRE,
UNITED KINGDOM
DIED: MARCH 30, 2004 (AGED 95),
NEW YORK, NEW YORK

The story of broadcaster and journalist Alistair Cooke's bones might have appeared in one of his own broadcasts. Like Laurence Sterne, Cooke was a victim of body snatchers, but this time they were the twenty-first-century type. The motive was the same as ever—money—but the destination had changed: instead of the dissecting table, the parts these body snatchers stole ended up inside the living.

During his lifetime, Cooke interpreted two countries for one another: he explained America to Britain, and

Britain to America. His BBC radio show *Letter from America* ran longer than any other radio speech show in history (1946–2004). In America, Cooke spent two decades as the host of *Masterpiece Theatre,* introducing delightfully stodgy British dramas to public television audiences. For many viewers, he was the very picture of an English gentleman: dignified, erudite, never without a considered opinion or a jacket and tie.

But ten days before Christmas 2005, Susan Cooke Kittredge, Cooke's daughter, received a disturbing phone call. The man on the other end of the line was a detective with the Brooklyn district attorney's office, who asked Kittredge if she had heard anything about the recent investigation into the illegal sale of body parts plundered from local funeral homes and crematoriums. Kittredge said she had not. Then the detective told her that one of the bodies picked apart by the thieves had belonged to her own father.

Kittredge would feel unsettled for months afterward. She had, she thought, helped to sprinkle her father's ashes in Central Park a year and a half before, tipping them out of a paper cup smuggled from a nearby Starbucks. That had been Cooke's last wish, carried out even though it violated New York City laws. But now it was clear that Cooke's remains had been used for something far worse, and Kittredge couldn't be sure exactly *what* she had poured out of that paper cup.

It was a Fort Lee, New Jersey, dentist who played the modern-day Resurrection Man. According to his February 2006 indictment, Michael Mastromarino spent four years leading a criminal ring that illegally harvested body parts from more than one thousand people. Mastromarino and his associates bribed funeral directors to give them access to cadavers, which they dissected and sold to tissue-processing companies for use in transplants and research. They forged consent forms and medical records, and in some cases even replaced stolen bones with plastic pipes to hide their handiwork before their victims' funerals.

In many cases, the forged medical forms allowed aged and diseased tissue to enter the supply chain. With Cooke, it turned out that the paperwork accompanying his body parts had listed him as an eighty-five-year-old who had died of a heart attack, instead of a ninety-five-year-old who died of lung cancer that had spread to his bones. And it was his cancerous arm and leg bones that had been removed from his body, or "harvested," in organ-donor parlance. They ended up at a Florida tissue-processing company, although it's unclear whether they ever made their way into a transplant patient.

According to the district attorney's investigation, Mastromarino claimed to have phoned Kittredge and received verbal consent for the removal of Cooke's bones. But Kittredge says that never happened. She also told reporters that her father would have been "horrified" to learn of the fate of his remains: "He had a very weak stomach," she said to CNN. "And it would make him sick."

No one is supposed to be selling body parts for profit, at least in America. But the government does allow tissue-processing companies to charge for "reasonable expenses," and there's been little effort to define what that means. Furthermore, advances in immunosuppressive drugs during the 1990s have created a thriving market not just for major organs, like hearts and kidneys, but also for muscles, tendons, skin, and bones. The industry is growing faster than regulation can keep up, and the burgeoning demand has created an ideal climate for criminal operation.

In 2008, Mastromarino pleaded guilty to 1,353 separate counts of enterprise corruption, conspiracy, theft of body parts, deceptive business practices, and corpse abuse. He was sentenced to eighteen to fifty-four years in prison and ordered to pay $4.6 million to the district attorney's office, which distributed the funds to victims' families. Several of Mastromarino's criminal associates were also sentenced to time behind bars. But that was little comfort for patients who received transplants using one of the twenty-five thousand pieces of stolen tissue and were forced to spend years wondering if they might develop a disease as a result. Some did: a man in Ohio contracted HIV and hepatitis C, while a widow, also from Ohio, developed syphilis.

There may, however, be a glimmer of a silver lining. The story of Cooke's corpse attracted headlines, which in turn led to greater scrutiny of the human tissue-processing industry. After the scandal made the news, the US Food and Drug Administration conducted an inspection blitz targeting 153 major tissue-processing firms. While the agency said they found no substantial issues, they did create a task force focused on tissue safety, whose recommendations (including better paper trails and more frequent inspections) have been incorporated into FDA practice. If greater regulation cuts down on modern body snatching, consider it Cooke's final contribution to the public good.

TED WILLIAMS

BORN: AUGUST 30, 1918,
SAN DIEGO, CALIFORNIA
DIED: JULY 5, 2002 (AGE 83),
INVERNESS, FLORIDA

He was as American as apple pie. Not many men can say they were a star baseball player, ace fighter pilot, and expert fisherman in their time, but Ted Williams could. He was inducted into the Baseball Hall of Fame, twice won baseball's Triple Crown, was named the American League's Most Valuable Player two times, and earned a dozen military medals for his service in the Marines. He was also the last major league player to bat over .400 in a single season—actually .406, thank you very much.

But at the end of his life, Ted Williams got caught up in that other famous American pastime—the quest for immortality. In his will, Williams asked for his body to be cremated and his ashes spread off the coast of Florida. But as his days on Earth dwindled, his son developed other ideas. John Henry Williams was fascinated by the speculative science of cryonic preservation, which is predicated on the idea that medical technology might one day be far enough advanced to bring properly preserved tissues back to life. "Properly preserved" tissues, by the way, are those soaked in preservatives, then chilled to minus 320 degrees Fahrenheit by being submerged in liquid nitrogen. The results look a bit like human Popsicles—corpsicles, if you will.

If that sounds a little nuts, it's because it is. But for some people, the only thing crazier is giving up a chance at immortality, no matter how slim. That's how John Henry felt. Within hours of his father's death from cardiac arrest, John Henry had the great athlete's body set on ice and flown by chartered jet to the Alcor Life Extension Foundation in Scottsdale, Arizona.

Some members of Williams's family were not pleased by John Henry's actions, to say the least. Williams's eldest daughter, Bobby-Jo Ferrell, sued in a Florida court to get her father's body removed from the Alcor facility, thawed, and cremated. But ten days after Williams's death, John Henry and his sister Claudia produced a note scribbled on a scrap of oil-stained paper. The note read "JHW, Claudia, and Dad all agree to be put into bio-stasis after we die. This is what we want, to be able to be together in the future, even if it is only a chance."

Bobby-Jo and others questioned the note's authenticity, but John Henry eventually got his way. After spending two years and $87,000 battling her brother and sister in court, in 2004 Ferrell agreed to drop her lawsuit; she said she had no money left to fight the case. But the controversy didn't end there. Today, some know Williams as much for the gruesome allegations about his corpse's treatment at Alcor as for the accomplishments of his career.

In August 2003, *Sports Illustrated* ran an exposé about Williams's fate at Alcor, based on information provided by the company's former chief operating officer, Larry Johnson. The revelations were not for the faint of heart: Johnson alleged that during the preservation process, Williams's head had been sloppily severed while a crowd stood around cracking jokes and taking photos. During the freezing, malfunctioning equipment had caused the tissues in the head to repeatedly crack. The article also said that John Henry had neglected to pay Alcor's bill in full, and as a result, employees had joked about throwing Williams's body away, selling it on eBay, or leaving it on John Henry's doorstep in a "frosted cardboard box."

It got worse. In 2009 Johnson published a tell-all about his time at Alcor called *Frozen: My Journey into the World of Cryonics, Deception, and Death.* The book presented the Williams saga in far more detail than the *Sports Illustrated* article did. Its most memorable passage described how Alcor employees used a monkey wrench to try to pry Williams's head from its pedestal—a Bumble Bee tuna can. "Little gray chunks of Ted's head flew off, peppering the walls, skittering across the floor and sliding under the machinery," Johnson wrote.

Alcor steadfastly denies all of these claims, and sued Johnson both in 2003 and in 2009, seeking damages for false and defamatory content in *Frozen,* among other issues. In 2012, Alcor dropped its case against Johnson after he declared bankruptcy and changed his tune on the treatment of Ted's head. In a public statement reprinted on Alcor's website, Johnson said, "When the book *Frozen* was written, I believed my conclusions to be correct. However, information unknown to me and a more complete understanding of the facts furnished by ALCOR contradict part of my account and some of my conclusions. . . . For example my account of the Ted Williams cryopreservation, which was not based upon my first-hand observation as noted in my book, is contradicted by information furnished by ALCOR. I am not now certain that Ted Williams' body was treated disrespectfully, or that any procedures were performed without authorization or conducted poorly."

At the time of this writing, Alcor was continuing their lawsuit against Johnson's coauthor on *Frozen,* as well as the book's publisher. It seems the truth of what happened to Ted Williams may never be known, but for now, the matter is evolving in that other beloved American institution—the courtroom.

CRIME

AND

PUNISHMENT

Obviously crime pays, or there'd be no crime.
—G. GORDON LIDDY (1930–)

More than one famous body has been stolen and held for ransom, but corpse-nappings rarely turn out well for the perpetrators—just ask the criminals who tried to make off with Abraham Lincoln, Elvis Presley, or Charlie Chaplin. Only the mysterious thieves who stole Alexander Stewart, the "Merchant Prince" of Manhattan, got what they wanted. Slightly more successful are bandits who steal bodily bits and pieces, like the bones of the poet John Milton or the skull of the Apache warrior Geronimo (if it was really his). And while there have been many snatchings in the name of love, science, or religion, the crimes recounted here were committed primarily for fun and profit.

JOHN MILTON

BORN: DECEMBER 9, 1608,
LONDON, ENGLAND
DIED: NOVEMBER 8, 1674 (AGE 65),
LONDON, ENGLAND

John Milton is often mentioned alongside Shakespeare as one of the most brilliant poets of the English language. But in at least one respect, Shakespeare was the smarter of the pair, because he had the foresight to place a curse on his tomb. The Bard's grave at Holy Trinity Church, Stratford, is engraved with the following lines:

> *Good frend for Jesus sake forbeare*
> *To digg the dust enclosed heare*
> *Blese be ye man yt spares thes stones,*
> *And curst be he yt moues my bones.*

If Milton's spirit survives, he probably wishes he'd done something similar.

Milton is said to have died "in a fit of the gout," but so quietly that no one in the room noticed. After his death, he was buried in a vault beneath the clerk's desk at St. Giles' Cripplegate, one of London's oldest churches. His grave marker disappeared shortly thereafter, and for most of the next century, no other monument marked the spot. During the ensuing decades, visitors who asked where Milton lay were shown the clerk's desk, even after it was moved during renovations. At least one parishioner who asked to be buried near Milton was interred beneath the clerk's desk where it was in the late eighteenth century, which was not the same as its location in the seventeenth century, when Milton passed away.

By 1790, parishioners were growing uneasy about this state of affairs, and about the lack of a church monument to Milton. So, in August of that year, officials took advantage of another round of church repairs to ask workmen to dig for Milton's coffin. Sure enough, a few days later workers reported that they'd found two coffins, one on top of the other, near where the clerk's desk was thought to have once stood. The clerk and the churchwarden in charge of the excavation were pleased, since they had been expecting two coffins: Milton was known to have been buried with his father. The clerk and warden measured and cleaned the uppermost coffin, but resisted the urge to peek inside. Unfortunately, not everyone exercised the same discretion.

After leaving the church that evening, the churchwarden, a man named John Cole, went drinking with some friends. History records their names as Laming, Taylor, Fountain, and Holmes, and their professions as pawnbroker, physician, tavern-keeper, and journeyman coffin-maker—occupations not unrelated to the events that followed. The talk that evening soon turned to the day's events, and the story of the discovery at St. Giles'. After hearing the intriguing news, Cole's friends asked to see Milton's coffin. Cole—perhaps a little proud of his church's most famous burial—told them that they could visit the church the next morning and see it for themselves.

The next day, Cole's friends went to St. Giles' and pulled the coffin from the ground. It's hard to say what motivated them: morbid curiosity? The desire for a memento or trophy? A healthy dose of alcohol still flowing through their veins? Whatever their reasons, the men cut open the coffin and pulled aside the shroud. At that moment, the ribs of the decaying skeleton fell down into a heap. The men began picking apart the bones, knocking the skull's teeth out with a stone, and pulling out clumps of the corpse's long hair. When it didn't come out easily enough, two of the men went home to get scissors.

Eventually, the group tired of the desecration and took their souvenirs home. But allegedly, the ghastly scene didn't end there. According to legend, the church gravedigger, a woman of an apparently entrepreneurial bent, decided to charge visitors a few pence each for a look inside the coffin. Even the church repairmen got into the act, charging visitors the price of a "pot of beer" to be let into the church. The show lasted until about four o'clock the following afternoon, when Milton's "relics," both real and spurious, began circulating through London. One newspaper reported that "several thousands" of Milton's teeth had been purchased in the days after the desecration.

Most of what we know about these events comes from a narrative written by Philip Neve, a barrister and Milton aficionado. Neve read a story in a newspaper soon after the desecration and launched an investigation, interviewing the participants and buying back as many of the relics as he could, with the goal of returning them to the grave. It's worth noting that while Neve believed the body in the coffin belonged to Milton, not everyone was convinced. An anonymously published article in a local paper claimed the body belonged to a female, but later scholars have suggested that the author of that article was George Steevens, a Shakespearean commentator and notorious hoaxer who liked to poke fun at "antiquarian" discoveries. Steevens had once faked the discovery of the tombstone of an ancient Danish king, and fooled a magazine into publishing an article about murderous Javanese trees.

The idea that the body belonged to a woman was repudiated by several physicians, but Steevens's eight (and later nine) "Reasons why it is improbable that the Coffin lately dug up . . . should contain the Reliques of Milton" were seconded by the church sexton and published repeatedly in various newspapers and journals. Just as persistently, Philip Neve continued to publish rebuttals.

It's unlikely we'll ever know whether the body desecrated that day belonged to the famous poet. But Milton scholar Carol Barton, who in 2004 made an exhaustive inquiry into these events, believes it is likely that Cripplegate officials engaged in a cover-up. Though the desecration was the talk of the British press for two months, coverage quickly died down, and Barton found no reference in local records to any punishment for the participants, nor any ceremony marking the reinterment of the remains. However, she did find an interesting record listed in the burial register for August 10, 1790, a few days after the coffin was opened. The entry reads: "James Milton, a child, convulsions."

Aside from the similarity of the name (not unusual for the time), Barton thinks it's notable that the record makes no mention of the child's parentage or age. Under the heading for payment, it simply notes "poor," which means the boy would have been buried at parish expense. Barton wonders if the church decided to take what was left of Milton and bury him quietly in a less expensive child's coffin. She speculates that church officials secured Neve's silence by agreeing to conduct a private but dignified reburial of all of the remains he'd purchased. Today a marble plaque and bust of Milton adorn one of the church walls, and an engraved stone at the foot of the altar (near where the clerk's desk is believed to have stood) proclaims his birth and death, but nothing indicates precisely where he is buried.

The poet William Cowper was one of those who believed it was Milton's body that was picked apart and sold. Soon after the reports of the desecration, Cowper wrote the following lines. Poets, and the rest of us, could do worse than placing a version of them on our own tombstones:

Ill fare the hands that heaved the stones
Where Milton's ashes lay,
That trembled not to grasp his bones
And steal his dust away!

ABRAHAM LINCOLN

BORN: FEBRUARY 12, 1809,
IN HARDIN COUNTY, KENTUCKY
DIED: APRIL 15, 1865 (AGE 56),
IN WASHINGTON, DC

Abraham Lincoln was the first president to be assassinated, the first to be embalmed, the first to get a state funeral, and the first to—almost—have his body stolen. For that "almost," we can thank the Secret Service.

Lincoln signed the legislation to create the Secret Service the day he was assassinated. That's not as eerie as it sounds, since the agency wasn't originally charged with protecting the president. For its first few decades, the mission of the Secret Service was to seek out and destroy counterfeiting rings. Counterfeiting was rife in nineteenth-century America: by the 1860s, almost half the nation's cash was funny money, then called "coney" or "queer."

In the Midwest, a Cincinnati-born engraver named Benjamin Boyd was one of the artists who kept forgery operations humming. His claim to fame was a five-dollar bill so accurate it fooled even experts. Not surprisingly, the Secret Service decided it had to take Boyd himself out of circulation. In 1875, he was arrested in Illinois and sentenced to a decade in the Joliet penitentiary.

Boyd's arrest left Midwest counterfeiters in the lurch, and there was one in particular who was very annoyed. James "Big Jim" Kinealy was the hard-drinking leader of a counterfeiting ring in central Illinois, and the silent owner of a Chicago saloon called The Hub. Not much is known about the man, but he must have been a pretty strange type, because the plan he came up with to get Boyd out of jail is one of the weirder schemes in American history.

Kinealy planned to kidnap Abraham Lincoln's body and hold it for ransom, demanding Boyd's safe release and a cool $200,000 cash (the real stuff). Where Kinealy got his inspiration we'll never know, although there is one strange tale, recorded by a Lincoln Memorial custodian, of a Springfield attorney who planned to kidnap Lincoln's corpse in 1867. His reasons have been lost to history, and the plan failed for want of accomplices willing to carry out the ghoulish task.

Big Jim had no such problem, but he did have trouble getting his men to keep their mouths shut. His first plan involved hiring a gang from the appropriately named town of Lincoln, Illinois, to steal the dead president's body and hide it in a hollowed-out log. The scheme failed when one of the conspirators blabbed about it to a local prostitute, who promptly informed the police. The criminals skipped town and left Big Jim in the dust.

Undeterred, Kinealy came up with a brilliant new scheme, or so he thought. He decided to hire some of the lowlifes who hung around his saloon to steal Lincoln's corpse and hide it in the sand dunes of Illinois, where the wind would erase all sign of their tracks. That may have seemed smart, except for the fact that the trip would require ten days of carrying the coffin in an open wagon—sure to arouse suspicion if headlines across the country were screaming that Lincoln's body had just been stolen.

Kinealy's lone stroke of genius was in planning the caper for the night of November 7, 1876, the date of an election so hotly contested it made Bush versus Gore in 2000 look like a Sunday picnic. While the rest of the United States was obsessing over Hayes versus Tilden, Kinealy's men boarded the train to Springfield. They waited until a few hours after dusk, then crept to Oak Ridge Cemetery and broke into Lincoln's tomb.

It wasn't a particularly difficult task. The only thing protecting the tomb was an ordinary padlock, which the would-be thieves used a file to cut through. Once inside, the criminals were momentarily mesmerized by Lincoln's pale marble sarcophagus, which must have given off a glow in the moonlit night. The gang's leader, a hard-bitten barkeep by the name of Terrence Mullen, snapped out of his daze first and raised his ax high. But just as it was about to come down on the sarcophagus lid, another member of the group, Lewis C. Swegles, told Mullen to stop. If they pried open the sarcophagus instead of smashing it, Swegles reasoned, they'd have a better chance of concealing the theft, giving them more time to get away. Mullen agreed, and the men pried open the sarcophagus. Unfortunately for them, the lead-lined, five-hundred-pound coffin inside was far too heavy to lift. Mullen ordered Swegles to fetch the getaway driver, hoping another pair of arms would help.

But instead of heading to the road, Swegles crept into the tomb's reception chamber, where he came face to face with a crowd of Secret Service agents. Swegles wasn't surprised: he'd planned it that way. He was an informant, a onetime petty crook who earned his bread snitching for the Secret Service. He'd finagled his way into Kinealy's plot when he heard it discussed at The Hub (these were not the smartest of criminals), and introduced himself as the "boss body snatcher of

Chicago." In fact he was no such thing, and *his* boss was actually Patrick D. Tyrrell, Chicago bureau chief for the Secret Service.

Tyrrell had been waiting in the chamber for three hours, alongside several other agents and Pinkerton detectives. After Swegles's signal, the men crept from the room and prepared to arrest Kinealy's gang. But as these were also not the smartest of detectives, one of the group cocked his pistol, which accidentally fired. The sound reverberated through the cemetery like thunder.

Tyrrell ran ahead, dashed into the tomb, and ordered the thieves to freeze. But they were already gone, spooked by the gunshot. To make matters worse, Tyrrell then mistook one of the detectives for a Kinealy thief, and the two began firing at each other. Neither was seriously wounded, but Tyrrell later called the evening "one of the most unfortunate nights I have ever experienced."

But the night wasn't a total loss, at least as far as the good guys were concerned, because Lincoln's coffin never left the tomb. And the criminals didn't get very far: after wandering across the countryside and haggling their way onto trains, the gang regrouped at The Hub in Chicago, where Tyrrell arrested them ten days later. Because the punishment for attempted body snatching was minimal, the men were charged only with attempted theft of the coffin. Their punishment was a year of hard labor in Joliet, alongside their old friend Benjamin Boyd. Kinealy remained free until 1880, when he was arrested for—what else?—counterfeiting.

After the break-in, the custodian of the tomb decided there was only one surefire way to keep Lincoln's remains safe: hide them. For several years, Lincoln's coffin lay beneath piles of lumber in the basement of the Lincoln Memorial, and between 1876 and 1901, it was moved at least sixteen times to foil would-be thieves.

By 1901, Lincoln's son Robert decided he'd had enough. Inspired by the burial plans of widely despised railroad car entrepreneur George Pullman, Robert ordered his father's coffin encased in a steel cage, lowered into a vault ten feet below the monument floor, and topped with four thousand pounds of cement. As far as anybody knows, Lincoln is still there.

Heads of State

Lincoln is the only president to have suffered an attempted theft of his corpse, but there was an earlier attempt on a presidential skull. In 1830, a disgruntled gardener fired by one of George Washington's heirs crept into the family vault at Mount Vernon and tried to make off with the Father of the Country's cranium. Instead, he accidentally stole a skull belonging to an in-law of one of the president's nephews. The head was returned the following day, and the next year George and the other residents of his vault were reburied in a new—and significantly more secure—brick tomb.

CHARLIE CHAPLIN

BORN: APRIL 16, 1889,
LONDON, ENGLAND
DIED: DECEMBER 25, 1977 (AGE 88),
CORSIER-SUR-VEVEY, SWITZERLAND

Though we usually think of actor, director, and comedic genius Charlie Chaplin cavorting across Hollywood stages, his life ended in Switzerland. Chaplin settled there after a trip home to England in 1952 was rudely interrupted by news that the US attorney general had revoked his reentry permit (he had never obtained American citizenship) because of Chaplin's alleged Communist sympathies, which were tantamount to treason in the era of Joseph McCarthy's witch hunts. Shocked and disgusted—he considered himself apolitical—Chaplin vowed he would never set foot in the United States again. (He did, to accept a special Academy Award, but it took twenty years.)

Several decades after moving to Switzerland, Chaplin

died of old age and was buried in the peaceful town of Corsier-sur-Vevey, perched on the northeastern edge of Lake Geneva. He'd lived there for twenty-five years, keeping more or less to himself. Townspeople knew who he was, but prided themselves on leaving him alone. That is, until three months after he was buried.

One morning early in March 1978, the local cemetery superintendent made a startling discovery. Where the body of Sir Charlie had lain for the past two months, there was now only a muddy hole, with tire tracks and footprints marring the neatly kept grass. The town was aghast: the police had no idea who would want to steal Chaplin's body, and neither did his family. The press speculated that the culprits were Neo-Nazis, anti-Semites, rabid fans, or possibly crazed Englishmen who wanted to return Chaplin to his native country. But within a few days, the real motive was revealed: money. The body snatchers telephoned Chaplin's house and demanded 600,000 Swiss francs in exchange for his corpse.

During his lifetime, Chaplin declared that he would never negotiate with kidnappers, and that no member of his family should pay any ransom money (there had been rumors of plots against his children). His devoted widow, Oona, stuck to her late husband's wishes and told the police she wouldn't cough up a cent. "A body is simply a body. My husband is in heaven and in my heart," she declared to her lawyer. But the police eventually convinced her that if she at least pretended to cooperate, they'd have a much easier time catching the culprits.

Chaplin's thieves got further than the would-be bandits who had tried to steal Abraham Lincoln, but they were no geniuses. In fact, they were two impoverished political refugees, one a Pole and one a Bulgarian, both of whom occasionally worked as auto mechanics. Their tactic was to call the Chaplin household from phone booths and harass Oona or her daughter Geraldine, sometimes threatening to harm one of the younger Chaplin children if the ransom money wasn't forthcoming.

It took eleven weeks, but the police eventually traced

the calls and staked out a series of public phone booths. After a call came through at its preappointed time on May 16, the police nabbed their men. The pair later confessed they had hoped to use the money from Chaplin's ransom to open up their own garage.

The thieves led police to a cornfield about fifteen miles from the cemetery, where they'd buried Chaplin's coffin three feet below ground. After police dug up the coffin, the farmer who owned the field marked the spot with a wooden cross decorated with a cane—a homage to the Little Tramp. Oona said the spot was even lovelier than Chaplin's original grave, and occasionally liked to visit it.

Roman Wardas, the twenty-four-year-old Pole, was sentenced to four and a half years' hard labor for his role as the "mastermind" behind the plot. Gantscho Ganev, the thirty-eight-year-old Bulgarian, was described as the "muscle man" and only got eighteen months. As for the coffin, it was reburied at Corsier-sur-Vevey beneath a ton of concrete.

THE WORLD'S MOST VALUABLE CORPSE

One of the few corpse-napping cases that worked out for the snatchers concerns the body of Alexander T. Stewart, an Irish immigrant-turned-"Merchant Prince" of Manhattan. When Stewart died in 1876, his department store empire had made him one of the richest men in the United States. At his death, he was said to be worth about $50 million ($50 billion in today's dollars). Two years after his demise, a group of sophisticated thieves broke into his vault in St. Mark's Cemetery, stuffed his body in a bag, and ran off. New York City police never solved the case, and in 1882, Mrs. Stewart paid $20,000 for a bag of bones she could only hope belonged to her late husband.

ELVIS PRESLEY

BORN: JANUARY 8, 1935,
TUPELO, MISSISSIPPI
DIED: AUGUST 16, 1977 (AGE 42),
MEMPHIS, TENNESSEE

For a corpse, Elvis is probably having more fun than anyone else in this book. Even though he's been gone for decades, he still rakes in millions each year, has hundreds of fan clubs throughout the world, and is reportedly living a life of leisure everywhere from Buenos Aires to Kalamazoo. His fans go on pilgrimages to his final home, and Memphis stages a weeklong festival on the anniversary of his death. Some scholars even say Elvis worship could develop into a full-blown religion. When it comes to life after death, no one is rocking it quite like the King.

It's certainly an improvement on his final years. By the time he died, Elvis was routinely seeking solace for physical and emotional pain in pills and peanut-butter-and-bacon sandwiches, which helped him balloon to more than three hundred pounds. He was prone to mumbling incoherently, splitting his pants, and falling asleep onstage during his rhinestone-studded Vegas performances. The night he died, he could barely make it to the bathroom by himself.

His death still came as a shock. His fiancée, Ginger Alden, awoke one afternoon to find him lying stiff and bluish in the bathroom. Elvis had apparently tumbled off the toilet and onto the floor, pajamas around his ankles. He was rushed to the hospital, even though rigor mortis had clearly set in. The cause of death, at least officially, was "cardiac arrhythmia" (an irregular heartbeat), but the full autopsy materials have never been released to the public, and today many believe Elvis died after taking one too many "daddy's little helpers." Other rumors still swirl: Elvis committed suicide because of his dwindling career; Elvis was murdered; Elvis faked his own death to go undercover for the DEA; Elvis was done in by aliens. Some claim the King never died at all: in 1988, a Michigan housewife said she saw Elvis eating a Whopper at a Kalamazoo Burger King, and the sightings haven't stopped since.

But on August 16, 1977, the grief in Memphis was real. As news of Elvis's death spread, a crowd of fifty thousand mourners gathered on Elvis Presley Boulevard in front of Graceland, where they stayed for two days. Vernon Presley, Elvis's father, allowed fans to pay their respects in the Graceland foyer, where Elvis's embalmed body lay in one of Vernon's white suits, with a white tie, a powder blue shirt, and his trademark TCB (Taking Care of Business) pendant. There is only one photo of the corpse, shot surreptitiously by a family member (or so it's said) and sold to the *National Enquirer* for $75,000.

After the funeral, a motorcade of more than a dozen white Cadillacs carried the body and mourners to Forest Hill Cemetery, where Elvis was buried in a mausoleum alongside his beloved mother, Gladys. According to witnesses, an anguished Vernon kept repeating, "Son, Daddy will be with you soon. Daddy will be with you soon." In fact, Vernon would join his son less than two years later—but first he had some business to take care of.

A few weeks after his son's death, Vernon applied to the county for permission to rebury Elvis and Gladys at the Graceland Mansion in Memphis. Because burials at private residences weren't permitted, Vernon had to apply for a zoning variance. In his application, he cited security concerns around the grave, including a recent grave-robbing attempt. Fortunately for him, the application was approved, and on October 2, Elvis and his mother were reburied beneath bronze markers near the swimming pool at Graceland, where they have rested ever since. But who had tried to dig up the King?

The plot never got very far. According to press reports, on August 29, 1977, four young men from Memphis climbed the gates of Forest Hill Cemetery shortly after midnight. They had just begun rattling the mausoleum door when headlights from a nearby car frightened them off. Three fled in a getaway car, while the fourth ran off and stumbled, injuring himself. Police—who had been tipped off beforehand—stopped the car and arrested all inside, but found no burglary tools either in the vehicle or nearby. The mausoleum remained unharmed, and three of the would-be grave robbers were charged with criminal trespassing. All the charges were later dropped.

Some say the grave robbers wanted to prove the tomb was empty because they believed Elvis was still alive. Others say the plan was to hold the body for a $10 million ransom, an echo of Lincoln's and Chaplin's stories. But twenty years later, one of the would-be robbers—a police informant by the name of Ronnie Lee Adkins—told a very different story.

Adkins claimed that the entire plot was cooked up by Vernon Presley in an attempt to prove to the county that Elvis was unsafe in the cemetery. Adkins told his story to FBI special agent Ivian Smith, who published it in his memoirs but said he hadn't been able to confirm it independently. If true, this wouldn't be the first time Vernon had played fast and loose with the law: during the Depression, he'd forged a check on a hog sale and had been carted off to jail. Granted, it would take a uniquely inspired criminal mind to come up with the idea of faking your own son's body-snatching just to get permission to rebury his corpse.

LAST LAUGHS

Groucho Marx died just a few days after Elvis, whose passing overshadowed his own. Five years later, the urn containing Groucho's ashes was stolen from the Eden Memorial Park in Mission Hills, California. It turned up about twelve hours later at the office of Mount Sinai Memorial Park in Glendale, twenty miles away. The crime has never been solved, but detectives from the Los Angeles Police Department guess it was probably a prank. Others say the culprit was an irate cemetery employee, who brought the ashes home to Burbank in defiance of Groucho's line "I would never be caught dead in Burbank."

GERONIMO

BORN: JUNE 1829,
NO-DOYOHN CAÑON, ARIZONA
DIED: FEBRUARY 17, 1909 (AGE 79),
FORT SILL, OKLAHOMA

Today most people know "Geronimo" as a cry hollered by skydivers, bungee jumpers, and small children leaping into swimming pools. But the Apache warrior was once one of the most feared men in the American Southwest, terrorizing residents in modern-day Arizona, Mexico, New Mexico, and Texas with bloody raids that earned him the nickname "The Human Tiger." He was one of the last Native American renegades, battling white settlers who wanted to swallow every inch of Apache land.

Geronimo finally surrendered in September 1886 at Skeleton Canyon, Arizona. He spent the rest of his days as a prisoner of war on a reservation near Fort Sill, Oklahoma, although the government occasionally released him long enough to appear in Wild West shows with Buffalo Bill. When he died, his body was buried in a prisoner of war cemetery on his reservation. His head, however, may be a prisoner somewhere else—at least if the stories about the nation's most notorious secret society are true.

The Order of Skull and Bones is an undergraduate student society at Yale founded in 1832 by William H. Russell and Alphonso Taft, father of US president William H. Taft. The group is often said to be the most powerful secret society in America, preparing its young members to take top posts in politics, law, and finance. Two presidents (both George Bushes) have been Bonesmen, as have an assortment of Supreme Court justices, secretaries of state, national security advisers, and a host of industry titans. Because of its elite connections, the group is a favorite target of conspiracy theorists, who say its members are secretly plotting to control the world (if they don't already).

Like many secret societies, Skull and Bones deliberately surrounds itself with a macabre iconography. Skulls appear not only in the group's name and logo but scattered, reportedly, throughout the halls of its ultrasecure windowless "tomb," or headquarters, in New Haven, Connecticut. The order has a reputation for stealing, and several of the skulls staring down at the tomb's revels are rumored to have been snatched from the graves of famous people, including Martin Van Buren, Che Guevara, and Pancho Villa. However, the skull that has received the most attention is said to belong to Geronimo; rumor has it that the feared Apache warrior's cranium is preserved in a glass case near the front door of the tomb, where all new initiates must kiss it.

The story of Geronimo's skull first came to light in the early 1980s, when the chairman of the San Carlos Apache Nation in Arizona, Ned Anderson, was campaigning to have Geronimo's remains transferred from Oklahoma to Apache ancestral land in Arizona. One day, Anderson received a mysterious letter from an anonymous source who claimed to be a Bonesman. According to the author Alexandra Robbins, who tells the story in her book *Secrets of the Tomb,* the letter said, "What you're seeking is not over at Fort Sill. It is in New Haven, Connecticut, on the Yale University campus."

As if that wasn't weird enough, a little while later

Anderson received a photograph showing a glass case containing a skull, bones, stirrups, and a horse bit. Accompanying the photo was an excerpt from a privately published history of Skull and Bones, written in the 1930s, which included an account of a grave robbery perpetrated by six Bonesmen stationed in Oklahoma during World War I. Among the main characters was Prescott Bush, father and grandfather of the aforementioned presidents.

The excerpt described how Skull and Bones members stationed at the artillery school at Fort Sill had launched a "mad expedition" to dig up the "skull of Geronimo the Terrible." The history quoted from a 1918 logbook, which described how the Bonesmen had used an ax to "pry open the iron door" of Geronimo's tomb. They then dug out the warrior's head, which had "only some flesh inside and a little hair," and cleaned it off with a liberal application of carbolic acid.

Not surprisingly, Anderson was more than a little alarmed by the letter. He arranged a meeting with Jonathan Bush (son of Prescott Bush and brother of George H. W. Bush), as well as Endicott Peabody Davison, descendant of another Bonesman named in the excerpt, and who also happened to be a Skull and Bones lawyer. According to what Anderson told journalists, Bush and Davison denied that Bonesmen had stolen Geronimo's skull, but they presented a glass case resembling the one shown in the photo, complete with a skull inside. However, Bush and Davison said this was no warrior's skull; according to them, it had belonged to an anonymous child. Anderson refused to take the case or the skull, and he also refused to sign papers asking him to keep the whole matter a secret.

Since then, Skull and Bones representatives have dismissed the story as a hoax—when they talk about it at all. But the 2005 discovery of a letter written from one Bonesman to another lends the story some weight. The letter, unearthed by the author Marc Wortman in a Yale library, was written in June 1918 from Winter

Mead to F. Trubee Davison, who was then at home recuperating from injuries sustained while training for war duty. Among other society matters, the letter reported that "The skull of the worthy Geronimo the Terrible, exhumed from its tomb at Fort Sill by your club & the K[nigh]t Haffner, is now safe inside the T[omb] together with his well worn femurs, bit & saddle horn."

Winter Mead was not at Fort Sill himself, and so the letter cannot prove the event occurred. But it does make it seem like Bonesmen in 1918 at least *believed* they had the skull of "Geronimo the Terrible," whether or not they actually did. There is reason to be skeptical: according to Oklahoma historians, Geronimo's grave was unmarked in 1918. Not only was there no "iron door," as described in the logbook's account of the theft, there was nothing there at all. Even today, the grave is marked with a stone pyramid, not a vault with an iron door.

Wortman, a Yale graduate himself, believes that Prescott Bush and his cronies did engage in a bit of skulduggery, but it's more likely they raided someone else's grave. According to Wortman, there are only two graves with tombs at Fort Sill: one belonging to Kiowa chief Kicking Bird, the other to Mark "Thomas" Perconnic of the Comanche Tribe, located a few miles away. The entrance of Perconnic's vault does look suspicious: the bricks don't match those used for the rest of the structure, and appear to fill in what once was a door. It seems plausible that the skull the Bonesmen believed to be Geronimo's in fact belonged to Perconnic, which means the future leaders of America may have been kissing the wrong head all along.

Nevertheless, in 2009 descendants of Geronimo filed a federal suit to get the contents of that glass case back into Apache hands. They were helped by former US attorney general Ramsey Clarke, who said his larger goal was to have all of Geronimo's remains reburied in New Mexico, as the warrior had wished. The lawsuit, which targeted the US government, Yale, and Skull and Bones, sought "to free Geronimo, his remains, funerary objects and spirit, from one hundred years of imprisonment at Ft. Sill, Oklahoma, the Yale University campus at New Haven, Connecticut and wherever else they may be found." The lawsuit was dismissed in 2010 on technical grounds, but some of Geronimo's relatives insist his spirit is still wandering for want of a proper burial. More than a century after losing the fight for his land, they say it's time for Geronimo to finally come home.

WAR AND PIECES

Geronimo was not the only Native American resistance leader to have left a valuable corpse. After the Sauk warrior Black Hawk died of an unspecified illness in Iowa in 1838, a local doctor stole his skeleton and wired it together for display in his office. The governor of the Iowa Territory managed to get the bones back, and installed them—with the permission of the warrior's family—at the Burlington Geographical and Historical Society. The skeleton was destroyed when the building burned down in the mid-1850s.

(Un)Solved
Mysteries

If a man die, shall he live again?

—JOB 14:14

(READ AT JESSE JAMES'S THIRD FUNERAL)

The mysteries of death are usually philosophical. But for some famous figures, they're practical. We don't know who's buried in Columbus's tomb, for example, especially since he has two of them. Jesse James had three graves (and might not have been in any of them), while it took a court case and an exhumation to prove that Lee Harvey Oswald was actually in his. And although we're fairly certain where Edgar Allan Poe lies, we don't know how he ended up dead in the first place, nor do we know the identity of the man who used to bring cognac and roses to his grave each year.

Edgar Allan Poe

Born: January 19, 1809,
Boston, Massachusetts
Died: October 7, 1849 (age 40)
Baltimore, Maryland

Edgar Allan Poe's death is his final mystery. It seems almost too fitting, as if the inventor of the detective story wrote his own ending. If he had, the story would be more outlandish, gruesome, and entertaining. Instead it's just strange and sad, a puzzle that biographers have been trying to solve for more than one hundred fifty years.

The problem with Poe's death is that he disappeared—on September 27, 1849, to be exact, after saying good-bye to his brand-new fiancée in Richmond, Virginia. Poe had been visiting Richmond on a lecture tour, but after rekindling an old romance had decided to stay. He told his fiancée that he would be gone for just a few weeks on a trip to Philadelphia and New York. But the next time anyone saw Poe was six days later in Baltimore, where he was found filthy, nearly unconscious, and wearing someone else's clothes.

On October 3, Poe appeared at Ryan's Tavern on Baltimore's Lombard Street. Some reports say he was drunk out of his mind, while others say he was clearly suffering from some kind of illness. Somehow, a young typesetter named Joseph Walker managed to get Poe talking long enough for the author to mutter the name of someone Walker knew. He then hurriedly wrote the following note:

Dear Sir—

There is a gentleman, rather the worse for wear, at Ryan's 4th ward polls, who goes under the cognomen of Edgar A. Poe, and who appears in great distress, & he says he is acquainted with you, and I assure you, he is in need of immediate assistance.

Yours, in haste, Jos. W. Walker

The note was delivered to one Dr. Snodgrass, an old friend of Poe's who lived close to the tavern. When Snodgrass arrived, he found his friend with a "bloated and unwashed" face, a gaze of "vacant stupidity," and an ill-fitting shirt "sadly crumpled and soiled." Poe had always been a snappy dresser, so this new look was particularly disturbing.

Snodgrass took Poe to Washington College Hospital, but there was little the doctors could do. When admitted, Poe had no idea where he was or who he was with. He soon lapsed into a delirium, conversing with "spectral and imaginary objects on the walls." After a few days of feverish dreaming, he began calling out the name "Reynolds," though no one knows why. After several hours his cries ceased, and on the morning of October 7, he murmured, "Lord help my poor soul." And then, as the *New York Herald* reported, "Death put a period to his existence."

So what happened to Poe? No one can say for sure. There are no reliable reports of his whereabouts on the days between September 27 and October 3. There was no autopsy, all the medical records have been lost, and newspaper articles of the time attributed his death to *mania a potu* (literally "mania from drink") or the usefully vague "congestion of the brain." Today, the popular theory is that Poe simply drank himself to death. But biographers disagree about Poe's alcohol habits; some say even a glass of wine made him ill.

In the beginning, Baltimore didn't do much to commemorate Poe. He was buried in the graveyard of the Westminster Presbyterian Church, but perhaps because of the unseasonably cold weather, the ceremony lasted for only three minutes and was attended by fewer than ten people. There wasn't even a eulogy. A passerby later reported that the ceremony "was so cold and unchristianlike as to provoke on my part a sense of anger difficult to suppress."

To make matters worse, for twenty-five years the grave had no headstone. In 1860, a cousin named Neilson Poe finally ordered one, but it was destroyed when a freight train derailed and ran into the sculptor's yard. Poe's stone was the only one irreparably broken, and his cousin had no funds with which to order a replacement.

The grave had to wait for a proper marker until 1875, when a local fund-raising drive called "Pennies for Poe" raised enough money to erect a marble-and-granite monument. The drive also managed to raise Baltimore's interest in the author, and local officials decided to rebury Poe in the front of the cemetery, alongside the remains of his beloved mother-in-law. In 1913, a headstone decorated with a raven was placed on the site of Poe's original grave.

That's where the second mystery begins. Starting in the 1940s and continuing every year for sixty years, a cloaked figure would steal into the Westminster Church cemetery in the wee hours of the morning on Poe's birthday and hurry to the writer's original grave. Face hidden by a scarf, the visitor would raise a glass of cognac, take a sip, and leave the bottle on the grave alongside three red roses. No one understands the significance of the cognac (amontillado would be more appropriate, given its appearance in Poe's work) but the roses are thought to represent Poe and the two people he is buried with: his wife, Virginia, and his mother-in-law, Maria Clemm.

For decades, the "Poe Toaster" was witnessed each year by a group of dedicated fans who kept an overnight vigil. But no one ever knew who the cloaked figure was. In 2007, the mystery temporarily seemed to have been solved after ninety-two-year-old Westminster Church historian Sam Porpora declared that he was the Toaster. Porpora claimed to have invented the "tradition" in the 1970s as a promotional gimmick for the church, which had then fallen on hard times. But Jeff Jerome, curator of the Poe House in Baltimore, has a collection of newspaper accounts of the Toaster that show the ritual dates back to 1949 (the one-hundredth anniversary of Poe's death). And there are other elements of Porpora's story that don't add up.

Some think that Jerome himself is the Toaster, a claim he vehemently denies. Others think the Toaster could be a distant relative of Poe's, a member of some secret society, or simply a fraternity kid playing an annual prank. To add to the intrigue, in later years the Toaster had a habit of leaving notes: one seemed to reference the Iraq War, while another predicted that the Baltimore Ravens would lose the upcoming Super Bowl—which they won.

The mystery might never be solved, because the Poe Toaster has stopped coming. On Poe's birthday in 2010 the usual crowd gathered overnight at the cemetery, but the man of the hour never arrived. He also failed to show in 2011 and 2012. Journalists speculated that the Toaster had become overwhelmed by the increasingly large gatherings awaiting his visit, but Jerome mentioned another possibility. After the two-hundredth anniversary of Poe's birth in 2009, perhaps it was time for him to rest in the peace that so often eluded him in life. As for the identity of the Poe Toaster, maybe it's as the writer himself once said: "There are some secrets which do not permit themselves to be told."

STUFFED ANIMALS

The raven that inspired Poe's most famous poem is preserved forevermore in a glass case at the Free Library of Philadelphia. "Grip" originally belonged to Charles Dickens, who featured him in his serialized novel *Barnaby Rudge*. Poe reviewed *Barnaby Rudge* in 1841 and 1842, and though he praised the book, he believed the talking bird should have been given a bigger role. Poe never admitted that Dickens's feathered friend inspired *The Raven*, but that's exactly what Poe scholars now believe. When Grip died in 1841 (after nibbling on some lead paint), Dickens had him preserved with arsenic and mounted in a Victorian-style diorama. The display was later sold to Poe collector Colonel Richard Gimbel, who bequeathed his collection to the Free Library. Since 1971, Grip has been keeping watch from the library's third-floor Rare Books Department, near one of Poe's original manuscripts for the poem that made his reputation.

JESSE JAMES

Born: September 5, 1847,
Kearney, Missouri
Died: April 3, 1882 (age 34),
St. Joseph, Missouri (or did he?)

History tells us that Jesse James died while dusting. One hot morning in 1882, the notorious outlaw was in his living room chatting with a new recruit to his gang, Robert Ford, when he noticed a needlepoint picture hanging askew. James stood on a chair to realign it, and as he was polishing the frame, Ford—forever after known as a "dirty little coward"—shot James in the back of the head. He died almost instantly.

James had learned how to rob and murder during the Civil War. He studied at the foot of "Bloody Bill" Anderson, a guerrilla leader who decorated his saddle with Union scalps. After the war ended, Jesse and his brother Frank smarted at the defeat of the South and continued the fight by other means—robbing banks, stagecoaches, and trains in an arc of terror that stretched from Iowa to Texas. It was said that they robbed from the rich and gave to the poor, but there is no evidence they gave to anyone but themselves. Yet the James brothers became heroes to a generation of rural Southern whites who saw them as champions in the fight against Northern oppression.

Many found James's death difficult to believe. The bandit had been reported dead before, and the public was used to a trail of misinformation where James was concerned. But there was something more going on than just commonsense skepticism. In the years to come, more than a dozen men would claim to be the outlaw, saying they had cheated death. Eventually it would require digging up James's grave to find out the truth.

In the days after his death, James's body was brought back to his hometown of Kearney, Missouri, by special train and buried in his mother Zerelda's front yard beneath a coffee bean tree. To replace some of the income she had lost with her son's death, Zerelda turned her house into a James family museum, where for 25 cents the curious could see heirlooms and even pluck a pebble off Jesse's grave.

Zerelda kept watch over the grave for twenty years, but when her health declined, the family decided to move the body to a nearby cemetery. In June 1902, in the middle of a rainstorm that turned the ground slick with mud, James's body was exhumed from Zerelda's yard. Jesse James Jr., the outlaw's son, confirmed the identity of the body by the bullet wound still visible on its face and the gold fillings in its mouth.

Not long after the body escaped Zerelda's watchful eye, the imposters started to appear. One of the earliest was a banker who suddenly arrived in Brownwood, Texas, in the 1880s. He never revealed anything about his life before that date—not even to his own son—and in the years after his death locals whispered that he must have been Jesse James. In the early 1930s another story emerged, about a recluse from the mountains of

Colorado who went by the name of James Sears. Sears loved to quiz townspeople on what they thought of Jesse James, and insisted that the outlaw's death had been a hoax. After he died, a friend revealed that Sears had confessed to being James himself. The physical resemblance was strong enough to convince at least some locals of the tale.

As memory of the real James faded further into the past, his imposters grew more bold. In the autumn of 1931, an old drifter appeared in Excelsior Springs, Missouri, and began telling anyone who would listen that he was Jesse James. The drifter, who also went by the name John James, was convincing enough that he managed to get local officials to accompany him to the capital to ask for a pardon for all the crimes that he, as "Jesse James," had committed. The somewhat perplexed governor refused, but Excelsior Springs residents remained enthralled by the man's claims until Jesse Jr.'s wife, Stella, came to town. Under Stella's questioning, John James failed to remember key details of Jesse's life—such as which of his mother's arms had been blown off years before. As her coup de grace, Stella asked John to try on one of Jesse's boots. The imposter's foot was far too large to fit inside.

John James died in an Arkansas mental institution in December 1947, and just a few months later the most famous—and persistent—of the imposters appeared. Incredibly, J. Frank Dalton claimed to be the one-hundred-year-old Jesse James. Even more incredibly, people believed him. Dalton did seem to know a great deal about James's life, even though some of his stories were riddled with holes. The promoters who flocked to him ascribed these gaps to the memory losses of old age, and exhibited him propped up in his hospital bed at state fairs. In 1950, a promoter named Rudy Turilli arranged what must have been one of the more surreal American scenes of the twentieth century: a 103rd birthday bash for Jesse James, with Dalton as the man of honor. There was at least one other imposter in attendance—an ancient Nashville man claiming to be the one-hundred-six-year-old bandit Cole Younger. (Never mind that Younger was reported dead in 1916.)

Dalton held on to his claim even after death. When he died in Granbury, Texas, in 1951, the Turilli family labeled his tombstone with Jesse James's name and birth date, alongside Dalton's death date and the words "Supposedly killed in 1882." The Turillis also created the Jesse James Wax Museum, which still exists in Stanton, Missouri. There visitors can see life-size wax mannequins of the James family, as well as an exhibit on Jesse James's ears, designed to show their resemblance to Dalton's.

In the 1990s, a George Washington University law and forensic science professor tried to put a stop to the imposters and end the speculation about Jesse James's death. Professor James Starrs had already made a name for himself in the weird world of historical exhumations by presiding over the digging up of Carl Austin Weiss (charged with murdering Louisiana governor Huey Long in 1935) as well as Frank Olson (who jumped out of a window in 1953 after the CIA allegedly dosed him with LSD). With this macabre but useful background, Starrs managed to win the support of the remaining James family members, as well as a court order that allowed him to dig up James's coffin.

Starrs's plan was to use mitochondrial DNA, which is passed down the female line, to test the relationship between the remains buried in the Kearney cemetery and descendants of Jesse's sister, Susan. The analysis would not be able to prove whether the remains in the grave were in fact James's, but they could at least show whether the body in the grave was a descendant of Jesse James's mother, and not some unrelated gang member or random typhoid victim, as several conspiracy theorists had claimed.

The exhumation, carried out in July 1995, soon turned into a three-ring media circus, complete with salesmen hawking "We Dig Jesse" T-shirts and a camera crew banished for drinking beer in the cemetery. Once the dig began, Starrs and his associates discovered that Jesse had been buried in a wooden coffin that had rotted and exposed the bones to groundwater—bad news for the DNA investigation. However, the team was able to pluck several teeth from the remains (teeth are particularly resilient repositories of DNA). They also found a tie pin that appeared to be the same one shown in an 1882 photo of Jesse's corpse, and a bullet from an 1851 Navy revolver, possibly the gun that caused Jesse's chest wound during the Civil War.

Starrs presented his final results from the dig at a February 1996 meeting of the American Academy of Forensic Sciences in Nashville. In addition to the thousands of scientists attending the conference, descendants of Jesse James, J. Frank Dalton, and several other men who had claimed to be Jesse showed up. During his presentation, Starrs revealed that the mitochondrial DNA extracted from the teeth in the grave matched samples taken from Jesse's sister's descendants. In addition, these DNA sequences matched those found in hair samples discovered in James's original grave during a 1978 excavation. In the published version of his results, Starrs concluded, "there is no scientific basis whatsoever for doubting that the exhumed remains are those of Jesse James."

Dalton's supporters left the hotel grumbling. Five years later, they tried to have Dalton's body exhumed for its own set of tests, but they dug up the wrong guy—a fact that became clear once they realized the corpse had only one arm. (The person they exhumed was named William Henry Holland, and his relatives were not amused.) Nevertheless, Dalton's believers have said they will try again to exhume him, just as soon as they can raise the money.

With the advent of the Internet, Dalton has acquired company. In the last few decades, several more people have come forward claiming to be descendants of the "real" Jesse James. There's no shortage of people who want to associate themselves with the iconic outlaw—perhaps his story is just too good to go to his grave.

THE WEIRD WEST: OTHER OUTLAW BODY DOUBLES

Jesse James is not the only bandit who is said to have cheated death. In the years after Billy the Kid was reported dead in 1881, at least twenty men came forward claiming to be him. One of the most famous was "Brushy Bill" Roberts, a central Texas man "discovered" by a probate investigator in 1948. Roberts said he wanted to come clean about his "real" identity so that he could be pardoned for his (the Kid's) crimes before he died. That never happened, but Roberts's tombstone in Hamilton, Texas, does include the words "a.k.a. Billy the Kid." A museum in Hico, Texas, tells his story; its motto is "Where Everybody is Somebody."

Butch Cassidy and the Sundance Kid also died under mysterious circumstances. While many historians believe the pair perished in a 1908 shootout with Bolivian soldiers and police, their bodies were never conclusively identified. Some researchers maintain that both men lived to a ripe old age, and Cassidy's sister said that she enjoyed at least one visit from him after his alleged death (then again, she might have been pulling the reporter's leg). Two skeletons thought to belong to Cassidy and Sundance were exhumed in Bolivia in 1991, but tests showed the bones belonged to some other poor souls.

LEE HARVEY OSWALD

BORN: OCTOBER 18, 1939,
NEW ORLEANS, LOUISIANA
DIED: NOVEMBER 24, 1963 (AGE 24),
DALLAS, TEXAS

If the posthumous reappearances of Jesse James high-light the appeal of the outlaw, the idea that Lee Har-vey Oswald had an imposter throws Cold War paranoia into sharp relief. Among all the theories suggested to explain John F. Kennedy's assassination, involving every-one from the CIA, FBI, and KGB to little green men, the idea that there was more than one Oswald has to be among the most bizarre—and it is the only theory that has led to disturbing the dead.

The notion that there were multiple Oswalds found its most forceful proponent in Michael Eddowes, a wealthy British author, lawyer, and restaurateur. Ed-dowes is best remembered for writing 1955's *The Man on Your Conscience,* in which he argued that a London laborer, Timothy Evans, had been executed for two mur-ders he didn't commit. The book led to a posthumous pardon for Evans, and lent support to the movement to abolish the death penalty in Britain. In 1975, Eddowes came out with *Khrushchev Killed Kennedy,* the first in a trio of books arguing exactly what the title suggests. Al-though it wasn't particularly unusual to suggest that the

Soviets were behind JFK's murder, Eddowes's innovation came in his account of their methods. He suggested that the Soviets had been involved long before that fateful day in Dallas.

Born in 1939, Lee Harvey Oswald spent many of his formative years in Texas, then enlisted in the Marines in 1956. He served for three years before moving to the Soviet Union. At a dance in Minsk he met a Russian woman named Marina Prusakova, whom he married shortly thereafter. He returned to the United States in 1962, with his wife and infant daughter in tow. After a string of menial jobs, the last of which was at the Texas School Book Depository, he shot the president (or so the FBI and the Warren Commission say) on November 22, 1963. Two days later, Oswald himself was shot to death on live television by Dallas underworld figure Jack Ruby.

According to Eddowes, the man Ruby shot was not the same person who had gone to Russia in 1959. Instead, after Oswald's arrival the Soviets had trained a KGB agent to assume his identity. This agent was the man who met and married Marina, then returned to the United States and killed the president. (It's unclear what was supposed to have happened to the real Oswald, but it probably wasn't pleasant.) Eddowes also claimed that the US government was aware of the conspiracy, but had chosen not to share its knowledge to avoid triggering World War III. For Eddowes, the imposture and its cover-up were part of a series of delicate and potentially deadly maneuvers between the Soviets and the United States, which arose as part of the fallout from the Cuban Missile Crisis.

The evidence Eddowes presented to support his theory, laid out in his 1977 book *The Oswald File,* was largely circumstantial. He noted that passport and Marine Corps application papers created before Oswald went to Russia listed his height as 5'11", while documents created after he returned reported his height as 5'9". Marina, when she met Oswald in Minsk, had at first believed she was speaking to a native Russian with a

Baltic accent. Upon Oswald's return from Russia, family members noted that he had lost some hair and weight, while his complexion appeared more ruddy. His autopsy records failed to match his Marine Corps records regarding the number and position of scars on his arms, and also failed to make note of a prominent scar from a childhood wound behind one of his ears.

(Eddowes wasn't the first to suggest there might have been more than one Oswald; government officials, including J. Edgar Hoover, had raised the possibility of an Oswald imposter before. But when the House Select Committee on Assassinations looked into photos of Oswald pre- and post-Soviet Union, forensic investigators felt sure they were the same person. For one thing, fingerprints taken before and after Oswald's trip to Russia matched up, although Eddowes explained this by saying the Soviets surreptitiously switched fingerprint files.)

For Eddowes, the best way to test his theory was to open up Oswald's grave. If the body in the coffin matched up with Oswald's Marine Corps records, all would be well. If not, the public had a right to know what was going on. Eddowes himself seemed pretty sure there would be a surprise in store. He told one BBC reporter, "[From] the documentary evidence as it stands today, the body in the grave should be that of an imposter."

Eddowes had a difficult time convincing Texas officials of his case. He initially approached the Medical Examiner's Office in Tarrant County, where Oswald was buried, but when his requests were denied he turned to Dallas County, where Oswald had been killed. Having managed to win over officials there, he triggered a six-month legal battle concerning which county had jurisdiction over Oswald's remains. The situation was more or less at a standstill when Eddowes gained the support of Marina Oswald, Lee Harvey's widow and legal next of kin. She agreed to go forward with the exhumation as a private case, with Eddowes to pay all of the expenses.

Marina had her own suspicions about the grave. Her concern stemmed from a 1964 visit by government officials, who asked her to sign a stack of papers without explaining what they meant. She knew that the papers had something to do with the grave, but not exactly what, and the odd encounter led her to believe that Oswald's remains had somehow been disturbed. Oswald's brother Robert battled in court to stop the exhumation, but eventually ran out of emotional and financial resources to continue the fight. On October 4, 1981, the exhumation at the Rose Hill Cemetery finally began. Eddowes would soon have his answers.

Once the digging started, it became clear that Oswald's concrete vault had cracked, and water damage had caused the casket lid to partially cave in, exposing the remains. The exhumation team had hoped to transport the entire vault to the Baylor Medical Center in Dallas, but its dilapidated condition persuaded them to remove only the coffin. Once the body arrived at Baylor, the exhumation team—led by Assistant Dallas County Medical Examiner Linda E. Norton—conducted a brief examination, which found the body in an advanced state of decomposition. But that didn't particularly matter, because the only thing they really needed was the corpse's head. The plan was to take a set of dental X-rays and compare them to a set produced while Oswald was in the Marines. The team also wanted to look for a small crater behind one of the corpse's ears, to see if it matched records of the scar left by Oswald's childhood mastoidectomy (a procedure used to repair skull damage after an ear infection).

The forensic odontologists who compared the corpse's teeth to Oswald's dental X-rays found that three of the teeth in the corpse's skull were exactly the same shape as in the documents, while three other teeth were very similar; the pulpal anatomy also showed comparable formation. In addition, the mastoidectomy scar was clearly present on the left side of the skull. At a press conference a few hours later, Norton stepped before the microphone and announced, "We, both individually and as a team, have concluded beyond any doubt, and I mean beyond any doubt, that the individual buried under the name Lee Harvey Oswald in Rose Hill Cemetery is, in fact, Lee Harvey Oswald."

Marina said she was happy to finally have some answers, and wanted to go on with her life. Eddowes, ever the gentleman, issued a statement saying that he was "surprised" by the results, but "in no way disappointed in the apparent disproving of my evidence of imposture."

Still, not everyone was convinced the body was Oswald's. During the examination at Baylor, Paul Groody—the mortician who had prepared Oswald for burial in 1963—had been asked to verify whether the body in the coffin was the same one he'd embalmed. At the time he agreed that it was, but later he had his doubts. A few days after the exhumation, Groody was discussing the events with his assistant, Alan Baumgartner, when both men realized they hadn't seen a key detail on the corpse's head. Neither had noticed the craniotomy line, a crevice created when morticians saw off the top of the skull to examine the brain. Both were sure that a craniotomy had been performed on Oswald in 1963, and indeed his brain weight is recorded on his autopsy report, which means doctors had to access his gray matter somehow. Yet neither Groody nor his assistant could remember seeing the telltale mark.

Groody shared his concerns with assassination researchers, and together they developed a theory that makes Eddowes's look uninspired. While Groody agrees that the *body* buried in Oswald's grave was the same one he embalmed, he's not so sure about the *head*. He thinks that the KGB, CIA, FBI, or someone else dug up the corpse in Oswald's grave before the 1981 exhumation, cut off the head, and replaced it with Oswald's real noggin, presumably rescued from somewhere in Russia. Fittingly, this is known as the "head in a box" theory.

This idea generated quite a bit of comment among conspiracy theorists, and debate was encouraged by the fact that it took three years for the Norton team to publish the official account of their work in a medical journal. In 1984, their report finally appeared in the *Journal of Forensic Sciences,* complete with a lovely photo of Oswald's rotting jaw. Among other observations, the report noted that the corpse's neck column was entirely intact, making any head switch unlikely. More importantly, the report said that the craniotomy line was evident on the skullcap, which was covered by patches of "mummified soft tissue." Today, some assassination researchers think that Groody and Baumgartner simply failed to notice the craniotomy mark during their brief time in the examination room.

But true conspiracy buffs know there's no reason to let evidence stand in the way of a good theory. The Internet and bookstores are rife with reports that the craniotomy mark was missing, or that the head was found rolling around inside the coffin. It's tempting to suggest that the authors of those theories reread Dr. Norton's article—but of course, she might be in on the conspiracy, too. Even though Oswald is long dead, the theories about his crimes have taken on a life of their own.

CHRISTOPHER COLUMBUS

BORN: *CA.* 1451
GENOA, ITALY (MAYBE)
DIED: MAY 20, 1506 (AGE 54),
VALLADOLID, SPAIN

Where did Christopher Columbus come from, and where did he go? Historians have long debated whether the man who "discovered" America was Genoese, Catalonian, Portuguese, or some combination thereof. We call the lands he found "America," but Columbus died believing he'd explored the Indies. The location of his final resting place is just as muddled: his bones might be in the New World, or they might be in the Old; they might even be in both places at once.

Columbus died (perhaps from complications of reactive arthritis) feeling like he'd been cheated out of his fair share of New World riches. Some say he wanted to be buried in the Americas just to spite the Spanish king, but that's not clear; his wills are as muddled as everything else about the man.

What we do know is that Columbus was first buried in a Franciscan monastery in the Castilian city of Valladolid, then transferred to another monastery in Seville in 1513. Around 1540, his daughter-in-law Maria moved his remains, as well as those of her husband, Diego, to the cathedral in Santo Domingo, capital of the modern-day Dominican Republic and the first permanent European settlement in the New World.

Unfortunately, the island of Hispaniola, which includes both Haiti and the Dominican Republic, has never been the most stable place in terms of either politics or plate tectonics. In the years after Columbus's burial, the Cathedral of Santo Domingo was plagued by pirates, earthquakes, poverty, and hordes of insects that chewed precious documents into lace. Any official record of Columbus's burial not gobbled by hungry ants was probably destroyed when the British privateer Sir Francis Drake raided the city in 1586.

Santo Domingo suffered yet another upheaval in 1795, when Spain ceded Hispaniola to France's republican troops. Unwilling to let Columbus's bones fall into foreign hands, the Spanish took his remains with them to their new headquarters in Havana. The commander of the Spanish fleet in the Caribbean took charge of the excavations, and after digging beneath the high altar, where the explorer's bones were long believed to rest, workers discovered a stone vault with bones and ashes inside. The commander and other Spanish officials deemed these the last earthly remains of Christopher Columbus, locked them in a gilt box, and sent them to the cathedral in Havana.

But when Cuba won its independence from Spain in 1898, poor Columbus was unearthed yet again, and shipped back to Seville—almost right where he started. His bones were reburied in the massive Cathedral of Seville, the largest Gothic cathedral in the world, where his elaborately carved tomb is held high by four ghostly figures.

At least that's the story the Spanish tell. Tourists in the Dominican Republic hear a different tale. That account goes back to 1877, the year a bishop at the Cathedral of Santo Domingo announced the discovery of a mysterious casket right next to where the bones deemed by the Spanish to be Columbus's had been unearthed in 1795. And unlike those bones, these ones came with labels.

The newly discovered casket included several inscriptions that seemed to reference Columbus, including one that said, *"Illtre. y Esdo Varon Don Cristoval Colon,"* which has been extrapolated and translated to "Illustrious and distinguished male, Don Christopher Columbus." The box was also marked with the letters "D. de la A. P$^{er.}$ A$^{te.}$" and "C.C.A.," which some say represent the Spanish for "Discoverer of America, First Admiral" and "Admiral Christopher Columbus." The casket also contained a small silver plate, engraved with words that have been translated as "Last of the remains of the first admiral, Sir Christopher Columbus, discoverer."

To Santo Domingo bishop Roque Cocchia, the situation was clear: the Spaniards had taken the wrong bones in 1795. Instead of moving Christopher Columbus to Havana, the Spanish had accidentally taken the body buried next to him. If Cocchia's story is true, the bones inside the elaborate tomb in Seville may belong to the great explorer's son Diego—a fine man, but not the one who "discovered" America.

The news from Santo Domingo in 1877 delighted the residents of the Dominican Republic, who felt blessed to have the bones of the world's most famous explorer in their midst. But Spanish scholars attacked Cocchia's claims, calling him an imposter who had committed a "pious fraud." Several were particularly critical of the inscriptions on the rediscovered casket, which don't seem like sixteenth-century products in either substance or style. But that's no guarantee of the date for the bones inside, since Columbus may have received a new casket during his long interment.

Fraud or not, Cocchia asked governments around the world to contribute funds for a monument to Columbus's true resting place. The monument was only completed in 1992—more than a century after the initial discovery of the bones, and just in time for the five-hundredth anniversary of Columbus's famed voyage. The remains that the Dominicans insist belong to Columbus now rest in the Columbus Memorial Lighthouse in Santo Domingo, a giant building that stretches for several city blocks and beams light in the shape of a cross into the night sky.

Yet the Spanish still maintain they have the real Columbus. In 2003, Spanish geneticists launched a project to use DNA testing to settle the questions about Columbus's origin and remains. But despite swabbing six hundred people in Italy, France, and Spain with last names similar to "Columbus," the scientists failed to find a conclusive match that would prove the explorer's ancestry. In 2006, they did manage to extract enough mitochondrial DNA from the bones in Seville to make a connection between Columbus and the undisputed bones of one of his brothers, who was also buried in Seville. The tests proved the bones definitely belonged to siblings, but there was no way to prove whether the mystery bones came from Columbus himself.

And there was a twist. When the scientists opened the tomb in Seville, they found only about 20 percent of a skeleton inside. That means that even if the bones there do belong to Columbus, the rest of him could lie elsewhere—perhaps in the Dominican Republic. In fact, a Yale orthopedic surgeon who studied the bones in Santo Domingo in 1960 noted that some of them were missing. To date, no one has determined whether the bones in Seville are the missing ones, but it may be that Columbus is divided between the Old World and the New.

In the absence of proof, anything seems possible. The Italian journalist and historian Gianni Granzotto has written of a theory that the Franciscan monks of Valladolid never gave up Columbus in the first place, and kept him buried in their monastery's crypt. Today the monastery houses a popular café, and the crypt has been transformed into a billiards hall—with bodies still supposedly buried beneath it. Perhaps the body of the world's most famous explorer never went traveling after all.

PARTS UNKNOWN

The Spanish painter Francisco Goya died in 1828 while in self-imposed exile in France. In 1901, the Spanish government decided to rebury him beneath the Church of San Antonio de la Florida in Madrid, whose frescoes Goya had painted. But when the Spanish consul to France had Goya exhumed, he found two skeletons in the grave—and only one skull. He dispatched a telegraph to Madrid, saying: "Goya skeleton without a head. Please instruct me." The ministry replied, "Send Goya, with or without head." Unable to tell which of the bones belonged to the great artist, the consul had the whole jumble of remains exhumed—and reburied together in Madrid.

D. H. LAWRENCE

BORN: SEPTEMBER 11, 1885,
EASTWOOD, NOTTINGHAMSHIRE,
ENGLAND
DIED: MARCH 2, 1930 (AGE 44),
VENCE, FRANCE

D. H. Lawrence, the British author who scandalized the English-speaking world with *Lady Chatterley's Lover,* died of tuberculosis in the south of France. He left behind neither a current will nor any instructions for his final resting place, but his widow, Frieda, felt certain that he had wanted to be buried at their ranch near Taos, New Mexico. Since she knew that transporting the body back to America wouldn't be an easy task, she first buried Lawrence in the small cemetery of the town where he died. His headstone bore an image of a phoenix, Lawrence's personal symbol, created with colored pebbles.

It would be five years before Lawrence made his way back to America—if he ever did at all. The man in charge of bringing Lawrence home was Angelo Ravagli, Frieda's second husband, whose affair with the formidable Frieda (begun some years earlier) likely formed the inspiration for *Lady Chatterley's Lover*. Ravagli left his wife and children for Frieda, but made periodic trips back home to Italy to visit his old household, and it was during one of these trips that Frieda asked Ravagli to bring Lawrence back home.

That's when the trouble started. First Ravagli had to tussle with French authorities to get permission to exhume Lawrence's body and transport it to Marseille, where it was cremated in March 1935. The following month, Ravagli accompanied the ashes, stored in an urn, on a steamer that sailed from Villefranche, France, to New York. But Ravagli was never sure he'd successfully navigated all the red tape required to take human remains out of France, and when he disembarked in Manhattan, it was clear he was not going to have an easy time at customs.

Officials looked askance at this foreigner bringing in a funerary urn on a tourist visa—Ravagli had nothing more permanent, since he had yet to marry Frieda. (Some biographers have also suggested that the officials wanted no part of Lawrence in their country, alive or dead, since his works had been banned.) The customs agents seized the urn, and only returned it after a family friend, photographer Alfred Stieglitz, intervened to help cut the red tape. No one knows exactly what Stieglitz did, but in a letter to the painter Dorothy Brett a few months after the events, he wrote, "Some day I'll tell you the whole story. Nothing quite like it has ever happened. Angelo really has no idea of what did happen."

Neither do we. To complicate matters, after Frieda's death Ravagli confessed to a friend, the Baron Prosper de Haulleville, over drinks in Taos that he had gotten so fed up with the bureaucracy and fees that he had never brought Lawrence over at all. Instead, he scattered the author's ashes in the ocean. He then transported the empty urn to New York, where he refilled it with ordinary ash. If that's true, Stieglitz rescued the remains not of a legendary writer, but of a fireplace.

In any event, after arriving in New York, the urn that was supposed to contain Lawrence's ashes accompanied Ravagli on a four-day train trip to New Mexico. At the end of it, Ravagli and his precious (or not) cargo detrained at Lamy, the nearest station stop to Taos, where they were met by Frieda and a pack of friends. Local legend says that the crowd was so overjoyed to see Ravagli after his six-month absence that they forgot the urn on the station platform. They were almost at Santa Fe when they realized what they had left behind, and doubled back to retrieve it.

But what was inside? A variant of the legend says that Lawrence's friend Witter Bynner, a poet who lived nearby, retrieved the ashes instead; he returned the urn to Frieda but kept the contents for himself, stirring a teaspoon of them into his tea each morning so that he might absorb some of Lawrence's genius.

Frieda maintained that she took the rescued urn on to Santa Fe, where the party stopped because it was then too dark to continue. The group held a festive welcome-home dinner party at the La Fonda Hotel, where yet another story has it that Bynner accidentally spilled the ashes into the food. After their (possibly cannibalistic) repast, the party journeyed on to stay the night at the house of Nicolai Fechin, an artist and Russian émigré. But when the group departed for home the next morning, they forgot the urn. Again.

Once back in Frieda's possession, the urn became the subject of a fierce disagreement between the former Mrs. Lawrence, Dorothy Brett, and Mabel Dodge Luhan, a wealthy patron of the arts who had brought the Lawrences to Taos and given them their ranch. All seemed to feel they had some claim to Lawrence and his memory, but they had very different ideas about what should be done with his ashes.

Frieda felt that Lawrence should be buried in a shrine Ravagli had constructed on their ranch, but Brett and Luhan thought the white plaster building was ghastly, and worried that Frieda planned to charge admission. "Is a mausoleum looking like a station toilet a fitting resting place?" Brett wrote to one friend. They felt that it would be far more dignified to scatter Lawrence's ashes over his ranch.

Apparently, Luhan and Brett concocted several plans to steal the ashes, although at other times they maintained the whole thing was a big joke. Brett wrote to Stieglitz, "Shall I steal the ashes and place them in a tree where they will never be found?" But she also later said, "I don't believe any of us took it very seriously . . . Most of it, believe me, was talk." Nevertheless, some visitors to the Lawrence ranch remember loud arguments among the three women over the issue of Lawrence's resting place.

A rumor later arose that Luhan stole the ashes and scattered them in the wind, replacing them with ashes from her hearth, and that Brett then stole *these* ashes and scattered them in the mountains near the ranch, replacing them with either piñon dust from her stove or the ashes of a dead dog.

It's not clear how much of this got back to Frieda, but she certainly knew enough to be concerned. So she came up with an ingenious solution: she mixed the ashes with concrete and used the resulting slab as the altar of the small memorial chapel on the ranch. In September 1935 Frieda presided over a dedication ceremony for the building, with local Native Americans performing a ritual dance around a fire at sunset. While it's true the event may have dedicated a chapel holding hearth ashes, piñon dust, or the remains of a dog, Frieda still believed the place was sacred. When she died at age seventy-seven after a stroke, her own body was buried just outside of it.

BODY

POLITICS

Alas, I suppose I am becoming a god.
—THE ROMAN EMPEROR VESPASIAN (9–79),
ON HIS DEATHBED

A dead political leader is an opportunity for major propaganda—just take a look at Lenin, whose mummified body has been on display in Moscow since the 1920s. But when regimes fail, things can get complicated. Consider the fate of Argentina's former first lady Eva Perón, perhaps the only corpse that deserves its own passport. The bodies of rebels and insurgents have also taken strange journeys: the location of Che Guevara's bones was a secret for decades, while the treatment of Osama bin Laden's corpse caused international controversy. And you don't have to be political in life to have a political postmortem—ask the family of athlete Jim Thorpe, who are fighting to have his body removed from the town named after his corpse.

**ALEXANDER
THE GREAT**

BORN: July 356 BCE,
Pella, Macedonia
DIED: CA. June 10, 323 BCE (AGE 32),
Babylon

Alexander the Great didn't like to think of himself as a mere mortal. After all, his mother said she was descended from the hero Achilles, and his father claimed descent from the hero Heracles and the god Dionysus. Alexander certainly must have *felt* immortal—in all his campaigns across the restive Persian Empire, the deserts of Egypt, and the mountains of the Punjab, he never once lost a battle. He once said that the only things that reminded him he was mortal were sex and sleep.

But Alexander was made of flesh and blood, and his mummy would go on to help establish a dynasty. As the creator of the largest empire the world had ever seen, he had the world's first truly famous political corpse. But like everything else about Alexander's life, the story of his body is steeped in myth and legend. Little of it can be considered irrefutable fact, although we can construct an outline.

In the spring of 323 BCE, during an all-night revel in Babylon, Alexander fell ill. Some sources say he sickened suddenly and with a piercing cry (which makes it sound like he was poisoned), while others record that he withered slowly from a fever (which makes it sound like he contracted a tropical disease). The Romans said he simply had too much to drink.

As Alexander lay there sweating, his generals must have eyed each other uneasily. There was no clear heir to the throne, and in this warrior culture, succession was decided by battle. Perhaps noticing their glances, Alexander is said to have slipped off his signet ring and handed it to his senior bodyguard, Perdiccas. But when another general bent down low and asked Alexander to whom he was leaving his empire, the dying conqueror whispered "*tôi kratistôi*"—"to the strongest." As the sun set over Babylon, he slipped from this world to the next.

Alexander must have known that his generals would fight to control his empire, but he couldn't have expected his corpse to become part of their prize. After his death, tensions ran so high he wasn't even given a funeral. The Egyptian embalmers brought to mummify his corpse—a first for a Macedonian ruler—were afraid to touch his body because it still seemed so fresh, radiating vigor and strength. But eventually they went to work, removing his organs and smearing him with resins. For two years Alexander's mummy lay in state in the palace of Nebuchadnezzar in Babylon, while his generals waged wars of succession that stretched across three continents.

The man who would take control of Alexander's corpse is known as Ptolemy—not the early Greek mathematician and scientist, but a childhood friend of Alexander's who had become his second most important bodyguard, after Perdiccas. Though not necessarily the smartest or the strongest of Alexander's men, Ptolemy was perhaps the most shrewd. He understood that no man but Alexander could sustain his vast empire, and set his sights on ruling only Alexander's richest prize: Egypt.

To do that, Ptolemy needed to prove his legitimacy to the Egyptians. In Macedonian culture, burial of the old ruler conferred power upon the new one, a fact that was doubly true in the afterlife-obsessed nation of Egypt. Furthermore, Alexander was worshipped as a god in some parts of Asia, and Ptolemy knew that his tomb would become a site of pilgrimage for seekers and soldiers alike.

An apocryphal tale has it Ptolemy was also influenced by a prophecy from the seer Aristander, who said that the land that possessed Alexander's bones would be unvanquished forever. Too bad the prophecy didn't come true: Ptolemy's dynasty lasted only until Cleopatra was bitten by an asp—ancient Egypt's last hurrah before Roman domination.

While Perdiccas was off fighting a minor battle, Ptolemy cozied up to the Macedonian official in charge of building Alexander's hearse, which looked like a magnificent temple on wheels. Already the governor of Egypt, Ptolemy convinced the official to bring the glittering hearse and its precious cargo to his base of operations in the ancient city of Memphis. When Perdiccas found out about the move he chased after the hearse, but his attempt to invade Memphis failed miserably, and he ended up stabbed to death by his own men.

With the body safely in Memphis, Ptolemy set about burnishing the cult of Alexander. With the help of a high-ranking Egyptian priest, Ptolemy created a new deity called Serapis, a fusion of Osiris, the sacred bull Apis, and Greek gods such as Zeus. The worship of Serapis was linked to the worship of Alexander, not least because Alexander was said to have called out to Serapis on his deathbed. Ptolemy ordered the creation of new temples, a new liturgy, and a new priesthood, all dedicated to the new god. Alexander's body may have even been buried near the entrance to the Serapeum, a temple that served as a vast necropolis housing the mummified remains of thousands of sacred bulls.

Alexander's body stayed in Memphis for two decades, before Ptolemy (or possibly his son) transferred it to Alexandria, the city Alexander had founded. There Alexander's tomb—often called the *soma* (Greek for "body") or *sema* (for "tomb")—became a fixture of antiquity. Legend has it that one of the Ptolemies replaced the gold coffin with glass, giving visitors a clear view of the mummy inside, and foreshadowing the tactics to be used in Lenin's display almost two millennia later. The tomb was a required stop for Roman emperors looking for an image boost: both Julius Caesar and Augustus visited, the latter accidentally knocking off Alexander's nose when he bent to kiss the corpse. Caligula was worse: he stole Alexander's breastplate to wear while parading around Rome, but justified the desecration by claiming to be Alexander reincarnated.

Caligula's visit is the last one historians are certain occurred. As the first millennium stretched on, Alexandria's status as a pearl of the ancient world declined, and in 365 CE, a ferocious earthquake and tsunami struck the city. No source records the destruction of the tomb, but that is no guarantee it survived. Around 400 CE, John Chrysostom (the Archbishop of Constantinople) poked fun at the pagans by writing, "Tell me, where is the tomb of Alexander? Show me, tell me the day on which he died." The city lapsed into ruins, a silence that echoed for centuries.

Alexander's tomb has since become one of the most sought-after objects in archaeology. Several times a century, someone claims to have found it. One of the most notable discoveries occurred after Napoleon's invasion of Alexandria in 1798, when French archaeologists found a green stone sarcophagus that locals said had once held Alexander's body. But once the Rosetta Stone unlocked the secrets of Egyptian hieroglyphs a few years later, scholars realized that the sarcophagus had been created for Nectanebo II, the last native pharaoh before the Ptolemies took over.

Today, the modern city of Alexandria overlaps only

in part with the city of Ptolemy's day, which lies partially underwater. Nevertheless, Egyptian authorities are regularly contacted by both amateurs and experts who say they know where Alexander's tomb is. Many still remember the enthusiasm of Stelios Koumoutsos, a Greek café waiter who lived in Alexandria during the 1950s and 1960s. Koumoutsos was just one of the so-called fools of Alexander, ordinary people who searched obsessively for the tomb in the mid-twentieth century. None of them got very far, but Koumoutsos in particular was noted for his determination, which extended to borrowing vast sums of money for (frequently unauthorized) digs around the city. Toward the end of his life, Koumoutsos finally decided he'd had enough, and offered to turn over all of his information to a patron in exchange for a pension and a Mercedes. Given that an empire was built on Alexander's remains, that could be a small price to pay.

Ancient Remains

The great Roman statesman, philosopher, and orator Cicero suffered a particularly grisly fate after his death in 43 BCE. As a champion of republicanism, he opposed both the despotic Julius Caesar and Marc Antony, who he thought was trying to take Caesar's place. In response Antony had Cicero declared an enemy of the state, hunted down, and murdered. Cicero faced his death valiantly: caught by a group of soldiers, he is said to have offered his neck and declared, "There is nothing proper about what you are doing, but at least try to cut off my head properly." The soldiers complied, and also sliced off his hands, on Antony's orders. Both head and hands were sent back to Rome and nailed above the speaker's platform in the Forum as a warning against further public criticism.

The Roman emperor Valerian was also noted for his unfortunate end. After a failed campaign against the Persian king Shapur I, he was captured and humiliated by being exposed to the crowds. From then on, whenever the king mounted his horse, he would use Valerian's neck as his stepping stool. Some say Valerian grew so tired of his humiliation that he offered to raise a huge ransom, but Shapur decided to pour molten gold down his throat instead, killing him. The Persian king then had his skin stuffed with straw and his body displayed in a Persian temple, where it stayed for many years, being given a proper burial only after a subsequent Roman invasion.

The first emperor of China, Shi Huangdi, is known for uniting his country, building much of the Great Wall, and constructing a lavish tomb for himself, complete with thousands of terra-cotta warriors. He died while traveling, and his chief minister, Li Si, became so concerned about the potentially destabilizing effect of his death that he hid it from the traveling party until they returned to the capital. During the two-month journey home, he visited the emperor's carriage daily (pretending as if the two were still having meetings), kept the shades pulled low, and ordered carts of rotten fish pulled before and after the carriage to disguise the corpse's smell.

VLADIMIR LENIN

BORN: APRIL 22, 1870,
SIMBIRSK, RUSSIA
DIED: JANUARY 21, 1924 (AGE 53),
GORKI, RUSSIA

Since 1924, Lenin's mummified body has been on display in a mausoleum in the middle of Moscow's Red Square. Even though he's soaked in formaldehyde and looks a little like a waxy prop from a Vincent Price film, lines of tourists still wait to visit him each day. He's the world's most famous political corpse and one of its most macabre tourist attractions. And though he wanted his political philosophy to live on forever, none of this was his idea.

Lenin's dying wish was to be buried simply near his mother and sister in St. Petersburg. As a dedicated atheist, he hated anything that smacked of religion, including the "worship" of human remains. But one of the many unfortunate things about being dead is that you no longer have a say over your body, and after Lenin died, Stalin turned his corpse into the ultimate piece of Communist propaganda.

When Lenin passed away at his country estate in Gorki (following a massive stroke), peasants poured in from across the snowy countryside to pay their respects. In Moscow, half a million visitors braved days-long lines and a vicious cold snap to see the founder of the Soviet Union lying in state at the Moscow Trade Union House. In fact, so many people came to see Lenin's corpse that a funeral scheduled for five days after his death had to be postponed. Scholars say the rituals drew on a tradition of visiting the tsar's remains after death—usually the only time a Russian leader and his subjects would ever come face-to-face.

On the day set for Lenin's funeral, party newspaper *Izvestiya* announced that "in accordance with the wishes expressed by many workers and peasants," party leaders had decided on the "long-term preservation" of Lenin's body. Other records show that Stalin suggested embalming Lenin even before he passed away, despite vehement opposition from both the family of the deceased and the commissar of health.

While not quite the political genius Lenin had been, Stalin knew that the fledgling Bolshevik regime needed any symbol it could find to create and sustain an emotional bond with the populace. The remains of Lenin, who was already the subject of a personality cult before his death, fit the bill perfectly. Russians were used to worshipping the remains of Orthodox saints, and it wasn't that much of a stretch to revere the dead body of a political leader—especially if that body did not decay. In both the Catholic and Eastern Orthodox churches, bodies of holy men and women that stay fresh after death—known as "incorruptibles"—are seen as evidence of divine grace. And while the Church was banished under Soviet communism, many of its ancient ideas remained. Consciously or not, Stalin likely hoped to capitalize on the reverence associated with ever-fresh corpses.

But absent an act of God, preserving a body permanently is no easy task. Lenin's first embalming, meant to last only until his funeral, began to fail as the weather turned warmer. Scientists called to examine his remains noticed dark splotches spreading across his skin, his mouth beginning to gape open, and his half-open eyes sinking back into their sockets. After seeing the decay, some of them told the Bolshevik brass that a permanent embalming was all but impossible.

In northeastern Ukraine, anatomy professor Vladimir Vorobyov heard about the scientists' remarks and told colleagues he disagreed. After all, his laboratory was filled with pickled anatomy specimens that had been sitting on his shelves for decades. Why couldn't the same preservation process he used be applied to an entire human body?

In those days Big Brother was always listening, and it wasn't long before Vorobyov found himself ordered to report to Lenin's "Immortalization Commission" in Moscow. His team of skilled embalmers labored over Lenin's corpse for four months in a dank cellar beneath a temporary mausoleum. The stakes were high: if they bungled the body, they could end up in the gulag—or worse.

Ilya Zbarsky, son of one of the embalmers (and eventually in charge of the corpse himself), later described the preservation process in a book called *Lenin's Embalmers*. According to Zbarksy, Lenin's inner organs were removed, his tissues fixed with a solution of formaldehyde and water, and his body washed clean with acetic acid. Next, cotton wool saturated with formaldehyde was pressed all over the corpse. Then Lenin took a series of baths in formaldehyde, alcohol, glycerin, and potassium acetate, with incisions made in his skin and muscles to help absorb the fluid. Lastly, the embalmers added fake eyeballs to keep the sockets from sinking, and sewed the eyes and lips shut. When the process was complete, Lenin's brother said the dead leader looked "as he did when we saw him a few hours after his death— perhaps even better."

Lenin's embalmed corpse went on display in a temporary mausoleum in August 1924, and was moved to the mausoleum tourists see today—a black and red constructivist wonder resembling an ancient Mayan temple—in 1930. The body has left the building only once: in 1941, it was whisked away to the tiny Siberian town of Tiumen for several years to keep it safe from the Nazis. For a time, Lenin's preserved brain was also on display alongside his body, but it now rests (in over thirty thousand tiny sections) farther down the street at the Moscow Brain Institute, near the brains of Stalin, Tchaikovsky, and the famous dissident Andrei Sakharov.

Since the fall of communism, a private firm called Ritual Service has taken care of Lenin's corpse. They are public about the upkeep it requires: an examination every Monday and Friday, a rubdown with antibacterial solution weekly, and a one-month-long beauty bath in potassium and glycerin every eighteen months. The maintenance is no longer state-funded, but supported by private donations and the freelance work Ritual Service performs for Moscow's deceased gangsters and nouveaux riches. Yet not everyone is sure Lenin's corpse is real: some scientists believe the necessary chemicals simply weren't available to the Bolsheviks of the 1920s, and the embalmers probably substituted a lifelike wax dummy. Zbarsky's account makes that seem unlikely.

In recent years, there has been a lot of talk about putting Lenin to rest six feet under, chemicals and all. It makes sense: he's the embodiment (literally) of a political system that many believe failed miserably. But when Boris Yeltsin tried to bury Lenin he was defeated by old-guard Communists, and successive leaders have refused to take action. Polling has shown that most Russians want Lenin below ground, but there seems to be a political reluctance toward making that happen. In 2001, Vladimir Putin said, "Many people in this country associate their lives with the name of Lenin. To take Lenin out and bury him would say to them that they have worshipped false values, that their lives were lived in vain."

Still, there's a vague sense in Russia today that the nation can't get back on track until Lenin's body is safely buried. At times, the sentiment seems mystical. In 1998 a liberal Russian politician, Boris Nemtsov, told a reporter he had a "feeling that as long as we don't bury Lenin, Russia is under an evil spell."

BLOOD(LESS) BROTHERS

Lenin would roll over in his grave—assuming he had one—if he knew that his permanently preserved corpse had started an international trend. In the decades after his death, the embalming process used to keep him forever young (or at least, forever middle-aged) became the procedure of choice for dead Communist leaders. In many cases, their preservations were carried out by the staff at Lenin's mausoleum, creating one of the world's strangest, and most exclusive, international clubs.

The first Communist leader so preserved was Georgi Dimitrov, the premier of Bulgaria, who died in office in 1949 while receiving medical treatment near Moscow. After his death, he was loaded onto a train with a team of Russian embalmers, who preserved his corpse in Bulgaria as a gift. His body went on display in the Georgi Dimitrov Mausoleum in Sofia, where it stayed until 1990, when the fall of communism removed his successors from office and his body from show. He was cremated and buried in a nearby cemetery.

In 1953, Stalin died and got the Lenin Mausoleum treatment himself. His embalmed body lay on display beside Lenin's in the Red Square mausoleum until 1961, when Khrushchev's de-Stalinization program kicked into high gear and the party decided the arrangement was "no longer appropriate." Stalin's remains were removed from the mausoleum in secret on October

31, 1961, and cremated, his ashes buried beneath the Kremlin wall.

Morticians at the Lenin Mausoleum have also applied their skills to the bodies of Czech Communist leader Klement Gottwald (died 1953, removed from display and cremated in 1956); Vietnamese leader Ho Chi Minh (died 1969, still on display in Hanoi); Angolan president Agostinho Neto (died 1979, buried 1992); Guyanese despot Linden Forbes Burnham (died 1985, embalmed, but never on display); and North Korean "Eternal Leader" Kim Il Sung (died in 1994 and still on display in Pyongyang). But it was Chinese scientists, not Russians, who embalmed Mao Zedong in 1976, and he is still on view in a crystal coffin at his mausoleum in Tiananmen Square. At the time this book was being written, "Eternal Leader 2.0" Kim Jong Il was being embalmed for display alongside his father, and reports from Moscow indicated the Russians were once again lending a helping hand.

BENITO MUSSOLINI

BORN: JULY 29, 1883,
PREDAPPIO, ITALY
DIED: APRIL 28, 1945 (AGE 61),
GIULINO DI MEZZEGRA, ITALY

During the twenty years that Mussolini ruled Italy as "Il Duce" ("The Leader"), he succeeded even more than most dictators in building a cult around his image. His face, all severe features and flashing dark eyes, appeared everywhere throughout the nation—in offices, schools, bakeries, drugstores, even on women's swimsuits. As one French journalist wrote after a visit to Rome in 1929, Mussolini's face directed "all circumstances of Italian life." Mussolini invited his subjects to identify his image with the nation's power and strength, and for the most part, it worked. It's little wonder, then, that when Fascism failed, his body was subject to so much abuse.

Mussolini spent the final years of his life as a puppet dictator in the German-backed Social Republic of Italy. When the Third Reich crumbled, he tried to flee Italy with several hundred retreating German soldiers. But members of the resistance movement who had staked out the highways recognized their former ruler, despite his disguise of a German greatcoat and helmet, and arrested him. They shot him the following day, alongside his young mistress, Clara Petacci, and a group of top Fascist officials. Mussolini faced death with his typical bravado; his last words are said to have been "Aim for the heart!"

In death Mussolini was silent, and the public spoke. The morning after the executions, the resistance members loaded the bodies of Mussolini, Petacci, and their dead associates into a moving truck, then drove them to a square in Milan known as Piazzale Loreto. The location was no accident: in August 1944, Fascists acting on SS orders had killed fifteen political prisoners and dumped their bodies in the same spot. By the time Mussolini's corpse arrived, the square had become heavily symbolic, and was known as the "Square of the Fifteen Martyrs."

The events that took place there on April 29, 1945, shocked the world. The bodies in the truck were dumped in Piazzale Loreto around three a.m. As the sun rose, a crowd gathered around them, first dragging the corpses into a pile and then kicking them, beating them, spitting on them. Gradually Mussolini's head, once practically a piece of sculpture, began to look more like a smashed pumpkin. One woman fired a gun into the ex-dictator's body, yelling, "Five shots for my five assassinated sons!" Soldiers tried to keep back the fray, but it was no use. Soon Mussolini, Petacci, and two Fascist officials were strung up by their feet from the roof of a gas station at the square's southwest corner. This too had symbolic resonance: in the preceding years, the Fascists often hung their enemies upside down, usually with meat hooks.

The bodies were cut down around one p.m., after complaints from a local cardinal and the US military command. Officials took the corpses to the city morgue, where an autopsy on Mussolini confirmed the damage his corpse had suffered: his face was all but unrecognizable, his skull and brain crushed, his upper jaw fractured, and one eyeball lacerated. His corpse was also riddled with bullets, including the four shots near the heart that had killed him. (American scientists later asked for, and received, a sliver of Mussolini's brain to study it for signs of syphilis; the results were inconclusive, and the fragment languished in Washington, DC, for twenty years before being returned to Mussolini's widow.)

In the months afterward, some members of the resistance sought to distance themselves from what had happened at Piazzale Loreto, though others felt it was an appropriate catharsis after so many years of repressive rule. One member of the National Liberation Committee later wrote, "I never went to see [the corpses], but it was necessary that people understood that justice had been done. And it was necessary also to cut short other acts of violence and vendettas that would undoubtedly have been unleashed if there had not been the clear sensation that the most important guilty ones had been punished and the chapter was closed." In his memoirs, Churchill wrote, "At least the world was spared an Italian Nuremberg."

From then on, Mussolini's body became a controversial issue in Italian politics. To prevent further incident, the government buried him and his executed compatriots in unmarked graves at Milan's Musocco Cemetery. But the location was an open secret, and in the liberation celebrations that summer, anti-Fascists danced on the graves with an accordion. (It's said one woman also urinated on them, to the applause of her friends.) Such actions enraged Mussolini's remaining followers—and one young man in particular.

Domenico Leccisi was a twenty-five-year-old journalist, activist, and former official in Mussolini's government. In later decades, he would go on to become a politician nicknamed "the Bodysnatcher"—for good reason. In the months after Mussolini's death, Leccisi frequently rode the train past the Musocco cemetery, and he was haunted by the fact that his idol had been buried in an unmarked grave. One sleepless night in 1946, he resolved to dig up the body. By his own account, he wanted to force Italy to confront its past and thereby bring about "closure." But it also seems that by digging up Mussolini's corpse, Leccisi hoped to resuscitate Fascism as a political force.

Leccisi and his neo-Fascist friends made their move on Easter Sunday 1946, when the police were conveniently distracted by a nearby prison riot. It helped that the cemetery was empty thanks to the holiday, and of course, the resurrection symbolism was perfect. The thieves had little trouble getting into the cemetery, and fortunately for them, Mussolini had been buried in a wooden casket, which Leccisi was able to pry open with his hands. Inside his coffin, the head of Il Duce was still recognizable, his upper lip drawn back in a grimace. Leccisi doffed his hat in respect.

The group lifted the body from the coffin and washed it in a nearby fountain, wrapping it in a sheet, and depositing it in a wheelbarrow, which they pushed to the getaway car. Before leaving the grave, they dropped in a note signed by Leccisi's "Democratic Fascist Party," which explained that the body had been stolen because it could no longer bear "the cannibal slurs made by human dregs organized in the Communist party." A few hours later, Leccisi phoned local newspapers to tell them that "from Musocco the dead have sprouted wings."

For the next hundred days, the Italian public had no idea where Mussolini's corpse was. That didn't stop the newspapers from reporting sightings on boats, airplanes, and even a hot air balloon. Eventually a police investigation nabbed Leccisi and his partners, who revealed that the body had first been stored in a garage in a mountain village, then moved to a Milan convent staffed by sympathetic friars. After some negotiation, the friars agreed to reveal the location of Mussolini's body if the authorities promised to give the corpse a secret and Christian burial. The police agreed, and the friars took them to the convent closet where the body had been stashed.

Having learned their lesson, the government kept the location of Mussolini's body a carefully guarded state secret for the next eleven years. The authorities were determined to prevent the gravesite from becoming a shrine for neo-Fascists, or being subject to further desecration. If anything, the secrecy only enhanced interest in Mussolini's resting place: his followers held memorial Masses attended by hundreds of people, and mounted a "Buried in Italy" campaign that asked each town to dedicate a small but visible spot to Mussolini's memory, so that he would have substitute tombs scattered throughout the country.

In 1957, after a concerted campaign by Mussolini's widow, Rachele, and the Italian Social Movement newspaper, Italian prime minister Adone Zoli agreed to return the body to Mussolini's hometown of Predappio. The body arrived in a wooden box marked "church documents." It hadn't been reburied at all, but instead spent the preceding eleven years in a Capuchin monastery, first near the altar, then in a cupboard after people noticed the smell.

Today the tomb in the San Casciano cemetery features a ghostly white bust of Mussolini's head gazing out over his crypt. Just as officials once feared, it has become a gathering spot for the neo-Fascist faithful—80,000 to 100,000 visitors arrive each year, some offering Fascist salutes to the grave. The tomb is especially packed on three annual occasions: the anniversaries of Mussolini's birth, death, and the "March on Rome" that brought him to power in 1922. Meanwhile, local merchants do a vigorous trade in Mussolini-themed accessories and figurines, including tiny versions of the head that once appeared in images throughout the nation, and suffered so much violence at Piazzale Loreto.

BORN: APRIL 20, 1889,
BRAUNAU, AUSTRIA
DIED: APRIL 30, 1945 (AGE 56),
BERLIN, GERMANY

At the end of World War II, Adolf Hitler was certain of one thing: he did not want to end up in enemy hands, alive or dead. With the Red Army only a few hundred meters from his bunker beneath the Reich Chancellery, he announced that he had decided to commit suicide, and instructed his aides to burn his body until nothing remained. He did not want his corpse to end up in some "Moscow waxworks," he declared, or in a "spectacle arranged by Jews."

Hitler and Eva Braun, his wife of one day, were alone in his study when Hitler shot himself and Braun took poison—if in fact that's how they perished. Historians have long debated the sequence of events surrounding Hitler's death, but according to Ian Kershaw, Hitler's most prominent modern biographer, the aides who opened the door to Hitler's study smelled bitter almonds (the telltale scent of cyanide) wafting up from Braun's corpse, and saw blood dripping from a bullet hole in Hitler's right temple.

After recovering from their initial shock, the men lifted up the bodies, wrapped them in blankets, and carried them up the steps to the garden of the Chancellery. Outside, Russian shells were raining down, and the aides had to move quickly to put down the corpses, douse them in gasoline, and set them alight. They did not stay to watch the cremation, and it's not clear how well it worked; one account from a guard who saw the bodies later said they were reduced to ash, while others reported that something more substantial survived the flames.

When the Soviets got to the Chancellery a few days later, they did find a corpse they claimed was Hitler's. According to Soviet intelligence files, the Red Army soldiers discovered the badly burned bodies of a man and a woman, as well as two dogs, buried inside a shell crater near the bunker's emergency exit. Their location—near where the remains of Hitler's right-hand man Joseph Goebbels and his wife, Magda, had already been found—suggested the identity of the bodies, a suspicion confirmed by one of Hitler's guards, who said he had witnessed the burning and a subsequent burial. (The dogs, by the way, were Hitler's beloved German shepherd, Blondi, and one of her pups, killed to make sure they also escaped the clutches of the Russians.)

The bodies in the crater became the sole responsibility of a counterintelligence unit called SMERSH—a Russian acronym for words meaning "death to spies." SMERSH officers packed the remains into wooden ammunition crates, adding in the bodies of Nazi chief of staff General Hans Krebs, Mr. and Mrs. Goebbels, and the six Goebbels children, all of whom had been found dead in or near the bunker. The officers then transported the bodies to a hospital in Buch, a suburb of Berlin, for autopsies.

Hitler's autopsy would prove controversial. Most of what we know about it comes from a 1968 book by Russian author Lev Bezymenski, and scholars have questioned the extent to which his information may have been censored, manipulated, or fabricated. According to Bezymenski, the autopsy was conducted by one Dr. Faust Shkaravaski, who found a badly charred male corpse with splinters of glass in its jaw. Part of the corpse's cranium was missing, as was the left testicle, even though the rest of the genital area seemed to be intact. The missing testicle is the most debated part of the autopsy, and possibly a piece of Soviet propaganda: despite the catchy World War II ditty about the private parts of the Nazi leadership ("Hitler has only got one ball, Göring has two but very small . . .") there is no other solid evidence that Hitler was abnormal below the belt.

Because the corpse was too charred to allow for identification based on facial features, Hitler's lower jaw and his bridge of gold teeth were given to some officers who were instructed to track down his dentist. A young translator attached to the team later wrote that she carried around Hitler's teeth in a cheap jewelry box for days while the group searched through Berlin. The dentist could not be found, but his assistant was, and she identified the teeth as Hitler's, as did a dental mechanic who had made the bridge and crowns for Hitler's mouth.

With the dental identification, Stalin had proof that Hitler was dead. But he wasn't interested in sharing it. Instead, he preferred to nurture the myth that Hitler had escaped, and deceived both his own generals and foreign officials to that end. In fact, the idea that Hitler had fled to safety remained official Soviet history for years. The story varied: Hitler had gone to South America by plane, or to Japan on a submarine; he was anywhere but below ground. Stalin gained political capital by sowing uncertainty on the issue, although according to Bezymenski,

Stalin kept the evidence in reserve just in case a fake Hitler appeared in order to resurrect the Reich. (People were more worried about this than you might think; for years after the war, Hitler was seen almost as many times as Elvis would be a few decades later.)

The truth is that Hitler's body never left Germany, but there are differing accounts of its destiny. Some historians argue that the shelling in the Chancellery garden was so severe that Hitler's remains were likely reduced to rubble before they could be found, which means the body in the crater belonged to someone else. By this account, Hitler's jaw—and perhaps some fragments of his skull—were the only things that ever traveled beyond the Chancellery.

However, Soviet files that came to light in the 1990s revealed that intelligence officials repeatedly moved remains they at least *believed* to be Hitler's. According to the files, Hitler's body—along with the others packed into the ammunition crates—was buried in three different spots in 1945 (near Berlin, near the city of Finow, and in a forest along a highway near the city of Rathenow). In 1946, the remains were moved to a military base in Magdeburg. When that base returned to German control, the KGB feared the remains would be discovered, so in 1970 they exhumed them again, ground them into dust, and dumped them into a tributary of the Elbe River.

The scattering in the Elbe also completed Hitler's last wish: there was nothing left of him to be found. Well, almost nothing. The jaw carried around in that jewelry box still rests in intelligence archives in Moscow, and there is another relic that survives in Moscow archives— actually, two of them.

In the spring of 1946, Soviet intelligence officials returned to the Chancellery garden to try to learn whatever they could about the circumstances of Hitler's death. There, in the same shell crater where SMERSH officials found the body they said was Hitler's, the team discovered two skull fragments—one with a bullet hole—alongside gasoline canisters, cloth, part of a shoe, and a braided dog collar. After forensic studies, the Russians decided that the skull fragments had belonged to Hitler, but 2009 tests conducted by University of Connecticut scientists showed the skull belonged to a woman.

The test results set conspiracy theorists aflutter; some said the only physical proof of Hitler's death had just been rendered worthless. That's not quite true: there is still that jaw sitting in the Moscow archives. But maybe Hitler got the last laugh after all. When a body is nowhere, it can be everywhere—swimming in Japan, shopping in Argentina, sipping wine in Spain. And it can never be captured.

EVA PERÓN

Born: May 7, 1919,
Los Toldos, Argentina
Died: July 26, 1952 (age 33),
Buenos Aires, Argentina

Eva Perón played many roles during her short life: child of poverty, radio actress, first lady of Argentina, charity maven, and finally, martyr. She was accused of being many other things as well: a prostitute, Fascist sympathizer, codictator, and harborer of Nazis. These days, she is most often remembered as the Evita of musicals and movies, a glamorous blonde who looks a lot like Madonna. But she played her longest, strangest role as a corpse.

Evita was embalmed for eternity in the same way that Lenin was, subjected to months of chemical baths and injections that turned her from an ex-person into a statue, or something in between. She was so tiny she looked like a doll—not even five feet tall, after the cancer and the chemicals. But despite her innocent appearance, her corpse was at the center of two decades of mayhem and madness.

While she was alive, Evita's image had always been about love. As first lady, she described herself as the "bridge of love" between her husband, Juan Perón, and the mass of Argentine poor, the *descamisados* ("shirtless ones") who had swept him to power. While her husband recoiled from human contact, Evita spent her days receiving long lines of the needy, embracing even the lice-ridden and syphilitic, and granting their requests for money or medicine. Through her eponymous foundation, she dispensed millions of gifts and built hospitals, orphanages, and schools. They called her "Lady Bountiful." She never rested, even when the doctors told her to. And when she died of uterine cancer at age thirty-three, her followers said she had sacrificed her life to the cause.

Within days, the Vatican was flooded with letters begging for her canonization. The Church wasn't interested, but that didn't prevent Argentina's poor from worshipping her at altars across the land. Meanwhile, Juan Perón—conscious of the fact that he had lost both the beautiful face and beating heart of his movement—decided to have his wife preserved forever.

Even before Evita died, Perón began holding secret meetings with an anatomy professor named Pedro Ara, a Spaniard famous in Buenos Aires for his work embalming the composer Manuel de Falla. Dr. Ara preferred to think of himself as an artist rather than an embalmer (he called himself a practitioner of the "art of death"), and carried the preserved head of an elderly peasant in his luggage to show off his skills.

Like Lenin, Evita was embalmed in two stages: once for a brief public viewing, and once for eternity. Ara got started on the first stage within an hour of Evita's death, and by the following morning, her body had been made "completely and definitively incorruptible," as he put it. Dressed in a white shroud and draped with the national flag, her body was placed in a glass-topped coffin and carried to the Ministry of Labor, which had long been her headquarters. There nearly two million people came to see her, bringing so many bouquets and wreaths that the flower shops of Buenos Aires were cleaned out. The three-day viewing period was extended to two weeks, but then Dr. Ara got nervous: if the president wanted Evita to last forever, Ara had to get to work.

Ara never revealed the precise formula he used in the embalming, but others have said that he worked by replacing the blood with glycerin or preservatives, injecting parts of the body with wax, and covering it with a layer of transparent plastic. The entire project took a year and is said to have cost the government $100,000. When it was done, Ara said the body still contained all its internal organs, and could last indefinitely. A visitor who saw it told biographers, "It was the size of a twelve-year-old girl. Its skin was wax-like and artificial, its mouth had been rouged, and when you tapped it, it rang hollow, like a store-window mannequin. The embalmer, Ara, hovered over it as if it was something he loved."

Evita's body was supposed to become part of a massive funeral monument, something like Napoleon's tomb at Les Invalides. The first lady herself had been planning the monument before she died, though originally it was meant to pay tribute to the idealized Argentine worker, not to her. She wanted it to be over four hundred feet high, taller than the Statue of Liberty, topped with a statue of a muscle-bound *descamisado* with a Perónist museum beneath. But in September 1955, three years after her death, Juan Perón was deposed in a military coup. The construction of the monument had not gotten beyond a massive hole in the ground.

Perón fled into exile on a Paraguayan gunboat, with little thought for his wife's corpse. At first, the new regime left Ara alone in his offices at the General Confederation of Labor. The professor had set up his embalming lab there, and spent most of his time watching over his masterpiece, repairing real or imagined defects.

But a few months later, curious officers started coming to see the body. In the beginning, they refused to believe it was real, even when Ara handed over X-rays. Finally the officers amputated part of a finger, and only then were they convinced they were dealing with an object that had once been a human.

And not just any former human: the female half of the deposed regime. The new rulers were so adamantly anti-Perónist that they'd banned images of the former first couple from the country, and scratched Evita's name off hospital beds and sheets before using them. Confronted with her corpse, the last thing they wanted was a burial site that followers would turn into a shrine. However, they also didn't want to harm the body; the new president, Pedro Aramburu, was a devout Catholic, and the Church had turned down a request for cremation even in this unique case.

It was obvious that burial was bad for Aramburu's political future, but the other options were bad for the future of his soul. So the president and his men decided on a secret burial. The location they chose was the Chacarita Cemetery, the largest in Buenos Aires, and the man they entrusted with the job was Carlos Eugenio Moori Koenig, the head of military intelligence.

One night in November 1955, Koenig appeared at the Confederation building to take the body away. Though he must have been concerned about the fate of his masterpiece, Ara had little choice but to help Koenig load the body into his truck. Afterward, Koenig was supposed to bring the body to the Chacarita Cemetery, but instead he went a little crazy. Or at least that was the judgment of his superiors.

It started when he parked the truck carrying Evita's body in the courtyard of a marine regiment for the night, then awoke to find the vehicle surrounded with candles and flowers. He then loaded the body into a different, unmarked, truck and drove it around the city, stopping in a different place each evening. But every morning brought the same thing: candles and flowers.

Clearly someone always knew where the corpse was, no matter how hard he tried to keep it a secret.

Spooked, Koenig hid the body in a box in the attic above his office at military intelligence headquarters. About a year later, he showed it to a friend, who let word get back to Aramburu. The president decided that Koening was suffering from a nervous breakdown, and dismissed him both from his duties as Evita's caretaker and from his job.

In 1957, the regime decided to try giving Evita another secret burial. This time, they planned to take the body out of the country, and therefore "outside politics"—or so they hoped. Under "Operation Cadaver," the body was sent to Italy, where it was buried under the name of an Italian who had died in Argentina, Maria Maggi de Magistris. The operation was so sensitive that even President Aramburu didn't know the details. He entrusted a letter with the corpse's location to his lawyer, with the proviso that it should be delivered to his successor four weeks after Aramburu's death, whenever that might be.

It was sooner than he hoped. In 1970, a group of militant Perónist guerrillas kidnapped Aramburu and put him "on trial" for his anti-Perónist activities. They interrogated him about the fate of Evita's corpse, but he couldn't tell them much, and he did not escape his captivity alive. After his murder, the guerrillas sent a communiqué to newspapers, refusing to give up his corpse until "the day the remains of our dear comrade Evita are returned to the people."

Aramburu's body was soon discovered by the police. But the current Argentine government had already decided to make peace with Perón, who retained a powerful hold on his followers even in exile. Since Aramburu was now dead, his lawyer delivered the envelope with Evita's burial details to the current leader, General Alejandro Agustín Lanusse. Lanusse shared the contents of the letter with a colonel and a priest, whom he dispatched to find Evita's body.

The letter contained nothing more than the names of a cemetery in Milan and a priest who had since passed away. There was nothing for the colonel and the priest to do but comb through the cemetery's records for 1956, the year of Evita's clandestine reburial. After some work, they zeroed in on Maria Maggi de Magistris, an Italian widow who had died in Argentina but was buried in Milan five years after her death. The enterprising colonel grew a mustache and, with the help of fake papers, posed as the brother of the deceased in order to get permission to exhume the coffin. Sure enough, the body inside was Evita's.

The corpse arrived at Perón's villa in Madrid in a bakery truck. Dr. Ara, summoned from retirement, restored his work to its former glory, while Perón's new wife, a former cabaret dancer named Isabel, restyled the hair in Evita's signature chignon. According to dinner guests, the refurbished Evita then went on display in the Perón family dining room.

Perón was elected for his third and final term in 1973, and everyone assumed he would return from Spain with Evita's body in tow. He didn't, and died after only a year in office. In 1974, his wife and successor, Isabel, finally brought Evita home, but only after guerrillas kidnapped Aramburu's corpse and again demanded Evita's in return. This time their plan worked, and Isabel had the body flown from Spain to Buenos Aires by chartered plane.

Isabel exhibited Evita's corpse in Buenos Aires next to her husband's closed coffin, and planned to build them both a giant monument. But like Juan's efforts, her plans were cut short by yet another military coup. She was deposed in March 1976, and later that same year the new regime finally returned Evita's remains to her family. Soon afterward Evita was buried in the fashionable Buenos Aires cemetery of Recoleta, near many members of the oligarchy she despised. Her embalmed corpse now rests twenty feet below ground in a steel vault said to be able to withstand a nuclear bomb.

The Hands of Perón

Evita and Aramburu weren't the only Argentine corpses of their era with adventurous afterlives. Juan Perón's tomb was also desecrated: in 1987, anonymous vandals broke into his grave at the Chacarita Cemetery and sawed off both his hands. The leaders of his political party later received a ransom note demanding eight million dollars, which they refused to pay, arguing that Perón's ideas mattered more than his bones. The crime has never been solved, and the hands remain missing.

JIM THORPE

BORN: MAY 28, 1888,
PRAGUE, OKLAHOMA
DIED: MARCH 28, 1953 (AGE 64),
LOMITA, CALIFORNIA

Jim Thorpe is the best all-around athlete America has ever produced. He rose from a childhood spent in federal Indian boarding schools to become a star football, baseball, and track athlete, earning success at both the college and professional levels. He caused a sensation at the 1912 Olympics in Stockholm, where he won gold in the pentathlon and decathlon and set records that remained unbeaten for decades. At the medal ceremonies, King Gustav of Sweden told him: "You, sir, are the greatest athlete in the world."

His later years were less golden. When he retired from football at age forty, it was just in time for the Depression to hit. At first he tried to make a living in Hollywood, playing Indian chiefs in B-grade Westerns, but when that dried up he joined the merchant marines, then drifted from job to job and wife to wife. A 1951 biopic briefly brought him back into the limelight, but he was felled two years later by a heart attack, his third in a decade.

He died broke, but friends came to the rescue. One of them called the Malloy Brothers Mortuary in Los Angeles, and the owner, a devoted baseball fan, claimed the body and handled all the arrangements for free. The money for Thorpe's coffin came from a committee of LA sportswriters. It seemed the world hadn't forgotten Thorpe after all, and when his embalmed body went on display at the mortuary, more than three thousand mourners came to pay their last respects.

Within days, offers came from several towns that wanted the honor of burying him. Bids arrived from Carlisle, Pennsylvania, the site of Thorpe's old college; from the American Indian Hall of Fame in Anadarko, Oklahoma; and from Shawnee, Oklahoma, where an oilman named Ross Porter launched a campaign to build Thorpe a huge memorial. To top it off, Shawnee officials also offered to pay all the funeral expenses and buy round-trip train tickets for Thorpe's family.

But Thorpe's third wife, born Patricia Askew, would have none of it. The last Mrs. Thorpe was her husband's manager in his final years, and did her best to maintain that role even after his death. She refused to send the body to Shawnee (or anywhere else) until plans for Thorpe's memorial were ironclad. But other family members outvoted her, and the body went to Shawnee after all—inducing years of family tension.

The plan was for Thorpe's body to be kept unburied in a cemetery north of Shawnee until $100,000 could be raised for his monument. Meanwhile, about two weeks after his death, members of the Sac and Fox and Potawatomi tribes gathered for a traditional funeral, a night of prayer, singing, and feasting that was to last until sunrise, when Thorpe's spirit would be released. It didn't quite work out that way. In the middle of the night, Patricia arrived with a hearse and police escort, declaring that her husband was "too cold" for the funeral to continue, whatever that meant. She took the body away before the ceremony was finished, leaving the rest of the family flabbergasted.

Things went even less smoothly with state officials. In the following months, Oklahoma's governor signed a bill approving a memorial commission for Thorpe, but with his state facing a budget deficit, he refused to fund it. Fed up, Patricia made another unannounced visit: one night in August, she showed up at the Shawnee cemetery where the body was being kept and demanded that workers load it onto a trailer. She drove the trailer to a cemetery in Tulsa, because she was somehow under the impression that officials there would give her husband the memorial he deserved. They didn't. Six months after Thorpe's death, he still didn't have a permanent resting place.

That's when the town of Jim Thorpe, Pennsylvania, was born. It started out as two towns: Mauch Chunk and East Mauch Chunk, collectively known as "the Chunks." Both had thrived in the nineteenth century thanks to the rich deposits of coal in nearby mountains, but by the 1950s, the towns were on life support. Their beautiful Victorian mansions and hotels, once teeming with visitors, lay vacant. With scant local industry and long-simmering ethnic tensions (Mauch Chunk was Irish, while East Mauch Chunk was German) the Chunks did little but glare at each other across a river bend.

Faced with this grim reality, an enterprising local newspaper publisher named Joseph Boyle hatched a two-pronged plan to help the towns pull themselves up by their bootstraps. The first prong was a "nickel a week" campaign, in which residents would save up for the construction of a factory to lure new industry. The second was more daring: by Boyle's calculation, the Chunks' best chance of survival was to avoid duplication of local services by merging into a single town. Not surprisingly, that idea was less popular; neither of the Chunks wanted to give up their name or distinct heritage.

But the nickel-a-week campaign took off, and the town's efforts caught the attention of a Philadelphia television producer. He made a documentary about the Chunks' efforts that aired on Philadelphia television in September 1953. One of the people who saw it was Patricia Thorpe, who decided that her husband's death could be the town's gain.

A few days later, Patricia went to Mauch Chunk and presented her proposal to Boyle. If the two towns were willing to consolidate and change their name to Jim Thorpe, she said, they could bury his body. Boyle must have been surprised, not least because Thorpe had no link to either of the Chunks; as far as anyone knew, he had never set foot in them. But with so few options for the town's survival, Boyle soon warmed to the idea.

As time went on, the plans grew: there would be not just a memorial monument but a museum, a heart and cancer foundation, a hospital, a stadium, a sporting goods factory. With Thorpe's body, they might even be able to win the bid for the Pro Football Hall of Fame. And by renaming themselves, the towns could start fresh, putting their old animosities aside.

Thorpe's body arrived in February 1954, eleven months after his death. Shortly thereafter the towns merged and named themselves Jim Thorpe. But just as before, the plans began to evaporate into the mountain air. The fraternal order that had offered to fund the mausoleum pulled out, and the town had to dip into its nickel-a-week savings. Townspeople started grumbling; some even wanted to dump the coffin on Boyle's porch in protest. It took three years, but finally a modest yet dignified rose granite sarcophagus was erected on a hill just outside town. On Memorial Day 1957, Jim Thorpe was finally laid to rest.

Unfortunately, the tourists never came. As one disgruntled resident famously (and controversially) put it in 1978, "All we saw were dollar signs, but all we got was a dead Indian." The Pro Football Hall of Fame was built in Canton, Ohio, instead, and none of the other projects materialized. Vandals smashed the sarcophagus with a hammer, and undertakers treated it as a repository for used funeral wreaths.

But then the town's fortunes reversed. It had nothing to do with Jim Thorpe, however, and everything to do with city boosters who wisely capitalized on the town's picture-perfect Victorian mansions and mountain scenery. Today, tourist brochures declare that Jim Thorpe is "the Switzerland of the Americas" and the "Gateway to the Poconos." The town is also a favored destination for bicyclists and whitewater rafters. When visitors come to partake in the town's pleasures, few stop at Jim Thorpe's grave.

Some of Thorpe's children are still unhappy about the arrangements Patricia made. They want to bring Thorpe's body to tribal land in Oklahoma, where they say he always wanted to be buried. At the time this book was being written, Thorpe's surviving two sons were fighting in court alongside the Sac and Fox Nation for the return of their father's remains. While they say they have nothing against the town of Jim Thorpe, they object to their father's body being used as a "tourist attraction." For now, the town is fighting the lawsuit. But if the suit succeeds, the place will no doubt survive the loss of the man—after all, it's the living who turned the town around, not the dead.

CHE GUEVARA

BORN: JUNE 14, 1928,
ROSARIO, ARGENTINA
DIED: OCTOBER 9, 1967 (AGE 39),
LA HIGUERA, VALLEGRANDE, BOLIVIA

For many people, Che Guevara is an image even more than he was a man. His face, as captured by the photographer Alberto Korda in 1960, has been reproduced endlessly on posters, T-shirts, flags, and countless items of radical chic. Of course, the capitalist system keeping Che's image alive is the same one he despised.

As a Marxist revolutionary, Che fought alongside Fidel Castro to bring about the Cuban Revolution, then tried to export his socialist ideals to the Congo and Bolivia. But he was never able to repeat the success he experienced in Cuba, and after months in the Bolivian wilderness, he was finally cornered, ill and emaciated, in a jungle ravine.

As with so many famous figures, controversy surrounds his final moments. The Bolivians reported that Che died in a firefight after declaring, "I am Che Guevara and I have failed!" But that unlikely story didn't last long, and it soon emerged that Che had been captured alive and executed by rifle the following day. According to legend, his last words were: "Shoot, coward, you are only going to kill a man."

A few hours after his death, his body was tied to the landing skids of a helicopter and flown to the nearby village of Vallegrande. In the laundry room of a hospital, soldiers propped his bedraggled corpse atop a cement washstand as locals crowded around. The nurses who washed Che's body thought he resembled the martyred Christ, and snipped off some of his hair as relics. (In fact, villagers would go on to pray to "Saint Ernesto" for healings and harvests.) The image of the dead Che, bloodied and prone, spread around the world.

With all the attention his corpse was getting, the Bolivian government decided to give Che a secret burial. As with the corpses of Mussolini, Hitler, and Eva Perón, officials were determined to avoid creating a shrine that could burnish a heroic myth. So early on the morning of October 11, two days after his death, Che's body and those of six other comrades-in-arms were unceremoniously dumped in a secret grave near the Vallegrande airport.

But officials were hesitant to bury their proof that Che was really dead. One Bolivian general, future dictator Alfredo Ovando Candía, had argued for decapitating Che and keeping his head as evidence. But some of the soldiers, and CIA operative Félix Rodríguez, felt that was "too barbaric," and advocated cutting off only a finger. In the end, the men compromised and decided to amputate Che's hands, so they could continue to have access to his fingerprints. Before the secret burial, his hands were sawn off and stored in jars of formaldehyde. Thanks to a sympathetic Bolivian interior minister, they reportedly ended up being kept by a succession of journalists, stored under beds and beneath floors. Eventually they made their way to Cuba, where at least one Latin American academic has said they are still kept at the Palace of the Revolution and occasionally displayed to visiting dignitaries.

The truth about Che's secret grave stayed hidden for thirty years. For a time, the official line was that Che had been cremated. But in November 1995, a retired Bolivian army general revealed the body's general location to a *New York Times* journalist. The resulting international coverage pressured the Bolivian government into a search for the remains, although it was Argentine and Cuban specialists who eventually found the body near the Vallegrande airstrip after a two-year search. The skeleton's missing hands made the bones easy to identify, although experts were also swayed by dental identification, facial bone structure, bullet wounds, and a tiny pouch of pipe tobacco hidden in a jacket buried beneath the body. A pilot remembered giving the pouch to Che before he died.

In October 1997, almost exactly thirty years after Che's death, his bones were finally laid to rest in Havana. Castro declared a week of mourning and homage, during which hundreds of thousands came to see Che's coffin on display inside a monument to José Martí, the father of Cuban independence. Afterward, Che's remains were transferred to a newly built mausoleum in the city of Santa Clara, the site of his decisive military victory. Thus the world's most iconic revolutionary was fully absorbed into the system that he helped to found. For a political corpse, that's about the best fate possible.

OSAMA BIN LADEN

BORN: MARCH 10, 1957,
RIYADH, SAUDI ARABIA
DIED: MAY 2, 2011 (AGE 54),
ABBOTTABAD, PAKISTAN

After all the death and destruction he caused, Osama bin Laden went down without much of a fight. The Navy SEALS who swarmed his compound in Abbottabad, Pakistan, were prepared for fierce resistance, an escape through underground tunnels, or wives wearing suicide vests. Instead they discovered the founder of al-Qaeda trapped in a pitch-black bedroom, with a few hundred euros and two telephone numbers sewn into his clothing. He had guns, but didn't reach for them. One of the SEALS fired a burst of bullets into his chest, and a second round into his head. Bin Laden's last words, uttered to his wife Amal, were: "Don't turn on the light."

On the same day sixty-six years earlier, the world had learned of Hitler's death. But bin Laden's postmortem journey was the opposite of Hitler's; for one thing, it lasted only a few hours, not decades. Less than twenty minutes after their helicopters landed at the compound, the SEALS were sliding bin Laden's corpse into a body bag. Eight hours later, after facial recognition analysis confirmed the identity of the corpse with 95 percent certainty, President Barack Obama addressed the nation from the White House. "Justice has been done," he declared, while cheering crowds erupted around the country.

As the sun rose on the other side of the world, bin Laden's body was loaded into a plane at the Bagram base in Afghanistan and flown to the USS *Carl Vinson,* an aircraft carrier sailing off the coast of Pakistan. About an hour and a half after the president's speech in Washington, the burial rites began on board the ship. Bin Laden's body was washed, wrapped in a white sheet, and placed in a weighted bag. An officer read Muslim prayers, which were translated into Arabic by a native speaker. Then the body was placed on a flat board and tipped into the North Arabian Sea, never to be seen again. Later the same morning, DNA from the corpse— checked against several bin Laden family members— proved without a doubt that the body had belonged to the terrorist mastermind.

The Obama administration emphasized that the rites had been carried out in accordance with Islamic law. They stressed that a watery grave had been necessary because no country was willing to take bin Laden's corpse within twenty-four hours, the maximum amount of time allowed between death and an Islamic burial. Yet some Muslim leaders outside America were quick to criticize the way the United States had dealt with the body. Sheikh Ahmed el-Tayeb, grand imam of Cairo's Al-Azhar Mosque, said, "Bin Laden's burial at sea runs contrary to the principles of Islamic laws, religious values, and humanitarian customs." Mohammed al-Qubaisi, Dubai's grand mufti, added: "If the family does not want him, it's really simple in Islam: you dig up a grave anywhere, even on a remote island, you say the prayers and that's it. Sea burials are permissible for Muslims in extraordinary circumstances. This is not one of them."

In fact, White House officials later admitted that a sea burial was necessary to prevent the creation of a shrine where bin Laden's followers might gather. Ever since Alexandria (and before), political leaders have understood how graves can become sites for commemoration and veneration. That's useful when the deceased is an ideological ancestor of current rulers, but problematic when he or she is part of a disgraced regime.

The grave of the last major enemy dispatched with US assistance, Saddam Hussein, is a case in point. After the former Iraqi dictator was executed in 2006, family members buried his body in a community center (redubbed "Martyr's Hall") in his native village of Al-Awja. The site has since become a gathering point for supporters. In 2009—after YouTube videos showed schoolchildren reciting pro-Hussein poetry at the grave—the Iraqi government banned organized trips, but as of 2011, the visitors were still coming.

Scattering ashes in water may be the most effective choice when a government wants to obliterate all memory of the deceased. That's how the International Military Tribunal dealt with the remains of the ten high-ranking Nazis executed after the Nuremberg Trials in 1946. Their ashes, as well as those of Hermann Göring (who committed suicide before he could be hanged), were scattered in the Conwentzbach River in Munich. The same method was used by the Israeli government to dispose of Adolf Eichmann, one of the major organizers of the Holocaust, after his execution in 1962. Eichmann's ashes were sprinkled in the Mediterranean, beyond the territorial boundaries of Israel, so that no trace of the man remained in the nation.

But cremation is forbidden by Islam, which means that governments must seek other options for preventing the creation of a shrine. (The Geneva Conventions require that enemy dead be buried according to the rites of their religion "if possible.") Unfortunately, even ordinary sea burials can nourish conspiracy theories about what happened to the deceased; in bin Laden's case, controversy was exacerbated by the fact that the US government refused to release photos of his corpse or the results of the DNA analysis. "We don't trot out this stuff as trophies," President Obama told *60 Minutes*. "The fact of the matter is, you will not see bin Laden walking on this earth again."

But sea burials aren't foolproof. In 2012, a California treasure hunter named Bill Warren said he had pin-pointed the location of the corpse at the bottom of the ocean, about two hundred miles west of Surat, India. At the time of this writing, Warren was trying to raise funds to take DNA samples from the corpse, because he doesn't "believe the Obama administration." He also said he'd been offered twenty million dollars for the body by a group in Pakistan. If Warren does find bin Laden's body, President Obama might wish he'd taken another route.

LOST

AND

FOUND

But who knows the fate of his bones,
or how often he is to be buried?
Who hath the oracles of his ashes,
or whither they are to be scattered?
—SIR THOMAS BROWNE (1605–82)

Famous graves and remains are lost for many reasons, including war, neglect, and redevelopment. Sometimes bodies are deliberately hidden, only to be rediscovered centuries later. More often, famous bodies are found because of the concerted efforts of an admirer, like the American ambassador to France who found John Paul Jones's body moldering in a Paris slum. Sometimes famous corpses are located by chance, which is what happened to the soldiers who found Frederick the Great stashed in a salt mine. Of course, not everything lost gets found; we don't know what happened to (most of) Descartes, for example, or what became of Thomas Paine.

JOHN PAUL JONES

BORN: JULY 6, 1747,
KIRKCUDBRIGHTSHIRE, SCOTLAND
DIED: JULY 18, 1792 (AGE 45),
PARIS, FRANCE

On the evening of September 23, 1779, the American naval commander John Paul Jones was locked in desperate battle against a British warship when he gave his famous cry, "I have not yet begun to fight!" The phrase came in response to a British taunt: was Jones ready to surrender? He was, after all, outgunned, outnumbered, and in enemy waters. The flag on his ship had just been shot down. But Jones would not give up, and after hours of battle during which his deck ran red with blood, the British were the ones who surrendered. The victory proved the strength of the American navy, and to this day, Jones is called the father of that force. But he died ignored, and it took a man with similar determination, more than a century later, to rescue his bones from oblivion.

The young American republic could not afford a peacetime navy, and so Jones went to France on an assignment to secure prize money due from captured ships. In Paris he found himself fêted as a hero for his humiliation of the British, but when his assignment expired, it was cash he needed, not elaborate dinners and ceremonial swords. His next offer of work came from Russia, where Catherine the Great made him a rear admiral in her ragtag navy of Cossacks and pirates. Jones fought valiantly against the Turks, and things seemed to be going well enough, until he found himself on Grigory Potemkin's bad side.

Potemkin saw Jones as a threat to his monopoly over both Russia's military and Catherine's affections. In a setup that Potemkin may or may not have helped orchestrate, Jones was accused of raping a young girl and left Russia in disgrace. He returned to Paris just in time to witness the first phase of the French Revolution, but the stress of his misadventures in Russia had badly weakened both his body and spirit. He died of kidney disease and pneumonia while trying to get from his favorite armchair to his bed.

The American minister to France, Gouverneur Morris, held little regard for Jones, whom he thought more than a little full of himself. Morris decided that Jones should be buried "in a private and economical manner" in the Protestant cemetery of Paris, without any of the "follies" of a grand funeral. But Morris was forced to apply to the French government for access to the plot, and the French felt that Jones deserved better. The commissary in charge of the cemetery decided that if the Americans wouldn't pay for a public funeral, the French would—making Jones the first Protestant ever given a public funeral in France. Morris, however, found that he was simply too busy to attend.

The cemetery closed six months after Jones's burial, and the grounds were soon covered over. The instabilities caused by the French Revolution prevented any thought of taking Jones back to America, even if Americans had been calling for such a move, which they weren't. Over time, the cemetery was turned into a garden, and then became part of a slum known as "Le Combat" due to the animal fights waged atop the graves. By the time the first serious proposals to bring Jones home were suggested by American officials in the 1840s, no one could remember exactly where he lay. They couldn't even remember the cemetery in which he'd been buried.

It wasn't until 1899, when an enterprising journalist named Julius Chambers claimed to have discovered Jones's grave, that plans for his homecoming were finally put into motion. Chambers's assertion turned out to be incorrect, but the publicity he generated was enough to inspire the American ambassador to France to take over the search. Horace Porter, a greatly mustachioed Civil War veteran who had served under Ulysses S. Grant, was a far different man than Gouverneur Morris had been. He would go on to spend six years and much of his own money searching for Jones's body. For Porter, the quest was a matter of honor. He would later write that he felt "pained beyond expression and overcome by a sense of profound mortification" at the treatment of Jones's grave. "Here was presented the spectacle of a hero whose fame once covered two continents," he wrote, "relegated to oblivion in a squalid corner of a distant foreign city."

The problem was, which corner? Porter had little information to work with. Jones's death certificate had been burned alongside other city records by the Paris Commune, and over the years, a variety of rumors had sprung up about his final resting place. Finally, Porter found a reprint of Jones's death certificate in an 1859 article written by an antiquary. The certificate stated that Jones had been buried in "the cemetery for foreign Protestants," which the antiquary believed meant the old St. Louis cemetery. After searching through local publications, Porter confirmed that St. Louis was the only cemetery that would have buried Protestants at the time of Jones's death.

After consulting old maps, Porter located the site of the cemetery in northeastern Paris. Thanks to a letter written by one of Jones's friends, Porter knew that Jones had been buried in a lead coffin, which Porter hoped would make the correct grave easier to find (lead coffins were expensive, and rare in that part of town). But just as Porter was getting ready to excavate, fabulous stories began to spread through the neighborhood about the high price the French government would pay residents for their land in order to carry out the search. Actually, the project was being funded out of Porter's own pocket, and he was forced to put the whole thing on hold for two years until the stories died down.

Finally, Porter succeeded in getting the right to dig at a price he could afford. A top Parisian mining engineer led the excavations, which began on February 3, 1905. The workers had their job cut out for them: the soil, which had been variously used as a dump and an animal burial ground in addition to everything else, was very loose, and the men had to build a network of timber around themselves just to keep from getting crushed. As Porter described the conditions, "slime, mud, and mephitic odors were encountered, and long red worms appeared in abundance." Bodies were stacked two and three deep, an indication of the poverty of most of the inhabitants.

As it turned out, Jones's was not the only corpse buried in a lead coffin in the cemetery. First one, then two such coffins were discovered, both with inscriptions proving they did not belong to Jones. Finally, a third coffin was found, better-constructed than the previous two and bearing no inscription. Porter decided to open the coffin, although the air at the site was so bad the men had to wait a week until they could create better ventilation. At the appointed hour, workers removed the coffin's heavy lid and were greeted by a strong alcoholic odor. The French had pickled the corpse inside with spirits.

A corpse of roughly Jones's height lay inside the coffin, wrapped in a winding sheet that still felt moist. Carefully, the men lit half a dozen candles and unraveled the sheet. To their surprise, the body inside was remarkably well preserved, its grayish-brown skin entirely intact and only slightly shrunken. The curls of the hair were still tightly wound in an eighteenth-century coif. Porter bent into the candlelight and compared a copy of Jones's congressional gold medal, which was engraved with his portrait, to the corpse. The broad forehead, the curve of the brow, the high cheekbones—everything matched up. "Paul Jones!" the men exclaimed all at once, and took off their hats.

The next night, the body was taken to the Paris School of Medicine for a complete examination. When the scientists unwrapped the sheet, they found the limbs partially covered in tinfoil, yet another aid to preservation helpfully placed there by the French. The scientists also found a linen cap embroidered with a curly letter "J" that became a "P" when turned upside down— a further sign of the corpse's identity. But it was the well-preserved internal organs that provided the most convincing proof: the lungs showed signs of pneumonia, and the kidneys evidence of the interstitial nephritis that had helped kill Jones. The scientists concluded that it would take a "concurrence of circumstances absolutely exceptional and improbable" for the corpse to be anyone other than Jones.

On hearing the news that Jones had been found, President Theodore Roosevelt sent four warships to Cherbourg, France. Officers carried Jones's remains, encased in a new coffin, to an American church in Paris for a patriotic service filled with flags and flowers. The service was held on July 6, 1905—exactly 158 years after Jones's birth. After a grand procession along the Avenue de l'Alma, the remains traveled by special train to Cherbourg and then steamed home on the USS *Brooklyn* to the US Naval Academy in Annapolis. Porter was offered a ride, but said he would make his own way home.

Congress eventually reimbursed Porter for all the money he had spent during his search, but Porter donated the funds to build a memorial to Jones. It took years for the memorial to be completed, but Jones was finally interred in the crypt of the US Naval Academy Chapel in 1913. He rests inside a twenty-one-ton sarcophagus of donated French marble, carved by a French sculptor and modeled on Napoleon's tomb. An honor guard stands watch whenever the crypt is open. Now that America finally has Jones's body, it has decided it had better take care of it.

"Tapping the Admiral"

Preserving a corpse in alcohol is not entirely unusual. A naval hero from the other side of the Atlantic was also pickled in spirits: Lord Horatio Nelson was submerged in brandy (others say rum) for his journey back to England after dying in the Battle of Trafalgar. Some say the sailors siphoned off a bit of the booze during the journey, and their supposed actions are the origin of the British phrase "tapping the Admiral," meaning illicit drinking. (Lord Byron was also shipped home in spirits, but no one suggests the sailors on his ship took a sip.)

DANTE ALIGHIERI

BORN: MID-JUNE 1265,
IN FLORENCE, ITALY
DIED: SEPTEMBER 14, 1321 (AGE 56),
IN RAVENNA, ITALY

We know Dante as a poet, but he was also a political leader who found himself on the wrong side of a schism in Florence. His party, the Guelphs, split in two, and in 1301 (five years before he started the *Divine Comedy*) the group Dante opposed staged a massive coup. The leaders of Dante's faction were exiled from Florence, and Dante himself was forced to spend most of the rest of his life wandering Italy, adrift "like a ship without sail or rudder," as he once wrote. If he tried to return to Florence, he would be burned alive.

His wanderings came to an end in Ravenna, where in 1318 the literary-minded local lord, Guido Novello da Polenta, invited him to stay. Dante was given complete freedom to finish his *Comedy,* but died (probably of malaria) shortly after writing the final lines. Guido Novello dressed Dante's corpse in scarlet robes and a laurel wreath and buried him in the church of a Franciscan order in what was planned to be a temporary tomb. But when Guido was ousted from his office the following year, the friars became the real guardians of Dante's bones.

In the centuries after Dante's death, Florence repeatedly requested the return of his remains, but the citizens of Ravenna had taken to their adopted poet and refused to let him go. (Italy was not yet a united nation, but a collection of city-states and principalities with intense rivalries.) In 1513, the Florentines got a lucky break when one of their own was elected Pope Leo X, and soon the letters about Dante started arriving on the pope's desk. One particularly insistent missive said that the president of the local Platonic Academy had been frequently troubled by Dante's ghost, which often visited him around sunrise demanding to be let out of his "odious tomb" in Ravenna. When that didn't work, a group of Florentines sent the pope a petition in 1519 with signatures from prominent citizens, including Michelangelo, who offered to sculpt Dante's tomb.

That must have done the trick, because the pope finally sent representatives to Ravenna later that year. One night, under the cover of darkness, a group of would-be bandits crept into Dante's tomb. They succeeded in lifting off the heavy stone lid of his sarcophagus, but their sweat was in vain—Dante's coffin was empty. The men reported back to the pope that "it is supposed that, as in his lifetime [Dante] journeyed in soul and in body through Hell, Purgatory, and Paradise, so in death he must have been received, body and soul, into one of those realms." The situation must have left the pope scratching his head, and the fact of the empty tomb was kept quiet for centuries.

A mundane accident three hundred years later brought the truth to light. In 1865, the church where Dante lay was renovated in honor of the sixth centennial of his birth. While workers were removing part of a wall outside the Braccioforte Chapel, just a few yards away from Dante's tomb, they came upon a decayed wooden chest hidden inside the masonry. When they tried to move it, human bones tumbled through the rotten wood. One of the interior planks on the chest bore the Latin inscription "Dante's bones, revisited anew June 3, 1677." An exterior plank bore Latin words meaning, "Dante's bones placed here by Fra Antonio Santi, October 1677."

The workers, and Ravenna officials, were stunned. If Dante's bones were inside the chest, then what was inside his tomb? Nothing, it turned out, except a few small bones that matched parts missing from the newly discovered skeleton. The investigation also uncovered a hole in the back of the tomb, accessible only from within the monastery, which had been plastered over to hide its existence. Once officials matched up the skull in the chest with a mask of Dante's face made on his deathbed, they felt sure that their poet had gone wandering again after death.

But why? Nineteenth-century Dante scholars who analyzed the discovery believed that the words "revisited anew" meant that Dante's bones were taken from his original resting place sometime *before* 1677, and periodically reinspected. They theorized that the friars were determined not to let Dante's bones return to the city that exiled him, and hid them when they got wind of what the Florentines were planning in 1519. The knowledge of Dante's true resting place was then passed in secret from generation to generation. The friars had long whispered that a "great treasure" was to be found in the Braccioforte Chapel, but no one had guessed it was a body.

In the days that followed the discovery, Dante's bones were reassembled into a skeleton and laid inside a glass sarcophagus for display in the chapel. Thousands of Italians came to see the remains during a three-day viewing. On June 26, 1865, a month after their initial discovery, the bones were returned to the sarcophagus in Ravenna from which they'd been surreptitiously taken more than three centuries before.

These days, the city that exiled Dante has finally stopped asking for his return, and Florence even pays for the olive oil that lights Dante's tomb in Ravenna. Meanwhile, Dante's spirit—and his work—now belong to the entire country, and to the world.

RENÉ DESCARTES

BORN: MARCH 31, 1596,
LA HAYE, FRANCE
DIED: FEBRUARY 11, 1650 (AGE 53),
STOCKHOLM, SWEDEN

One of the strange coincidences of history is that Descartes, author of the modern mind-body split, has lost his head. Granted, he probably doesn't care now that he's dead, unless it's true that our minds really are separate from our bodies—in which case perhaps we're capable of mourning our own fates.

Descartes died in Stockholm, far from his native France, during the city's coldest winter in sixty years. He'd arrived there at the invitation of Sweden's Queen Christina, an intellectual monarch who wanted Descartes to give her private philosophy lessons. Christina was an unusual ruler, known for her fierce intelligence as well as her penchant for men's clothing (they called her the "Girl King"). She demanded her lessons at five in the morning, even though Descartes had to travel for an hour through the freezing darkness to reach her castle.

Descartes had never been an early riser, and some scholars think these rude awakenings made him more susceptible to the pneumonia he caught from the French ambassador. He had always hated doctors and bloodletting, but this time consented to both. It was no use. Soon his physician heard the telltale wheezing and sputtering of the death rattle, and saw "black sputum" dribbling from his mouth. In the middle of one February night, the philosopher breathed his last—no more thinking, no more being.

Queen Christina was racked with guilt. To honor Descartes's memory—and to appease her own conscience—she wanted to bury the philosopher in Riddarholm Church, the ancient resting place of Swedish kings. But her plan had one major flaw: Descartes was Catholic, and Riddarholm, like all of Sweden's churches, was Lutheran.

Instead, the French ambassador suggested laying Descartes to rest in a cemetery for unbaptized children, whose awkward religious status matched the philosopher's. So it was that Descartes was buried in the yard of the Adolf Fredriks Church in central Stockholm. The ceremony was brief, and the mourners were few. But Descartes did get to rest in one place for sixteen years, the longest stretch of repose his intact remains have ever had.

While Descartes's physical body deteriorated, his body of work lived on. His theories (materialism, rationalism, "I think, therefore I am") traveled throughout Europe, igniting both excitement and controversy. By 1666 Cartesian thought was on the rise, and France wanted its native son back. A group of French Cartesians wrote a letter to Hugues de Terlon, the new French ambassador to Sweden, asking him to exhume Descartes and send his remains back to Paris. Terlon was happy to comply, and also happy to take home a souvenir: the philosopher's right index finger, which he called the "instrument in the immortal writings of the deceased." Terlon asked permission from local priests, but the same can't be said for one of his employees, who stole something far more valuable.

After an eleven-month carriage trip (disguised as a bundle of rocks to thwart bandits), Descartes's remains received a hero's welcome in Paris. A procession of Cartesians, clergy, and ordinary citizens carried the coffin on a torch-lit parade through the streets to the city's highest point, the Gothic splendor of the Church of Sainte-Geneviève-du Mont. There, after prayers and celebrations, Descartes was reburied in a vault of honor next to the remains of Sainte-Geneviève herself, the patron saint of Paris.

This time, Descartes—or most of him—got to rest a little longer. But in 1792, a mob of revolutionary rebels attacked Sainte-Geneviève. Its desperate abbot begged a conservator named Alexandre Lenoir to save the church's relics, including the bones of Descartes. According to Lenoir, a team of his men spirited the bones from the church and took them to Lenoir's new Museum of French Monuments, which some call the world's first history museum. Descartes's remains lay in an Egyptian sarcophagus in the museum's *jardin élysée,* next to the purported bones of Molière. Lenoir later wrote that he carved some of Descartes's bones into rings, which he distributed to "friends of the good philosophy."

But there was just one problem. Years later, when the Museum of French Monuments was no more, officials decided to bury Descartes (for the third time) in Saint-Germain-des-Prés, the oldest church in Paris. Unfortunately, when the assembled dignitaries opened the coffin in 1819, they discovered that Descartes was missing his head. In fact, he was missing almost everything, except for some small bone fragments and bits of bone powder. Many of the assembled were scientists, who claimed that Descartes's remains should have survived in a far better state of preservation. The extent of the decay was a mystery—and it remains a mystery today.

Sure, you can walk into the shadows of Saint-Germain-des-Prés in Paris and see the black marble plaque said to cover the remains of Descartes. But what lies beneath is a matter of debate. Russell Shorto, a writer and historian who traced the remains of Descartes in his book *Descartes' Bones,* thinks Lenoir never saved Descartes at all. For one thing, Lenoir's notes, usually meticulous, make no mention of the philosopher's remains among the artifacts rescued from Sainte-Geneviève. Asked later to describe the removal, Lenoir reported digging in the wrong place, and described finding a copper coffin (Descartes was buried in a wooden one). If Descartes was never rescued from Sainte-Geneviève, the philosopher's remains were likely destroyed by revolutionary rebels in 1792, or when the church was demolished in 1807.

But not all of Descartes's remains left Sweden in the first place. We know this strange fact thanks to Swedish chemist Jöns Jacob Berzelius, famous for determining the atomic weight of every element then known. Shortly after completing that mammoth task, he suffered a nervous breakdown. While recuperating in Paris in 1819, friends at the French Academy of Sciences suggested he join them in attending Descartes's reburial ceremony. As a man who knew something about the properties of matter, Berzelius was puzzled by the missing skull. As a Swede, he was horrified when someone suggested the skull had come to harm in Stockholm.

Berzelius never forgot about the missing skull, and two years later, the almost-empty coffin leaped back into his mind one day while he was reading the paper. According to an article, "the skull of the famous Cartesius" had just been sold at an auction. After asking around, Berzelius discovered the cranium had been sold to a casino owner who planned to use it as decoration. Fortunately for Berzelius, the man was willing to sell the skull to him for the same price he'd paid at the auction. The chemist sent the skull to his friends at the Academy, with a note explaining the strange turn of events.

The men at the Academy were skeptical about whether

the cranium had once belonged to Descartes. But the skull carried its own special kind of evidence: all across its light brown surface were the signatures of former owners. Like the graffiti taggers of today who scrawl their names on highway overpasses, the previous owners of the skull had marked their territory.

With the help of a government archivist, the Academy discovered a seventeenth-century text describing a chain of ownership that matched the skull's scrawls. According to the text, the skull had been secretly severed by one Isaak Planstöm, captain of the squad of soldiers hired to guard Descartes's remains when they were exhumed in Sweden in 1666. It's hard to know exactly why Planstöm stole the skull, though he may have simply wanted a memento from the century's most famous philosopher. Greed might also have had something to do with it; the skull of the famous Cartesius would fetch a pretty penny.

After extensive debate, the Academy finally concluded that the skull probably did belong to Descartes. The object is currently in the collection of the Musée de l'Homme in Paris, but the controversy continues. There are at least four other skulls around the world that people say belonged to the philosopher—a mind-body split that even Descartes would have found unlikely.

LOST SOULS

Danish philosopher Søren Kierkegaard died of mysterious causes in 1855 in Copenhagen. Despite a history of scathing attacks on the Danish Church, he was given an official funeral, which degenerated into a spectacle at the cemetery when his hotheaded nephew loudly denounced the Church and began quoting from his uncle's works. Because of family tensions, Kierkegaard's brother refused to mark his gravesite for twenty years. By that time, no one could remember where the body had been buried.

FREDERICK THE GREAT

BORN: JANUARY 24, 1712,
BERLIN, GERMANY
DIED: AUGUST 17, 1786 (AGE 74),
SANSSOUCI, GERMANY

There was only one picture hanging on the wall of Hitler's last study: an oil portrait of Frederick the Great, king of Prussia from 1740 to 1786. As the Red Army approached Berlin in the final days of World War II, Hitler spent several nights in his bunker staring at the painting by candlelight. He idolized Frederick as an iron-willed commander who had doubled his kingdom's territory, and hoped that just as Frederick had enjoyed an unexpected victory during the Seven Years' War, he, too, would find a way to persevere.

But there was more to the Prussian king than militarism. A patron of the arts, Frederick composed flute music, wrote poetry, and corresponded with Voltaire, who once said the king "has written more books than any of his contemporary princes has sired bastards." Frederick's lack of progeny may have had something to do with his (reputed) homosexuality—a rumor that Hitler conveniently ignored.

Frederick's enlightened side was often at odds with the military society around him. As a child he preferred the arts, and at age eighteen attempted to escape his father's harsh discipline by fleeing to England. But he was betrayed, and forced to watch as his coconspirator (also likely his lover) was executed on his father's orders. It was only years later, after ascending the throne in 1740, that Frederick accepted his military destiny.

His last will and testament was more in keeping with his genteel sensibilities. He asked to be buried on the terrace of his summer palace in Potsdam, Sanssouci, alongside his beloved greyhounds, whom he called the "Marquises de Pompadour" to irritate the French king. "I have lived as a philosopher and wish to be buried as such, without circumstance, without solemn pomp or parade," he wrote.

His nephew and successor, Frederick William II, ignored his last wishes and buried him in the Potsdam Garrison Church, which he considered a more appropriate resting place for the "soldier-king." There Frederick lay next to his father, Frederick William I, who had so successfully molded him into a military man. In deference to the summer heat, the burial was rushed and private. A state funeral with a dummy coffin was held the following month.

Father and son rested in the Garrison Church until Hitler's rise, which twisted the old Prussian militarism into grotesque new forms. Anxious to claim Frederick the Great as part of his symbolic lineage, one of Hitler's first public events as chancellor was a parliamentary inauguration ceremony at the Garrison Church, where the German president, Field Marshal von Hindenberg, placed a golden crown of laurels on Frederick the Great's coffin.

But we know what happened to Hitler's Reich. And when he knew time was running out, he tried to keep Frederick and his father safe from enemy hands. During the war Hitler transferred both coffins into an underground bunker to protect them from bombs, and in March 1945, he moved them to a salt mine in the village of Bernterode, deep in the forests of central Germany, to protect them from the advancing Soviets.

The coffins stayed at the mine for barely a month. On April 27, 1945, American soldiers hunting for munitions stored in the mine made a curious discovery. Alongside 400,000 tons of ammo, they found a masonry wall that looked suspiciously fresh in one of the corridors near the mine entrance. After breaking through the wall, they discovered a treasure trove containing hundreds of paintings, books, and military banners, plus assorted swords and crowns. In the middle lay four coffins.

The soldiers knew they had stumbled on something important, so they turned the trove over to the Monuments, Fine Arts, and Archives section. The Monuments Men, as they were called, were a group of Allied museum curators, artists, and art historians who had volunteered for the difficult task of preserving the cultural treasures threatened by the war. Toward the end of the conflict, the group had turned their attention to recovering some of the estimated five million treasures that had been seized by the Nazis.

The American sculptor Walker Hancock was given the task of exploring the mine's secret room. He found labels written in crayon Scotch-taped to the coffin lids, identifying the bodies inside as Field Marshal von Hindenberg, Frau von Hindenberg, Frederick William I, and Frederick the Great. Of all the bounty the Monuments Men discovered during the war, this was surely the strangest.

The Monuments Men spent four days packing up all the goods in the vault, and then a full day bringing the coffins the nearly two thousand feet to the surface.

Frederick the Great's body went up last, since the men feared the coffin's twelve-hundred-pound bulk would break the mine's pulleys. It didn't, and the coffin rose to the surface just as a nearby radio began blaring "God Save the King." It was May 8, 1945, V-E day, and the Germans had just officially surrendered.

The coffins were taken to the cellar of a castle in Marburg while the soldiers awaited further instructions. The US commander in Europe sent word that the bodies were to be given a dignified burial that would reflect well on the liberating forces, but German war heroes, even dead ones, were not a hot commodity at the time. Neither Britain nor France wanted the bodies in the territory they controlled, and it took over a year for the Americans to find a suitable spot. In 1946, the four coffins were buried in Marburg's St. Elisabeth's Church, after being given new funerals.

For some of the deceased, including Frederick and his father, it would be only a temporary arrangement. In 1952, Frederick's descendants brought the remains of the two kings to their ancestral seat in southern Germany, Hohenzollern Castle, which they considered a more fitting resting place. But in 1991, Chancellor Helmut Kohl decided he wanted to celebrate Germany's reunification by bringing the Fredericks back to Potsdam, in the former East Germany. Some pointed out that Frederick's corpse was once again acting as a prop for a gesture of German nationalism, but in the process, Kohl fulfilled Frederick's last wish.

At midnight on August 17, 1991, both Frederick and his father were laid to rest at the palace of Sanssouci in Potsdam. Frederick William I was buried in a mausoleum at the "Church of Peace" on the Sanssouci grounds, while his son was finally placed beneath a simple stone slab on the terrace, next to his dogs, just as he'd always wanted.

THOMAS PAINE

BORN: JANUARY 29, 1737,
THETFORD, ENGLAND
DIED: JUNE 8, 1809 (AGE 72),
NEW YORK CITY

Without Thomas Paine, there might never have been a United States of America. Paine coined the country's name (or at least was the first to capitalize it), but he also did something far more important: his pamphlet *Common Sense* provided average Americans with the intellectual kindling for their revolution. Paine did away with the Latin and heavy philosophy of his predecessors, offering the colonists a powerful set of arguments for independence presented in a clear, straightforward style. Nearly every literate American read *Common Sense,* and it was read aloud in taverns and meeting halls for those who could not read themselves. Soon the tide of public opinion turned against British rule, and the ranks of the Continental Army swelled.

But then Paine went too far. Beginning in 1794, he published a series of pamphlets called *The Age of Reason,* in which he attacked organized religion and the Bible. His words still have the power to sting: "All national institutions of churches," he wrote, "whether Jewish, Christian or Turkish, appear to me no other than human inventions, set up to terrify and enslave mankind, and monopolize power and profit."

Paine admitted that he had gone "marching through the Christian forest with an ax." It soon became clear that his ax had also cut down his circle of supporters. Mark Twain later said, "It took a brave man before the Civil War to confess he had read *The Age of Reason*." In the years that followed, Paine found himself ostracized and denied a pension. By the time he was dying of gout in Greenwich Village, even his wish to be buried in a Quaker burial ground (the sect of his birth) was denied.

But after his death, a rebellious Quaker minister and five other mourners buried Paine at the writer's farm in New Rochelle, New York. A simple tombstone identifying the deceased as the author of *Common Sense* was the only monument, and even that didn't last. People walking by pelted it with stones, and eventually a neighboring tavernkeeper embedded what was left of the tombstone in her wall. It wasn't long before local drunks started chipping off flakes as souvenirs.

Ten years later, an unlikely ally came to Paine's rescue. William Cobbett was an Englishman who had once written loyalist pamphlets under the pen name "Peter Porcupine" while living in America some years before. Paine had been a frequent target of his venom: Cobbett called him a "sacrilegious monster, a seditionist, a rascal, a blasphemer, a wretch who beat his wife." (In turn, Paine called him "Peter Skunk.")

But then Cobbett changed his political stripes: after returning to England in 1800, he was baptized by the fires of English radicalism and reinvented himself as a champion of the working class. Eventually he began reading Paine's work, and realized that the man he'd so often abused was actually a kindred spirit.

Cobbett decided to make amends. And so he went

back to America, where at dawn one September morning in 1819 he dug up what was left of his former enemy. "The Quakers, even the Quakers refused him a grave!" Cobbett wrote in his *Political Register*. "I found him lying in the corner of a rugged, barren field!"

Two months later Cobbett arrived at the dock in Liverpool with a large trunk full of Paine's remains. He wanted, he said, to give his former enemy a beautiful funeral on streets lined with flowers, and then to build him a magnificent mausoleum. He hoped the project would be a stirring call to radicals throughout the British Isles—and also allow Cobbett himself to sleep a little more easily.

The plan backfired. British newspapers had a field day, calling Cobbett the "bone grubber" and printing cartoons that showed him dressed like a tramp with Paine's bones slung in a sack on his back. In the days of the "Resurrection Men" (see Laurence Sterne's story on pages 28–31), a body snatcher was a very bad thing to be. By Cobbett's own account, he was denounced by three hundred newspapers. Speaking in the House of Lords, Earl Grosvenor asked, "Was there ever any subject treated with more laughter, contempt, and derision than the introduction of those miserable bones?"

To make matters worse, King George III died on Paine's birthday, the same day Cobbett had planned to hold a fund-raising dinner. From then on, support for Cobbett's cause was extremely unfashionable. Discouraged, Cobbett left the bones to rot in a corner of his house while he turned to other pursuits, like tax reform and gardening.

Cobbett died in 1835, and because he was in debt, his goods were auctioned off—except for one large trunk. The auctioneer handling his estate refused to deal in human remains, and so the trunk containing Paine's bones went to Cobbett's neighbor, a farmer named George West. West had no clue what to do with it, and so around 1844 he sent it to Cobbett's former secretary, a man named Ben Tilly.

Tilly was by then working as a tailor in London, with barely the means to keep body and soul together, let alone bury Thomas Paine. Not knowing what else to do with the trunk, he sat on it. Literally. The trunk acted as a stool in Tilly's tailor shop, at least until his economic situation got so bad he was also forced to auction off all his goods. Tilly's auctioneer was more comfortable handling remains, and he sold the trunk to a radical publisher named James Watson. Watson made inquiries about burying Paine's bones, but no one is quite sure what he did with them. After Watson died in 1874, a Unitarian minister named Alexander Gordon said he'd gotten hold of the trunk and buried its contents, although he wouldn't provide any further details. That was the end of the trunk—though it wasn't the end of Paine.

In 1864, an American abolitionist named Moncure Conway had moved to England to advocate for the North during the Civil War. As an admirer of Paine, and later the author of Paine's first authoritative biography, Conway made it his mission to track down his bones. In 1876, after giving a lecture about Paine, Conway got a letter from a London bookseller who remembered a customer once bragging about owning Paine's skull and right hand. The customer thought he was boasting anonymously, but in fact the bookseller recognized him as the Reverend Robert Ainslie, a very conservative London minister. Conway quickly penned a letter to Ainslie, but it had the bad luck to arrive just after Ainslie died. His son, it turned out, had inherited Paine's skull and hand, but had recently thrown them out in the trash.

Conway nourished the hope that the skull, at least, had not been consigned to oblivion. As he put it, "Every physician must possess a skull, which is worth more than a wastepaper dealer would pay . . . it is probable that Paine's skull is now in some doctor's office or craniological collection." Since then, Paine's skull has been reported in a few different locations, even as far away as Australia.

At least one part of Paine did make its way back to

America. In 1833, while still working as a secretary for Cobbett and packing up for a move, Tilly took a souvenir out of his boss's trunk. From the pile of bones, he plucked out a hard, blackish lump—all that was left of Thomas Paine's brain. Tilly wrapped it in cloth and neatly labeled it, attaching a note about its provenance. After he died, both brain and note were found in his rooms. Conway tracked them down, and purchased them (for five pounds) in 1900. By then, the brain was only about the size of a fist, and "quite hard."

Conway brought the brain back to America, and in 1905 the Thomas Paine National Historical Association, which Conway helped establish, buried it in a secret location on the grounds of Paine's old farm in New Rochelle. (One rumor says Paine's brain is actually inside a monument on the grounds, in a hollow portion below the bust.)

Throughout the twentieth century, bits of Paine have been reported around Europe, and the Association has recently mounted what it calls the "Citizen Paine Restoration Initiative" to buy up as many of these remains as possible. The Association plans to subject them to DNA testing, and—if they are indeed parts of Paine—bury them together in the country he helped to found.

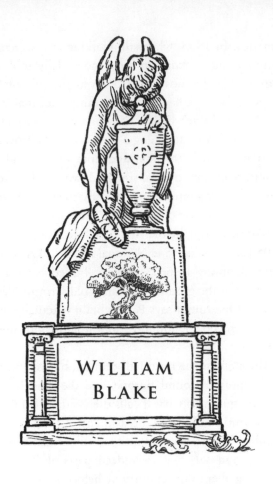

**WILLIAM
BLAKE**

BORN: NOVEMBER 28, 1757,
LONDON, ENGLAND
DIED: AUGUST 12, 1827 (AGE 69),
LONDON, ENGLAND

William Blake was a mystic who believed in a divine reality that existed beyond the material world. From the age of four onward, he experienced visions and spoke frequently to angels, as well as to a dead brother. This disturbed more than a few people, and some of his contemporaries wrote him off as insane. It took decades after his death for Blake's star to rise, but today we revere the transcendent imagery of his paintings, engravings, and poetry.

When death came to Blake, he was joyous. "I glory," he said, "in dying, and have no grief but in leaving you," he told his wife. As he lay on his deathbed, he began singing, then expired "like the sighing of a gentle breeze." After he died, a friend closed his eyelids "to keep the vision in."

Following a simple funeral, Blake was laid to rest in an unmarked grave at Bunhill Fields, a London burial ground for Nonconformists (Protestants who did not belong to the Church of England). But while the grave went unmarked, it was not unrecorded: at the time, Bunhill Fields noted the location of all of its graves using a series of directional coordinates. It was this information that would later prove essential to a pair of amateur London sleuths, because while Blake's grave has been in the same place for nearly two hundred years, for a large chunk of the twentieth century no one knew where to find it.

In the years after Blake's death, most of the public forgot about his grave. It wasn't marked until 1927, the centenary of his death, when the Blake Society finally erected a tombstone. But the inscription they used contained some mysterious language: "Nearby lie the remains of the poet-painter William Blake . . . and of his wife Catherine Sophia." As it turned out, the "nearby" part referred to Blake's wife, buried about seventy-five yards away. At the time, the stone did mark the spot of Blake's grave, but not for long.

In 1960, the City of London received permission from Parliament to clear away a portion of the tombstones from Bunhill, which had long been closed to new burials. The purpose of the removal was to repair damage from the Blitz and create a new lawn (now a popular place for office workers to take lunch). During the move, Blake's headstone was relocated about twenty yards away, next to the grave of the writer and journalist Daniel Defoe. Blake's body remained untouched, but with nothing marking his grave, its whereabouts were forgotten. The wording on the Blakes' gravestone continued to puzzle tourists for decades, and most who visit Bunhill Fields today have no clue where the poet is buried.

One London couple hopes to change that. Luis and Carol Garrido have long been attracted to Blake's work, even before they became involved in a spiritual movement known as Sahaja Yoga, which reveres Blake as a kind of saint. When they visited Bunhill in the late 1990s, the Garridos were disappointed to discover the imprecise wording on Blake's tombstone, and confused about where his grave might be. But as they walked around the cemetery, they began to notice a strange fragrance filling the air. The couple later wrote, "It was no ordinary fragrance, as we could feel ourselves becoming uplifted, joyous and silent." There was no obvious source for the odor, no flowering shrubs or trees anywhere nearby.

On a follow-up visit to Bunhill, the cemetery groundskeeper introduced himself to the couple. They asked what he knew about Blake's grave, and he responded that it had been lost. However, he also said that an old man he knew remembered the grave being located next to a large plane tree on the lawn—the same place the Garridos had detected the strange aroma. Seeing the enthusiasm on the couple's faces, the groundskeeper invited them into his office and began telling them about the history of Bunhill.

The Garridos grew determined to find Blake's grave. They put themselves to work hunting through records kept in London archives and libraries, as well as piecing together the clues left by Blake's biographers. While they soon discovered the existence of Bunhill's coordinate system, most of the reference points that had once stood on the cemetery's walls had been lost or heavily damaged. In addition, many of the older graves marked by the system were gone. Eventually, the Garridos were able to use the coordinates of two graves still standing to establish the location of Blake's resting place. It was right next to the plane tree.

The Garridos hope to mark Blake's original grave so that it will never be lost again. Through the Friends of William Blake (a society they founded), they have received planning permission from local authorities to lay a memorial stone at the site of the grave. They will also place paving stones between the grave and the site of the original tombstone. If all goes as planned, the paving stones are to be carved with the following lines from Blake's "Songs of Experience":

Hear the voice of the Bard!
Who Present, Past, & Future, sees;
Whose ears have heard
The Holy Word
That walk'd among the ancient trees.

DOROTHY PARKER

BORN: AUGUST 22, 1893,
LONG BRANCH, NEW JERSEY
DIED: JUNE 7, 1967 (AGE 73),
NEW YORK CITY

Dorothy Parker was one of the few female members of the Algonquin Round Table, a group of 1920s writers (read: drinkers) who regularly met for lunch at Manhattan's Algonquin Hotel. There, highball in hand, Parker flung some of her most famous barbs and dazzled the group with her quips. Once, during a word game in which she was challenged to use the word "horticulture" in a sentence, she replied, "You can lead a whore to culture, but you can't make her think."

Parker penned short stories and reviews for the *New Yorker*, worked as a critic for *Vanity Fair*, and later went off to Hollywood, where she earned an Oscar nomination for the screenplay of *A Star Is Born*. She also published several collections of stories and verse, and in

1929 won the O. Henry Prize for her devastating short story "Big Blonde." People followed her around at cocktail parties, just waiting for her to say something sharp.

But Parker had a tendency to turn her caustic humor against her intimates; she often criticized people the moment they walked out of the room. In her later years, most of her friends were estranged or dead, and she died alone at the Volney residential hotel on New York's Upper East Side, with only her poodle for company.

Afterward, friends discovered that she had willed her estate to a man she'd never met. Granted, he wasn't just any man. A fervent civil rights advocate, Parker had willed her entire estate, including all copyrights and royalties, to Martin Luther King Jr. According to Parker biographer Marion Meade, King was meeting with Southern Christian Leadership Conference members in an Atlanta restaurant when he got the news. Puzzled yet grateful, King announced to the table that Parker's gift "verifies what I have always said, that the Lord will provide."

Unfortunately, the Lord didn't provide instructions on what to do with Parker's remains. Parker's executor, the playwright Lillian Hellman, had arranged for Parker's cremation on June 9, 1967, but never told the crematorium what to do with the ashes, even when they repeatedly sent reminders for her unpaid storage bill. The ashes remained at the Ferncliff Cemetery crematory in Hartsdale, New York, until 1973, when Hellman finally told the crematorium to mail the urn to her attorney, Paul O'Dwyer. O'Dwyer didn't have any idea what to do with Parker either, and so he kept her remains in a box in the filing cabinet of his Wall Street office for fifteen years.

It was while researching her biography of Parker in 1987 that Meade discovered Dorothy had never been properly interred. Her discovery spurred O'Dwyer to action, and he called a meeting at the Algonquin to brainstorm ideas for Parker's final resting place. Some suggested using her ashes as part of a mural on a wall inside the Algonquin, or putting them on display in one of the hotel's bars. But both the Algonquin and the *New Yorker* declined to give Parker a final home, and it was the National Association for the Advancement of Colored People—which inherited Parker's estate after King was assassinated—that finally came to the rescue.

On a windy day in October 1988, twenty-one years after her death, Parker was finally laid to rest in a pine grove at the NAACP's Baltimore headquarters. The plaque on her gravesite says the spot is "dedicated to her noble spirit which celebrated the oneness of humankind, and to the bonds of everlasting friendship between black and Jewish people." It also includes her suggested epitaph: "Excuse my dust."

FINDING ZORA

The African-American author and anthropologist Zora Neale Hurston died in obscurity in 1960 and was buried in an unmarked grave in a segregated cemetery. Thirteen years later, author Alice Walker made it her mission to track down her grave. After getting directions from the funeral home that had handled Hurston's burial, Walker braved the snakes and waist-high weeds of an overgrown cemetery in Fort Pierce, Florida. When she finally found what seemed to be Hurston's grave, Walker had it marked with a headstone calling Hurston "A Genius of the South." Walker later wrote, "[T]here was nothing grand or historic in my mind. It was, rather, a duty I accepted as naturally mine—as a black person, a woman, and a writer—because Zora was dead and I, for the time being, was alive."

COLLECTIBLE

CORPSES

From ancient times to modern museums, humans have been using remains in ways nature never intended: as decorations, trophies, exhibits, and collectors' items. Because of their durability (not to mention portability), skulls have often been the most sought-after items, but that's not always the case—a few famous collectibles have come from a significantly more delicate part of the (male) anatomy. While that might seem grotesque, the urge to connect with famous figures by owning, handling, seeing, or displaying their bodies runs throughout history.

Born: January 27, 1756,
Salzburg, Austria
Died: December 5, 1791 (age 35),
Vienna, Austria

Mozart began composing music at an age when most of us are still learning how to tie our shoes. It's a good thing he started early, because he didn't have long; at age thirty-five, he was stricken with a fatal illness that has never been conclusively diagnosed. He kept on working until the very end, composing his own funeral anthem. But though it obsessed him, he never finished the *Requiem*. In the delirium of his final hours, he would inflate his cheeks and try to make the sounds of the kettledrums.

Like most Viennese dead of his day, Mozart was buried in a common grave. And like most other graves of the time, his was cleared ten years later to make way for new bodies. Fortunately, there was one person willing to save at least a part of Mozart from the trash.

We don't know for certain who rescued Mozart's head. According to one story, it was the sexton at Vienna's St. Marx cemetery, where the composer was buried. The sexton is said to have been a music lover who had admired Mozart since childhood and who had once been moved to tears by his work. When the composer's body was brought to the cemetery, the sexton made note of where it was buried, some say by twisting a piece of wire around the corpse's neck. And when the plot was cleared in 1801, he saved Mozart's skull as a personal memento.

The sexton is said to have kept the skull until the end of his life, and it later passed into the hands of another Viennese music lover, engraver and amateur musician Jakob Hyrtl. By one account, Hyrtl began paying regular visits to the St. Marx cemetery shortly after his mother was buried there. He struck up a friendship with the sexton's successor, who was nearing the end of his own life, and who decided to give Mozart's skull to someone who would appreciate it. But Hyrtl seems to have been a bit spooked by the gift; on at least one occasion, he thought about throwing it into the Danube.

Hyrtl's brother Joseph was a little more comfortable around human remains. Joseph, who inherited the skull when Jakob passed away in 1868, was one of the most popular anatomy teachers in all of Europe, a pioneer in anatomical preparations who had amassed a collection of skulls from around the world. When he added Mozart's skull to his specimens, he attached a red label that told the story of the sexton's rescue and his brother's prior ownership. Hyrtl may also have been the one who added the inscription on the skull's right temporal bone: "*musa vetat mori*," "the muse prevents death"—part of a line from Horace's *Odes*.

After Joseph's death in 1894 the skull was briefly lost, but in 1902 a cranium said to be Mozart's was donated to the International Mozarteum Foundation in Salzburg, Austria. The skull was now reduced to a skullcap, with the lower jaw and skull base missing, allegedly because of an anatomical investigation Joseph undertook when he was nearly blind.

Throughout the twentieth century, a succession of anatomists, anthropologists, and other scientists have examined the skull to try to establish its authenticity, as well as to find clues to Mozart's untimely death. Every few years the skull is conclusively linked to Mozart, only for the tower of evidence constructed by one scientist to be dismantled by another. In the meantime, 118 causes of Mozart's death have been proposed, everything from poisoning to heart disease.

In 2006, scientists hired by an Austrian television station sought to find out once and for all whether the skull belonged to Mozart. But after comparing DNA samples from the skull with bones, hair, and teeth belonging to Mozart's dead relatives, they concluded that the latter samples were from people biologically unrelated to one another—let alone to the owner of the skull. As a scientific paper published about the results put it, "the dead took their secrets to their graves."

The skull said to be Mozart's still belongs to the Mozarteum, but it was removed from display in the 1950s. Some say tastes changed, and museum staff felt the display was no longer appropriate. But others say the skull had a disturbing effect on visitors, who would sometimes weep at the sight of it. Some even said they heard it scream, or heard faint music emanating from the bones—perhaps the final strains of the *Requiem,* lost forever inside Mozart's head.

NAPOLEON BONAPARTE

BORN: AUGUST 15, 1769,
AJACCIO, CORSICA
DIED: MAY 5, 1821 (AGE 51),
LONGWOOD, ST. HELENA

Let's get one thing out of the way: Napoleon was not that short. At 5'6", he was average height for a French man of his day. That means the Napoleon Complex—in which short men act like despots to compensate for their lack of stature—has been misnamed. But there may have been other things Napoleon was trying to compensate for, and one of them apparently ended up 3,600 miles away from Paris, in Englewood, New Jersey.

The story of Napoleon's remains begins on the island of St. Helena, where he was exiled after his defeat at the

Battle of Waterloo. St. Helena is one of the most isolated places in the world, and the British installed Napoleon in a dank, moldy house overrun by rats. They also placed him in the care of the island's governor, Sir Hudson Lowe, whom Napoleon believed despised him. No wonder the ex-emperor's health, which had never been robust, deteriorated even further.

In the last months of his life, Napoleon suffered from a mysterious stomach ailment. He said he felt like he was being stabbed by a razor, although Lowe dismissed the ailment as "slight anemia." But Napoleon knew he was dying, and wrote out a detailed will. Ever the emperor, he even dictated his own death announcement, with a blank space for the date, to be filled in once the event had occurred.

Napoleon's will asked for his body to be buried on the banks of the Seine, "in the midst of the French people, whom I have loved so well." But Lowe had no intention of letting that happen, and he ordered that Napoleon be buried on St. Helena. The ex-emperor died one spring evening at around six p.m., "out as the light of a lamp goes out," according to his valet.

It was during the autopsy that pieces of Napoleon started disappearing. When Napoleon's Corsican doctor, a man named Francesco Antommarchi, cut into the emperor's stomach, he found an ulcer big enough to stick a pinky finger inside. The rest of the organ was riddled with what looked like cancer, although experts today are divided about whether cancer or ulcer complications ultimately killed the man. During the autopsy, Antommarchi cut out Napoleon's heart and his stomach, placing them in separate silver vases filled with spirits. The heart was supposed to go to Napoleon's second wife, Marie Louise, but it's not exactly clear where the stomach was destined to end up.

After Napoleon's corpse was sewn back together, it was dressed in his battle uniform and placed within four nested coffins, perhaps to deter grave robbers. On the orders of the British, the vases of viscera were placed within the innermost coffin, along with some of Napoleon's good silverware. Then each coffin was soldered tight, and the man who had ruled most of continental Europe was sealed away, never to be seen again. The funeral cortege wound its way across the island to a peaceful willow grove, where the body was laid to rest. Twenty years later, the French brought Napoleon's remains back to Paris, where they were given a state funeral and entombed in the crypt of Les Invalides. But other parts of his body made less dignified journeys.

According to one story, Antommarchi made an extra snip or two during the autopsy: he cut off Napoleon's penis. It's not impossible—the room was crowded, noisy, and probably stank, and you could forgive the onlookers if they got distracted toward the end. Antommarchi had been frequently abused by the ailing Napoleon, and it's possible he decided to extract some revenge. According to the gossip of the day, the doctor was ignorant, inept, and disrespectful, though it's unclear if he was really the kind of guy who would steal another guy's penis.

The organ first appeared in the possession of Napoleon's priest, Father Ange Paul Vignali. Vignali succeeded in taking a number of Napoleon's personal effects home to his Corsican village, including a copy of the emperor's will, his waistcoat, some hair, and a pair of his breeches. These artifacts went on to form the Vignali Collection, which had a far more illustrious history than Vignali himself. The priest, who was said to be uncouth and illiterate, died in a blood feud seven years after leaving St. Helena.

The collection stayed in Vignali's family until 1916, when it was put up for auction in London. An anonymous buyer purchased the entire lot, including the penis, gracefully described by the auctioneers as a "mummified tendon." The collection then went to the famed London antiquarian booksellers Maggs Bros., who sold it in 1924 to Philadelphia book collector Abraham Simon Wolf Rosenbach. In 1927, Rosenbach allowed the penis to go on display at the Museum of

French Art in New York City. A reporter from *Time* magazine said it looked like a "maltreated strip of buckskin shoelace or a shriveled eel."

Rosenbach sold the collection in 1944, and it passed among various American collectors until 1977, when it went up for sale in Paris. Most of the artifacts joined Napoleon's body at Les Invalides, but the French government has always refused to acknowledge the "mummified tendon" as genuine. The little hunk of flesh, stored in a dark blue leather box, was eventually purchased by a top American urologist named John K. Lattimer, who brought it home to New Jersey. Some say Lattimer wanted to take the object out of circulation so it would stop being ridiculed, but it probably also made a nice addition to his collection of macabre historical artifacts. These included Abraham Lincoln's blood-stained collar, leather from the car JFK was riding in when assassinated, and Hermann Göring's cyanide vial.

Lattimer kept the penis in a suitcase underneath his bed until he passed away in 2007. Before he died, he did clear up some of the object's mystery by taking a series of X-rays. These revealed that the sliver of flesh, though it may look like a shoelace or an eel, is actually *someone's* penis. Of course, whether it once belonged to "the little corporal" is anyone's guess.

LORD BYRON

BORN: JANUARY 22, 1788,
DOVER, ENGLAND
DIED: APRIL 19, 1824 (AGE 36),
MESOLÓNGION, GREECE

With his extravagant tastes in clothes, his sexual magnetism, and his devotion to the cult of himself, the poet Lord Byron was the first modern celebrity. He even got fan mail: women regularly wrote him letters offering praise and adoration, and sometimes even their own bodies. His wife coined the term "Byronmania" to describe the frenzy of his fans, anticipating the term "Beatlemania" by more than a hundred years.

But eventually Byron went too far. After his brief marriage failed miserably, he left Britain in 1816 amid rumors that he had forced his wife to perform "unnatural acts" and carried on an incestuous affair with his half sister, Augusta. In retreat, he first traveled to Switzerland, where he participated in the house party that inspired Mary Shelley to write *Frankenstein,* and then to Italy, where he sailed with Percy Shelley and bedded Mary's half sister, Claire. His next adventure was in Greece, where in 1823 he joined that country's fight for independence from the Ottoman Empire. Byron tried to bolster the disorganized Greek forces with financial and organizational support, but only a year after arriving, he was confined to his sickbed. The cause, at least according to many modern experts, was malaria contracted in the Greek marshlands.

His doctors didn't understand the root of his illness, and had Byron been given quinine in time, he might have been saved. Instead he was fed castor oil and antimony, and bled repeatedly despite his protests. "Have you no other remedy than bleeding?" he shouted at his physicians as they pulled pints of blood from his temples and jugular. None of it did any good. Byron died just after six in the evening, as a thunderstorm was breaking over the city. Superstitious locals interpreted the wrath of the heavens as a sign that a great man had died.

The city of Mesolóngion, where Byron's life had ended, was plunged into despair. The morning after his death, thirty-seven guns were fired from a nearby fortress, one for each year of his life. Black-bordered notices distributed throughout the city ordered Easter Week celebrations canceled and all nonessential shops and public offices closed. Meanwhile, Byron's friends debated what to do with his body. Throughout his life, the poet had left conflicting wishes. At times he asked to be buried in England, while at other times he refused. In 1819 he'd written to his publisher, "I am sure my Bones would not rest in an English grave—or my Clay mix with the Earth of that Country . . . I would not even feed your worms—if I could help it." And the day before he died,

Byron declared: "Let not my body be hacked, or be sent to England."

Both requests were denied. The doctors who "hacked" Byron's body during the autopsy found a congested brain, a flabby heart, and a diseased liver (no surprise, given that Byron lived on alcohol). Before stitching him back up, the doctors removed his heart, brain, and other internal organs, placing them in four urns. A mistranslated funeral oration has led to a story that the heart stayed in Greece, but in fact the Greeks got a different set of organs: his lungs and larynx. Pietro Capsali, the man in whose house Byron died, said, "We wished to have his lungs and larynx because he had used his breath and voice for Greece." But the urn with Byron's lungs disappeared when Mesolóngion fell to the Turks in a siege two years after the poet's death.

The British establishment was considerably less reverent than the Greeks, in part because Byron's support of Greek independence contradicted British foreign policy. One official said that Byron's body should be burned, a message conveyed back to London with multiple exclamation points. However, Byron's friends decided that the most honorable thing to do was to send the poet back to England, regardless of his wishes. They shipped his embalmed corpse and the urns containing his organs back home on the *Florida,* which had just arrived from Britain carrying the first installment of a large loan Byron had negotiated for the independence forces.

When London newspapers heard Byron's body would be coming to England, they reported on plans for a burial in Westminster Abbey. But the dean of Westminster, who still remembered the "unnatural acts" scandal of 1816, refused. He told one of Byron's executors that the best thing to do was "to carry away the body, and say as little about it as possible." In fact, it would not be until 1969 that church officials finally agreed to a memorial for Byron at Poets' Corner in Westminster Abbey.

Despite the establishment's cold shoulder, the public still loved their poet. Sir Walter Scott said the news of his death "stunned" the nation, while to a young Tennyson the "whole world seemed to be in darkness." When the *Florida* arrived in July 1824 carrying Byron's body (preserved in one hundred eighty gallons of spirits), spectators crowded the banks of the Thames. At one point, a little boy was caught below deck trying to cut off a piece of Byron's shroud. Thousands, many of them weeping women, came to see the body as it lay on view for a week in a house in London.

With no burial in Westminster Abbey forthcoming, Byron's executors and half sister decided to bury the poet at his family vault in Hucknall Torkard, Nottinghamshire. Byron was laid to rest in the church's vault, joining his father "Mad Jack" Byron, grandfather "Foul-Weather Jack" Byron, and dozens of other relatives with less colorful nicknames. Almost thirty years later, the vault was closed for good following the burial of Byron's daughter, Ada Lovelace, a celebrated mathematician.

But the public fascination with Byron's life and death only grew, and in 1938 his family vault was reopened. Officially, the reopening was motivated by a search for an ancient crypt, and to put to rest rumors that Byron's body had been stolen. However, the chief impetus seems to have been the personal curiosity of the Hucknall vicar, Thomas Gerrard Barber. Barber was passionate about both Lord Byron and local archaeology, and it was only a matter of time before he came up with a way to get into Lord Byron's tomb. In 1938 he received permission from the government, as well as the Byron family, to do just that.

In order not to attract undue public attention, the reopening was carried out after dusk, and the participants sworn to secrecy. One warm evening in the middle of June, about forty people gathered in the church, including stonemasons, an antiquarian, a surveyor, and a photographer. Once the vault had been opened, Barber allowed the assembled to take their measurements and photographs. But he made sure to return at midnight for a more leisurely personal viewing.

Descending the steps into the three-hundred-year-old vault, Barber found a small room littered with bones and decaying wood. In the center stood three tiers of coffins, newer and more ornate boxes flattening the older ones beneath. At the base of the stairs, Barber noticed a seventeenth-century infant's coffin partially crushed by a well-preserved chest. On the lid of the chest, Barber saw a brass plate identifying the contents:

Within this urn
Are deposited
The heart and the brain
Of the deceased
Lord Noel Byron

Turning his attention to the center of the room, Barber noticed two coffins topped with coronets from which the ermine and pearls had long since disappeared. Barber believed that the two coffins belonged to Byron and Lovelace, and indeed Lovelace's coffin still bore her ornate brass nameplate. The other coffin, wreathed in faded purple velvet and decorated with hundreds of brass nails, showed no signs of identification. To his horror, Barber discovered that the lid of the anonymous coffin was loose.

"Dare I look within?" Barber wrote in his account of the evening's events. "Yes, the world should know the truth—that the body of the great poet was there—or that the coffin was empty. Reverently, very reverently, I raised the lid, and before my eyes there lay the embalmed body of Byron in as perfect a condition as when it was placed in the coffin one hundred and fourteen years ago."

Barber allowed himself a glance only long enough to establish that the body was perfectly preserved, and that Byron's clubfoot—whose location biographers had long debated—was his right one. (The foot had become detached from the leg and lay at the coffin's bottom.) His curiosity satisfied, he closed the lid with a prayer for Byron's soul.

Earlier in the day, churchwarden Arnold Houldsworth and several workmen, left alone with the coffins while Barber took supper, also could not resist the urge to take a peek. Most likely, they were the ones who had cut open Byron's coffin earlier that day. Like Barber, they noted that the poet's face and torso were well preserved, but added that his extremities had been "skeletonized," as the warden would later write. No part of the body escaped their scrutiny: Houldsworth also noted that Byron's "sexual organ showed quite abnormal development."

Biographers have long wondered about this "abnormality," but Houldsworth, interviewed by a British journalist in the 1960s, cleared up the confusion. "I've been in the Army, I've been in bathhouses, I've seen men," Houldsworth said. "But I never saw nothing like him. . . . He was built like a pony."

GRIGORI RASPUTIN

BORN: JANUARY 22, 1869,
POKROVSKOYE, TYUMEN OBLAST,
RUSSIA
DIED: DECEMBER 29, 1916 (AGE 47),
ST. PETERSBURG, RUSSIA

In 2004, a disturbing image began circulating on the Internet. A middle-aged Russian man, wearing a lab coat and a bemused expression, held aloft a fluid-filled jar with a long column of flesh floating inside. According to news articles accompanying the image, the flesh had once dangled between the legs of famous mystic Grigori Rasputin, "Russia's greatest love machine," if you believe musical act Boney M. Like Einstein's brain and Shelley's heart, this relic symbolizes its original owner's best-known attributes—in this case, an enormous lust for women and power, both of which led to Rasputin's demise.

Though often called the "mad monk," Rasputin had no formal affiliation with any religious order. He's perhaps best understood as a faith healer known for his seemingly miraculous cures, and for his most famous client, Russia's last tsarina. Though most of Russia didn't know it, Alexandra Romanova's only son, Alexei, suffered from hemophilia, a disease in which any scrape can turn into a life-threatening hemorrhage. The existence of a son was a matter of stability for the empire, and Alexei's hemophilia was a closely guarded secret. Rasputin was the only person who was reliably able to heal Alexei, and the deeply religious Alexandra believed he had been sent to her by God.

The Russian public had a different idea about what was going on. After Rasputin arrived in St. Petersburg, his appetites—for fish soup, Madeira wine, and women—became legendary, and there was no shortage of bored bourgeois wives in the capital willing to satisfy them. Soon Rasputin's power went to his head, and he grew increasingly drunk and lecherous in public. Once, at a posh Moscow nightclub in 1915, he smashed furniture, attacked his female companion, and unbuttoned his trousers, waving his penis around. He also shouted out that he'd slept with the tsarina—which by that time is what most of St. Petersburg thought anyway.

The rumors of an affair were probably false, but the damage had been done. The Siberian mystic became a convenient scapegoat for the unraveling imperial government, whose many failures were blamed on Rasputin's malevolent sway over the tsar and tsarina. It wasn't long before a band of patriotic nobles decided that getting rid of Rasputin was the only way to save Russia from ruin. In those heady days before the revolution, it seemed worth trying anything that might make the tsar more popular.

One icy December evening in 1916, Prince Felix Yusupov, Russia's second-richest man, lured Rasputin to the basement of his magnificent palace. The pretext was a meeting with Yusupov's beautiful wife, Irina, who was in fact in the Crimea. Yusupov said she was just out at a party, and he entertained Rasputin while pretending to wait for her, and while he mustered the courage to take care of the evening's real purpose—Rasputin's murder.

Yusupov urged Rasputin to partake of the pastries and wine laid out before them, neglecting to mention that they had been poisoned. According to Yusupov, Rasputin consumed several cakes and goblets of wine but remained utterly unaffected. After growing increasingly frantic, Yusupov pulled out his gun and shot Rasputin at close range, but even that didn't work. The prince watched in horror as Rasputin's eyes blinked open, and then he ran screaming as his would-be victim staggered out into the snow.

Finally, another member of the murder party (who had been hiding upstairs) killed Rasputin with several more shots into his back, and the gang of murderous nobles dumped his body into the Neva River. Stories have long persisted that Rasputin died only when plunged into the frigid water, but more recent forensic analysis of the autopsy report shows it was a bullet in the forehead that got him.

So how did his penis end up in the newspapers? According to Rasputin's daughter, Maria, her father was castrated just before his murder. She says Yusupov killed Rasputin because the mystic resisted his sexual advances; the prince was known to play for both teams, but Rasputin not so much. In revenge for turning him down, Yusupov raped Rasputin, or so Maria says, and then he or one of his conspirators severed Rasputin's penis and flung it across the room.

The penis only came to the public's attention in the 1970s, when a writer named Patte Barham (then coauthoring a book with Maria) said she had seen it in the bedroom of a Russian émigré living in Paris. According to Barham, the émigré's sister had been married to a servant who worked at the Yusupov palace, and who found the penis while cleaning up after Rasputin's murder. Barham described it as resting in a polished wooden box, and looking like "a blackened, overripe banana, about a foot long, and resting on a velvet cloth." A coterie of

Rasputin's former followers apparently gathered at the émigré's apartment weekly to worship Rasputin's, ahem, memory.

When Rasputin's daughter discovered his penis was being kept in some strange woman's bedroom, she demanded it back. Her request was successful, but after her death, the item ended up sold alongside other effects to the London auction house Bonhams. The auctioneers were only too happy to receive Maria's manuscripts and photographs of her father, but they were a little more suspicious of the banana-shaped item. It turns out they had good reason: tests conducted at the Imperial College London showed it was actually a sea cucumber.

For his part, Igor Knyazkin—the man in those photos from 2004—says the penis he purchased was found in an abandoned house in a Parisian suburb in the late 1990s. Knyazkin purchased the item for his erotic museum, which he runs out of his prostatology clinic in St. Petersburg (apparently, the exhibits take people's minds off their medical troubles). Knyazkin says his prize possession is about thirteen inches long, and that he helped reconstruct it by steaming it and filling the inside with gel. That length would tally with Maria's description of her dear dad's member while he was alive—although one wonders how she would know.

Today there's no way to examine Rasputin's body for evidence. After his autopsy, his corpse was buried beneath a church constructed by one his devotees. Three months later, he was exhumed on orders of Russia's new revolutionary regime, who feared his grave might become a place for worshippers to spread monarchist propaganda. His body was driven to a nearby forest and burned. Eyewitnesses said that Rasputin sat up in the flames, giving the Russians one final spook. Perhaps his spirit wanted to be remembered—though who knows how he would feel about the idea that it was his penis that survived the grave.

INDECENT EXPOSURES

In 1968, King Tut's penis was reported missing. X-rays discovered the pharaoh to be bereft of his phallus, even though the mummy had been reported intact at the time of its discovery in 1922. Rumors blamed Harry Burton, the British expedition's official cameraman, and the only one who had ever been left alone with the boy king. Burton's name was cleared in 2006, however, when a CT scan found the missing member lying in the sand around King Tut's body. Archaeologists breathed a sigh of relief—one less reason to be concerned about the mummy's curse.

In the relics-mad Middle Ages, no fewer than a dozen churches and monasteries in Europe claimed to have Jesus's foreskin, also known as the Holy Prepuce. Like all good Jewish boys, Jesus was circumcised at eight days old, and some Christian writings hold that when he ascended to heaven, the results of his bris were left behind. The Holy Prepuce first appeared in the historical record in AD 800, when Charlemagne supposedly gave it to Pope Leo II, but went missing when Charles V's troops sacked Rome in 1527. The relic was discovered a few decades later thirty miles north in the town of Calcata, where its display turned the spot into a must-see pilgrimage destination. In 1983 it was reported stolen, and while the culprit has never been apprehended, some think the Vatican got sick of the attention and stole it themselves.

Pity the poor people who work at the Smithsonian. Every so often, a visitor comes in asking to see John Dillinger's penis. The story goes that someone, perhaps J. Edgar Hoover, nicked the notorious bank robber's prized appendage after his death and donated it to the nation's premier historical institution, in part because of said appendage's enormous size. Not surprisingly, the Smithsonian denies the story. As for the size issue, some say the rumors go back to a 1934 morgue photo, in which Dillinger's arm was raised beneath a sheet at an angle that made him appear particularly well endowed.

OLIVER CROMWELL

BORN: APRIL 25, 1599,
HUNTINGDON, CAMBRIDGESHIRE,
ENGLAND
DIED: SEPTEMBER 3, 1658 (AGE 59),
LONDON, ENGLAND

Oliver Cromwell ruled England as a military dictator for less than five years, but his head had a far longer career in English public life. Treated with reverence, rage, curiosity, and finally embarrassment, its fortunes waxed and waned in accordance with Cromwell's own reputation.

Cromwell died at the height of his power, of complications from a bladder infection. Though he had refused to wear the crown during his life, conservative members of his regime gave him a funeral fit for a king. His embalmed corpse lay in state for two months at Somerset House, near an effigy clad in royal purple velvet robes and a crown. In fact, the preparations for his funeral took so long that by the time the event occurred, Cromwell's corpse had already been buried at Westminster Abbey. The thousands who lined the streets of London to watch the funeral procession saw a £4,000 hearse carrying an empty coffin.

But while Cromwell was buried as a king, he was exhumed as a criminal. When the monarchy was restored in 1660, Charles II wanted to punish those responsible for his father's death. Ten remaining "king-killers" swung from the gallows, but it wasn't enough. In December 1660, Parliament ordered the bodies of Cromwell and several associates exhumed from their coffins. They were to be hanged at Tyburn, the execution spot normally reserved for common criminals.

In January 1661, a dozen years to the day after Charles I's demise, Cromwell's body was dragged to Tyburn on a sledge. Crowds jeered as the corpse was hanged from the notorious "Triple Tree" gallows, alongside the dead bodies of Henry Ireton (Cromwell's son-in-law) and John Bradshaw, who had presided over the court that tried Charles I. A Spanish merchant who witnessed the scene said Cromwell looked "very fresh," while Ireton "hung like a dried rat."

After dangling until the late afternoon, the trio's bodies were cut down and their heads hacked off. Workers buried their decapitated corpses below the Triple Tree, but the heads were impaled on twenty-foot oak spikes and mounted on the roof of Westminster Hall, part of the Houses of Parliament. They remained there for more than twenty years, visible for miles around as a warning to those who would dare cross the monarchy.

But during a furious storm toward the end of the seventeenth century, or so the story goes, Cromwell's head came tumbling off the roof and landed at the feet of a guard. The guard may not have known exactly whose head he was looking at, but he evidently knew enough to take it home and hide it in his chimney. He must have realized the true origin of his grisly gift when signs around London began offering a reward for the return of

Cromwell's head, but he chose to keep his discovery a secret until his last days. Only on his deathbed did he tell his wife and daughter about the unusual object wedged in their flue.

His daughter seems to have decided the head was not an appropriate family heirloom, and so she sold it, although we don't know to whom. The head next appeared in history around 1710 in the collection of one Claudius Du Puy, a French-Swiss calico printer who owned a well-stocked cabinet of curiosities. According to one German visitor, Cromwell's head was the star attraction in four rooms packed full of shells, herbs, magnets, snakeskins, coins, medals, mummies, and twenty wax dolls wearing nun's habits. By this point, Cromwell's head had clearly been stripped of its political significance, and reduced to nothing more than a macabre curio.

After Du Puy passed away, the head came into the possession of a failed comedian and drunkard named Samuel Russell, who exhibited it in a stall near London's Clare Market around 1780. Russell couldn't manage either his drinking or his possessions very well, and around 1787, a jeweler named John Cox swindled Russell out of the head by loaning him money and demanding the head as repayment. Cox's intentions were purely financial: he suspected he'd be able to sell the head for a tidy sum. He was right, and a few years later he sold it to three brothers named Hughes for twice what he'd paid.

The brothers mounted a public exhibition on Bond Street, charging two shillings and sixpence to see the head and other items of Cromwellania. But the show was a bust: almost no one came. Some say the entrance fee was too high, and the details about the head's provenance too sketchy. It also didn't help that the publicist quit halfway through. Strangely, all three brothers then perished in quick succession—sparking rumors of a Cromwellian curse.

The daughter of the last surviving Hughes brother tried to sell the head to museums, but no one would take it, perhaps because the days of exhibiting human heads were on their way out. When the proprietor of the Piccadilly Museum asked then Prime Minister Robert Jenkinson whether or not to purchase the head, Jenkinson stated the "strong objection which would naturally arise to the exhibition of any human remains at a Public Museum frequented by Persons of both Sexes and of all ages." Never mind that a century and a half before, human heads had been exhibited on pikes for the whole city to see.

In 1815, the Hughes daughter finally sold Cromwell's head to a private collector, a Mr. Josiah Henry Wilkinson of Kent. Wilkinson was proud of his relic, taking it out during dinner parties and bringing it on trips. His son and grandson also made no secret of their possession, and the head was a not-infrequent topic of conversation in Victorian drawing rooms. This became particularly true as the public rediscovered Cromwell through the work of Thomas Carlyle, although Carlyle himself dismissed the head as "fraudulent moonshine" (even though he never actually saw it).

Others shared Carlyle's opinion, and in the late nineteenth century, scientists began asking Wilkinson if they could study the skull to determine its authenticity. Wilkinson resisted such entreaties until 1875, when he allowed an Oxford professor to examine the skull alongside a rival claimant from the Ashmolean, one of Oxford's museums. After comparing both heads to a mask made of Cromwell on his deathbed, the professor concluded that the Ashmolean skull was clearly a fake, and the Wilkinson was the genuine article.

But it wasn't until the 1930s that the scientific community was convinced the Wilkinson skull was the real deal. In 1934 statistician Karl Pearson and anthropologist G. M. Morant measured a host of Cromwell busts, life masks, and death masks, and when they compared the average of these measurements to the Wilkinson skull, they found a nearly perfect match—down to the depression on the Wilkinson head at the site of a prominent wart. The pair concluded that there was a "moral certainty" that the head had belonged to Cromwell.

Soon afterward, the Wilkinson family decided they were tired of their odd inheritance and the media interest it inspired. In early 1960, Horace Wilkinson (a descendant of Josiah) contacted Sidney Sussex, the Cambridge college Cromwell had attended. On March 25 of that year, Cromwell's head was buried somewhere on the college grounds. A plaque in a college antechapel says the burial occurred "near to this place," but the precise location of the skull's interment has been kept secret. After three hundred years of display, it's time for Cromwell's head to finally rest in peace.

NED KELLY

BORN: *CA.* JUNE 1855,
BEVERIDGE, VICTORIA, AUSTRALIA
DIED: NOVEMBER 11, 1880 (AGE 25),
MELBOURNE, VICTORIA, AUSTRALIA

If there's one lesson to be learned from the story of Ned Kelly's remains, it's that you can't believe everything you see in a museum. Those little white labels beneath the models and the fossils may look reassuring, but they're only as accurate as the human beings who wrote them. Like all human beings, museum curators like a good story—but that doesn't mean their stories are true.

Ned Kelly was the Australian Jesse James, a handsome young sharpshooter born to rural poverty who justified his robberies and killings with the rhetoric of rebellion against oppression. To some, Kelly was a cold-blooded murderer, but to others, he was a hero who made his

Irish ancestors proud by standing up to a corrupt British establishment. Today, Kelly is one of the best-known characters in Australian history, and his image (clad in the homemade tin armor he wore during his final siege) appears on everything from stamps to mailboxes to mints.

Kelly's years on the run came to an end on June 27, 1880, during a fierce shoot-out at a hotel in Glenrowan, Victoria. Despite their armor, Kelly's gang perished in the firefight, but police took Kelly alive by shooting him repeatedly in the legs. After the battle, he was tried and condemned to death, a sentence that was carried out despite a petition with more than thirty-two thousand signatures calling for a reprieve. His last words on the scaffold are said to have been, "Tell 'em I died game," a phrase now enshrined in Australian popular culture.

After the execution, Kelly's corpse dangled from the gallows for half an hour, until officials were certain no life remained. Then his body was turned over to the proprietor of a Melbourne waxworks, who sheared off Kelly's dark hair and full beard before smearing his face with plaster of Paris. The resulting death mask looks strangely serene, though Kelly's brows are furrowed as if he were concentrating on something at the moment the noose tightened.

Today, Kelly's death mask (kept at the National Museum of Australia) is the nearest we can come to seeing the outlaw in the flesh. But for years, Australian institutions displayed another object intimately connected to the nation's most famous criminal: his skull. Or at least, what they said was his skull.

The story goes back to 1929, when the Melbourne jail where Kelly had been executed was closed. Part of its grounds were turned over to the nearby Working Men's College (now the Royal Melbourne Institute of Technology) to create a new engineering school. Authorities believed that the skeletons of the dozens of executed criminals buried at the jail had long since disintegrated, since the bodies had been well covered in quicklime. But despite what movies and TV might have you believe, quicklime doesn't disintegrate bone. When the workmen began digging to lay a new foundation, they were horrified to discover the ground packed full of skeletons.

At first, they covered up their disgust and kept going. But when a steam shovel accidentally cracked open a coffin near a stone wall labeled "E.K.," all hell broke loose. Both the workers and pupils from the college believed the initials stood for Edward (better known as Ned) Kelly, and they made a mad dash for souvenirs, pocketing bones, teeth, and several skulls from the coffin and those nearby. Some of the bones circulated among the Australian public for years, although most were returned a few days later, when the police threatened punishment. One of the items returned was a skull said to be Ned Kelly's.

But the skull never made its way back to Kelly's coffin. It spent about five years at the Victorian Penal Department, where rumor says it was used as a paperweight. In 1934 it was taken to the Institute of Anatomy in Canberra, and by the 1940s a cast of it had become one of the institute's most popular attractions (the real skull was kept in the basement). In 1971 the institute closed, and the skull made its way back to the Melbourne jail, which had by then transformed itself into a museum. The cranium went on display next to Kelly's death mask, just a few paces away from the place where the outlaw himself had been hanged almost a century before.

The skull stayed there until 1978, when it was stolen again. Staff at the jail museum were baffled: the glass cabinet remained locked, and showed no signs of tampering. But the skull was gone. The curator called the theft an "absolute mystery."

It stayed that way for two decades. But in the late 1990s a sandalwood farmer from the remote Kimberley region of Western Australia, Tom Baxter, came forward saying he had Ned's head. Baxter did seem to have the skull, or at least *a* skull: he showed it off to journalists, though he made sure to hide it whenever the police came around, storing it underground or inside a hollow tree. It helped that Baxter lived deep in the bush; as one journalist noted, you could hide a jumbo jet in the wilds that served as Baxter's backyard.

Baxter refused to say whether he had stolen the skull himself (at times he blamed the son of an unnamed local politician), but he took his role as its custodian seriously. He objected to the fact that the skull had been on display as a "police trophy," and refused to return it until the government agreed that the skull would be returned to Kelly's family for a Christian burial. After all, that had been Kelly's last wish, dictated in a letter the day before he died.

It took a decade of negotiations, but Baxter finally struck a deal with authorities. He handed over the skull in November 2009, the 129th anniversary of Kelly's hanging. But officials weren't taking any chances on the skull's authenticity, and weren't swayed by the "E. Kelly" someone had scrawled on one side. They wanted to know for sure whether the skull had belonged to the famous outlaw. To find out, they turned the cranium over to the Victorian Institute of Forensic Medicine, a group renowned for their work identifying victims of tsunamis, terrorist attacks, and deadly Australian bush fires.

The skull was the institute's first historical mystery. To solve it, scientists began comparing the skull with archival photographs and a cast made in the 1930s. But they weren't sure whether the skull had been stolen from the Melbourne jail in 1929 until a young man walked into the institute carrying a small wooden box.

The man was the grandson of Alexander Talbot, a laborer who worked on the 1929 construction at the jail grounds and participated in the free-for-all that followed. Old news photographs showed Talbot holding the skull said to be Kelly's, and articles recorded his theft of a tooth from the same item. The tooth had stayed in Talbot's family, at least until his grandson learned that the forensic institute had appealed to the public for help.

After the scientists opened the small wooden box, they discovered that the tooth slid perfectly into the socket of one of the skull's molars. Since the roots of every tooth are unique, the perfect match convinced the scientists that the skull in front of them had been stolen from the jail in 1929. Meanwhile, comparisons with historical photographs and the cast proved the skull was the same one that had been on display for decades, and that was stolen in 1978.

But that didn't prove it had belonged to Ned Kelly. For that, the team turned to DNA analysis. They tracked down one of Ned's sister Ellen's descendants—a Melbourne schoolteacher named Leigh Oliver—who agreed to shed a little blood to help solve the mystery. A finger prick later, the scientists had the evidence they needed to help figure out whether the skull was Kelly's.

The skull itself was too decayed and contaminated for direct testing, but the tooth that had been shown to come from the skull proved to be a rich repository of DNA. The scientists took samples from the tooth and compared them with Oliver's DNA, waiting with bated breath for the results. The tests showed a mismatch, leaving the scientists to conclude that the skull had not belonged to Kelly after all. For all those years, Baxter had been protecting someone else's skull.

There was a suggestion of who the skull's original owner might have been. As part of their investigation, the scientists examined the death masks of the dozen men buried in the same part of the jail cemetery as Kelly. Of the twelve, only two matched the contours of the mystery skull: Ned Kelly's, and a mask belonging to Australia's first serial killer, Frederick Deeming. As if being a country's first serial killer isn't bad enough, some think the English-born Deeming may have been Jack the Ripper. He was said to have been seen in the Whitechapel area of London during the notorious murders, and fit the description of the fiend.

With the aid of 3-D modeling software, scientists discovered that Deeming's death mask was a perfect match with the skull. Furthermore, the researchers discovered that Deeming had been buried right next to Kelly after his execution in 1892, which means the workers and pupils hunting for souvenirs in 1929 could easily have confused the bones of the two criminals. It would not be Deeming's first case of mistaken identity: throughout his life traveling in England, South Africa, and South America, he had constantly switched names and personae to conceal his crimes.

Kelly's real skull remains at large, but the rest of him has been found. As part of their investigation, the Institute of Forensic Medicine scientists examined bones that archaeologists had uncovered in 2008 while exhuming Pentridge Prison—the place where the bodies from the Melbourne jail cemetery ended up. The dig had uncovered two dozen skeletons buried in a mass grave, and while Kelly's bones were thought to be among them, nobody knew for sure. Thanks in part to Oliver's DNA, the scientists were able to identify Kelly's remains.

Two months after the results were announced, the Australian government said it would turn the bones over to the family for a private burial, just as Kelly had wanted. At the time this book was being written, the Kelly family was debating the best location for the outlaw's grave—one that they hope will be his last.

LOVE

AND

DEVOTION

If love may in life be brief, in death it is fixed forever.
—EDWARD BULWER-LYTTON (1803–73)

Death isn't necessarily the end of a relationship, even if it does make it a bit one-sided. The families and friends of some famous figures have demonstrated their devotion to the dead in unusual ways, either by taking extraordinary steps to safeguard their remains, or by creating some rather macabre mementos—the type that might get you locked up today. Some have also played posthumous pranks, as in the case of the actor John Barrymore, whose pals couldn't let him go without one last drink.

GALILEO GALILEI

BORN: FEBRUARY 15, 1564,
PISA, ITALY
DIED: JANUARY 8, 1642 (AGE 77),
ARCETRI, ITALY

It's common to think of Galileo as the lone man of science who fought the Church and lost. But Galileo himself was not antireligion. His trial in 1633, at which he was found "vehemently suspected of heresy" and sentenced to prison "at the pleasure of" the Church, disturbed him so deeply that for nights afterward he awoke neighbors with his cries and moans. As a devout Catholic, Galileo believed in the Bible; he just didn't believe in taking every word literally.

In the days following his trial, he had but one main comfort: the tender letters of his eldest daughter, Sister Maria Celeste, sent from her convent near Florence. Maria Celeste's letters helped reassure Galileo that his science was not an affront to God.

But the strains of Galileo's trial weakened Maria Celeste's already poor health, and in 1634 she died of dysentery at the age of thirty-three. Her distraught father poured himself into his work, despite his own poor health, failing eyesight, and the difficult fact that he was under house arrest. Four years later, when Galileo was totally blind, he was allowed an assistant: a sixteen-year-old Florentine math prodigy named Vincenzio Viviani.

While Viviani could never replace Maria Celeste, Galileo grew to love the boy as a son, and the two spent hours talking through all the problems of the universe. They had only four years together: in the final months of 1641 Galileo took to his bed with a fever and pain in his kidneys, and in January 1642 he passed away.

The Grand Duke of Tuscany, Ferdinando II, wanted to bury the astronomer in the Basilica of Santa Croce in Florence, with a marble mausoleum and all the pomp of a public funeral oration. But that was not to be. Pope Urban VII, a domineering man who once had the birds in the Vatican gardens killed because they annoyed him, sent word that such honors would be setting a bad example for a man who gave "rise to a universal scandal against Christianity." Instead, the grand duke had Galileo entombed in a closet-sized room beneath Santa Croce's bell tower, where his body rested for nearly a century.

Viviani, who succeeded Galileo as the grand duke's court mathematician, spent the rest of his life trying to give his mentor the burial he deserved. But while Ferdinando II had been sympathetic to the Galilean cause, his successor, Cosimo III, was too busy persecuting the Jews and taxing Florence into the ground to be of any help. Finally, Viviani took control of the only thing he really could: his own house.

Viviani turned the facade of his home into a monument to Galileo, complete with a bust of the astronomer crowning the entrance and huge stone scrolls lauding his achievements decorating either side of the door. The building is now a landmark in Florence, where it is known as the Palazzo dei Cartelloni, or Palace of Scrolls.

But home decor was not enough for Viviani. With his wishes thwarted in life, he made plans to triumph in death. Before he died in 1703, he left designs—and funds—in his will to build Galileo a sumptuous new marble tomb in Santa Croce. He also ordered his own body buried with Galileo, even if that meant decades interred in the closet beneath the bell tower, which it did.

By 1737 the memory of Galileo's trial had dimmed, and a Florentine pope was in power. That year the senator who inherited Viviani's property finally received permission from the Holy Office to carry out his benefactor's grand plans. And so, at six p.m. on March 12, 1737, Florence's elite gathered in the room beneath the bell tower to exhume Galileo. The timing was no accident: 173 years before, at the same hour and on the same day of the year, Michelangelo's body had been interred at Santa Croce. While singing his master's praises, Viviani had more than once mentioned the fanciful idea that Michelangelo's spirit had leaped into Galileo's body, which arrived in the world three days before Michelangelo left. Now, Galileo's remains would be brought to rest forever near the man whose brush depicted the heavens almost as beautifully as Galileo's telescope.

Amid the glare of torches and candles, the men began to break open the brick tombs of the tiny room. Viviani's was opened first, and his wooden coffin was taken to the novice's chapel, where a lead plate was discovered beneath the coffin lid that confirmed the body belonged to Galileo's last disciple. Next, the men broke open the bricks of Galileo's tomb, where they found a surprise: the tomb held not one coffin, but two.

No one had been expecting this. The men carried both bodies into the chapel, where the grand duke's personal physician examined them. Fortunately, they could not have looked more different: one had belonged to a very old man, and one to a very young woman. It seems that Viviani, unable to fulfill Galileo's wish for a proper burial in Santa Croce, buried him with Maria Celeste, whose bones would have been far more precious to him than any marble monument.

No DNA testing has confirmed the identity of the second set of bones, but many scholars feel sure they belong to Galileo's daughter, and Florentine officials reburied them alongside Galileo in his new tomb. That is, after they helped themselves to their own little gifts. Several of the assembled plucked mementos from Galileo's skeleton: three fingers, a tooth, and a vertebra were taken home from Santa Croce that day. The vertebra ended up at the University of Padua, while Galileo's middle finger has been on display (to the snickering delight of schoolchildren) for decades at Florence's Galileo Museum.

Galileo's other digits and his tooth were long considered lost, but in 2009 a Florentine collector purchased them at an auction where they were being sold as anonymous relics. The collector bought them on behalf of his daughter, a relics enthusiast who happened to be doing her graduate thesis on Galileo's tomb. Intrigued, the family turned the relics over to several experts, including one from the Galileo Museum, who confirmed they had indeed belonged to the great astronomer. In 2010, the rediscovered molar and digits joined Galileo's middle finger on display in Florence.

Because this is a story of love and faith, the collector doesn't believe he stumbled onto the remains by accident. "More than by chance," he told the *New York Times,* "things are also helped along a bit by the souls of the dead."

THOMAS MORE

BORN: *CA.* FEBRUARY 7, 1478,
LONDON, ENGLAND
DIED: JULY 6, 1535 (AGE 57),
LONDON, ENGLAND

A brilliant lawyer, statesman, and author, Thomas More was also a Catholic so pious he wore a hair shirt beneath his clothes and occasionally whipped himself. When Henry VIII passed the Act of Supremacy in 1534, making himself head of the English church, More refused to go with the Reformation flow. He was thrown into the Tower of London, tried, and convicted of treason. His punishment: beheading.

Fortunately, More had a daughter just as intelligent and strong-willed as he was. Margaret, known as Meg, was fluent in Greek and Latin, and later became an author in her own right—nearly unheard of for a woman of her time. Meg clearly had her father's spirit, and his willingness to defy authority. And though she could not save her dear dad's life, she was able to preserve one part of him. While some daughters might save their father's pocket watch or a favorite tie, More's daughter saved his skull.

After his execution, More's body was buried in an unmarked grave at the Tower, while his head was parboiled, tarred, and impaled on a pole on London Bridge. Poor Meg visited the bridge frequently, watching as her father's noggin was moved down the poles every few days to make way for other unfortunates. Some say that she kept track of the cranium, which must have been all but unrecognizable after the boiling and tarring, by means of a missing tooth.

An oft-repeated tale goes that after a month, when it was time for More's head to be thrown into the river, the resourceful Meg came along in a boat. "That head has lain many a time in my lap," she said to no one in particular. "Would to God it would fall into my lap as I pass under!" When the head was thrown over the bridge, lo and behold, Meg caught it—helped along by fate, a breeze, or perhaps a bridgemaster with newly filled pockets.

Smart as she was, Meg was no match for the king's chief minister, Thomas Cromwell. He hauled her before his private council and accused her of keeping her father's head as a "sacred relic," as well as concealing his papers. Meg answered like a good lawyer's daughter, saying merely that she had tried to keep her father's head from becoming "food for the fishes" and that she had saved only a few of his personal letters. (In fact, the documents she saved have become a key source for scholars trying to understand More's life.) Meanwhile, More's head—which Meg packed with spices as preservatives—rests today in her family vault at St. Dunstan's Church in Canterbury. She asked for it to be buried in her arms.

Memento Mori

The explorer, scholar, and adventurer Sir Walter Raleigh was in and out of the Tower of London throughout his adult life; one contemporary called him "fortune's tennis ball." His luck finally ran out in 1618, when he was executed on the orders of King James I. His body was buried in St. Margaret's Church, next to Westminster Abbey, while his head was sent to his widow, Elizabeth, in a red leather bag. She had it embalmed, and kept it in a special case for the rest of her life. After her death the head is said to have passed to her son, Carew, and according to tradition, it now lies with him at St. Mary's Church in West Horsley, Surrey.

PERCY SHELLEY

Born: August 4, 1792,
Field Place, West Sussex, England
Died: July 8, 1822 (age 29),
Viareggio, Tuscany, Italy

Shelley belongs to that tragic class of artists who die before age thirty and whose lives are always interpreted through the dark prism of their deaths. The poet has long been characterized as too good to live, an angel "beating in the void his luminous wings in vain," as the critic Matthew Arnold put it. Mary Shelley contributed to this characterization, calling her husband an "eternal spirit" who "could not adapt himself to this clay shrine."

Percy and Mary eloped when the latter was only sixteen, even though Percy had done the same thing with another sixteen-year-old just a few years before and was not yet divorced. After finding that England was an inhospitable place for a poet who promoted both free love and atheism, the Shelleys moved to Italy in 1818, where they joined a circle of other free-spirited expatriates that included Lord Byron.

While in Italy, both Byron and Shelley came to love sailing the Mediterranean, a pursuit nurtured by their adventurous friend Edward Trelawny, a self-described ex-pirate. On the first day of July in 1822, Shelley and his friend Edward Williams sailed Shelley's boat, the newly refurbished *Don Juan,* from their home in Lerici down the coast to Leghorn. The purpose of the trip was to greet their friend Leigh Hunt, newly arrived in Italy, with whom Shelley and Byron planned to start a liberal magazine. The trip was a success—until the journey home.

About three hours after the *Don Juan* set sail for Lerici, a violent squall approached from the west. The men barely had time to react. No one knows what happened on board, but when the storm cleared about twenty minutes after it had begun, there was no sign of the boat, or its passengers, anywhere nearby.

It was more than a week before the bodies washed ashore, each in a different location. Shelley was identified only by his nankeen trousers, white silk socks, and Hunt's volume of Keats bent backward in his pocket. In the months that followed, conspiracy theories suggested that the *Don Juan* had been rammed, or that Shelley had committed suicide. But the best explanation is that the sudden storm overwhelmed the poorly designed boat, which had too much ballast and not enough buoyancy. It didn't help that Shelley, his head always in the clouds, had never learned how to swim.

Trelawny was the one who identified Shelley and broke the news to a distraught Mary. Because of local health regulations, the corpses could not be transported as they were, and had to be cremated on the beach. The ever-capable Trelawny also took over the cremations, ordering the construction of a portable iron cremato-rium and velvet-covered boxes to hold the ashes. The group decided that Williams's remains would be brought home to England, while Shelley's would be buried in the Protestant Cemetery in Rome, the same place Keats had been buried the year before.

On August 15, Williams's body was pulled from his quicklime-filled pit in the sand and cremated, with wine, sugar, salt, and incense poured on the flames. Feeling overwhelmed, Byron stripped off his clothes and went swimming. "Don't repeat this with me," he told Trelawny. "Let my carcass rot where it falls."

The next day, Shelley's body was burned. Byron again couldn't face the scene and went swimming, while Leigh Hunt stayed in his carriage. Only Trelawny and some lo-cals witnessed Shelley's badly decomposed corpse being dragged out of the sand. As Trelawny described the scene, "more wine was poured over Shelley's dead body than he had consumed during his life. This with the oil and salt made the yellow flames glisten and quiver. The corpse fell open and the heart was laid bare. . . . [T]he brains literally seethed, bubbled, and boiled as in a caul-dron, for a very long time."

Shelley was buried at the Protestant Cemetery in Rome beneath the words "*Cor Cordium*" ("Heart of Hearts"), as well as his beloved (and appropriate) lines from Shakespeare's *The Tempest*:

Nothing of him that doth fade
But doth suffer a sea change
Into something rich and strange.

But one organ refused to burn. The heart, or what Trelawny thought was the heart, resisted the flames while oozing an oily fluid. Seeing this, Trelawny reached into the fire and plucked out the organ. "My hand was severely burnt," he later wrote, "and had any one seen me do the act I should have been put into quarantine."

Medical historians have long debated whether

Shelley's heart could have survived the fire, or whether it was the poet's liver, a more solid organ, taken home from the beach that day. Of course, both would have been equally important to Shelley in life—even if one is a slightly less fitting memento for a Romantic poet.

Trelawny gave the heart to Hunt, who wrote that he kept it in "spirits of wine." When Mary asked to have it, Hunt wrote her a strange letter saying that his love for Shelley negated "the claims of any other love, man's or woman's." Finally, Williams's wife, Jane, prevailed, after she wrote Hunt a letter about how sad it was that Shelley's remains had become a source of bitterness between his closest friends. Hunt relented and the heart went to Mary, who kept it until she died in 1851.

A year after her death, her son and daughter-in-law finally opened the traveling desk she had always kept closed. Inside, they found Mary's journal and her copy of *Adonais,* Shelley's poem composed on the death of Keats. One of its pages had been folded into an envelope, which contained a silk bag filled with brown dust. It was all that remained of Shelley's heart, plucked from the flames thirty years before (and presumably dried out after swimming in Trelawny's jar of spirits). It's widely believed that when Mary's son, Percy, died in 1889, the dust was added to the family vault in Bournemouth, England. But it is Trelawny who rests forever beside Shelley in Rome.

THE HEART OF THE MATTER

For famous figures of the Romantic era, having your heart buried in a particular location was a way of demonstrating your affections for a special spot. One of the last major instances of heart burial came after the death of English poet and novelist Thomas Hardy, who passed away in 1928. Hardy's friends mounted a (successful) campaign to have his ashes interred in Westminster Abbey, even though his will ordered his body to be buried in his hometown of Stinsford, Dorset. When the town discovered that the body was going to be taken to London, they pitched a fit, which led to a compromise between Hardy's friends and town officials. The night after the author's death, a local surgeon cut out Hardy's heart and carried it home in a biscuit tin. Some say a cat gobbled it up, but all evidence suggests the organ was buried intact in a Stinsford churchyard, where it remains to this day.

DAVID LIVINGSTONE

BORN: MARCH 19, 1813,
BLANTYRE, LANARKSHIRE, SCOTLAND
DIED: MAY 1, 1873 (AGE 60),
CHIEF CHITAMBO'S VILLAGE
IN WHAT IS NOW ZAMBIA

David Livingstone has the dubious distinction of being remembered for a single phrase, and it wasn't even something he said. "Dr. Livingstone, I presume?" was a question asked by the American reporter Henry Morton Stanley, who found the supposedly lost Livingstone in 1871 after a two-year search through central Africa. American and British audiences thought the line was hilarious: who else could this old white man in the middle of the African jungle possibly be?

Livingstone had become famous throughout the English-speaking world as a rugged missionary and explorer bringing Christian civilization to "darkest Africa." The truth is, Livingstone was a failure as a missionary and earned only one convert, who later lapsed. His fame now rests on his scientific and geographic discoveries, which filled in the long-blank European maps of Africa's middle. Among other discoveries, he "discovered" and named Victoria Falls, the world's largest waterfall.

But in his later years, Livingstone was obsessed with a different body of water: the Nile. His search for the source of that river was both an end in itself and a means to something else. More than anything, Livingstone's goal in Africa was to end the slave trade. He hoped that by finding the source of the Nile, sometimes called "the holy grail of Victorian geography," he would earn enough political clout to finally achieve his aims.

He never did find the source of the Nile, but he died trying. Two years after meeting Stanley, he succumbed to dysentery and malaria in a village southeast of Lake Bangweulu, in what is now Zambia. Two servants, Abdullah Susi and James Chuma, took tender care of him in his final hours.

The pair had been with Livingstone every day since 1866. Susi, the elder, was a former Zambezi riverman, while Chuma had been rescued from slavery at age eleven by Livingstone, who supposedly sawed off the boy's chains with his own hands. Neither Susi nor Chuma were always model servants; occasionally their fondness for women and "bange" (marijuana) won out over working. But when Livingstone fell ill, the two kept watch over him, and after his death, they performed a heroic feat.

At the time, many tribes in central Africa considered corpses dangerous objects. Transporting a dead body through a central African village was a great way to bring on heavy fines at best, and violent attacks at worst. Nevertheless, in the hours after Livingstone's death, Susi and Chuma decided that the only proper thing to do was to bring Livingstone's body back to his own people in England, even though that meant a journey of more than a thousand miles to the coast.

When the local chief found out about Livingstone's death he didn't punish the pair, but he did try to talk some sense into them. Instead of risking their lives, he reasoned, why not bury Livingstone right there? But Susi and Chuma would not be deterred.

The pair knew a journey to the coast would take many months, and so they quickly turned their attention to preserving Livingstone's body. After a two-day funeral with drumming and dancing, they constructed a fortified hut that would let them work on Livingstone's body while keeping the corpse safe from animals. Another member of the party, who had once worked for a doctor in Zanzibar, cut out Livingstone's heart and other internal organs, which were buried beneath a tree (its bark is now kept at the Royal Geographical Society in London).

Then Susi and Chuma stuffed the body with salt and left it to dry in the hut for two weeks, after which they applied brandy to the face and hair as an additional preservative. Next its legs were bent back to make the body shorter, and the corpse was stuffed inside a cocoon of calico, bark, and sailcloth. As a finishing touch, the whole thing was tarred to make it waterproof and then lashed to a pole. To an outsider's eye, there was no sign the bundle contained a body.

But local superstition wasn't all the party had to fear. Soon after starting the trek to the coast, they lost a whole month to illness. After recovering, their trials weren't over: at least one village denied them entry, while at another a brawl flared up over an imagined offense, and the group had to fight their way out. By the time they reached Unyanyembe about six months later, ten of the sixty men in the original party had died of injury or disease.

At Unyanyembe, the group ran into a party of Englishmen sent to find and assist Livingstone. After hearing the news of his death, the leader of the party,

Lieutenant V. Lovett Cameron, again tried to convince Susi and Chuma to bury the body immediately. The pair refused; they had not traveled all this way to give up now. Cameron relented, though not before stealing Livingstone's scientific instruments.

At last, five of the remaining men, including Susi and Chuma, reached Bagamoyo on the coast. The acting British consul for Zanzibar, Captain W. F. Prideaux, had little idea what to do with them, so he paid their wages (from his own pocket) and dismissed them.

Only Jacob Wainwright, the missionary-educated servant who could read and write, was allowed to accompany the coffin back to Britain; the Church Mission Society paid his way. Livingstone's body, alongside the books, maps, and other effects the group had carted through Africa, was loaded onto the disturbingly named HMS *Vulture* for the trip from Bagamoyo to Zanzibar, and reached Southampton in April 1874.

After lying in state for several days in the Royal Geographical Society's map room, the body was buried in Westminster Abbey. Both Wainwright and Henry Morton Stanley were pallbearers. Carved on the tombstone was a line decrying slavery that Livingstone had written to the *New York Herald* in 1872: "All I can add in my solitude is, may Heaven's rich blessing come down on every one, American, English, or Turk, who will help to heal this open sore of the world."

JOHN BARRYMORE

BORN: FEBRUARY 15, 1882,
PHILADELPHIA, PENNSYLVANIA
DIED: MAY 29, 1942 (AGE 60),
LOS ANGELES, CALIFORNIA

It's one of the most macabre tales in Hollywood, a town with its fair share of skeletons in closets. It's been denied almost as many times as it has been told, but the story is just too good to fade away. You'll find it in dog-eared biographies and late-night TV specials, with multiple variations but the same basic plot: John Barrymore, a notorious alcoholic, returned after death for one last drink with his friends.

Barrymore, a grandfather of actress Drew, lit up the stage and screen in his youth with a commanding presence, athletic physique, and a face that earned him the nickname "The Great Profile." He is often remembered for his Broadway performances as Richard III and Hamlet in the 1920s, with at least one drama critic praising him as the best Hamlet ever—a fact that adds a certain resonance to the tales of his afterlife.

Although Barrymore acted right up until his death, by his forties he had become what his friends called "a bottle man." In May 1942 he collapsed during rehearsals for a radio program and was rushed to Hollywood Presbyterian Hospital, where he was diagnosed with pneumonia, lung congestion, and cirrhosis of the liver. He soon fell into a coma, although he managed to revive long enough to flirt with the nurses and swig contraband gin from an eyewash bottle. After a week and a half in the hospital, he passed away one night at a little after ten. Friends were surprised he'd lasted so long, and the doctor who performed his autopsy noted that the case was one of "WINE WOMEN SONG."

Even though he'd been disintegrating for decades, Barrymore's death was a blow to his friends and drinking buddies. Actor Errol Flynn was particularly hard hit, especially because the penniless Barrymore had spent the last few weeks of his life living at Flynn's house. If there was one man in Hollywood more fond of wine and women than Barrymore, it was Flynn, and it's said that the younger actor idolized the older one. In his memoir, *My Wicked, Wicked Ways,* Flynn recounts what may be the genesis of the Barrymore corpse caper:

"A group of us gathered at a bar called The Cock and Bull for a general expression of our sadness at the passing of the great romantic," Flynn wrote. "I was particularly sad. I had come to know John pretty well in his declining days and had even felt favored by the three horrible weeks he had invaded my place. With our group was the great and imaginative director, Raoul Walsh, a man with an offbeat sense of humor."

Flynn goes on to describe how Walsh excused himself early by saying he was so upset about Barrymore's death he needed to go home. In fact, according to Flynn, Walsh and two friends went to the Pierce Brothers Mortuary on Sunset Boulevard, where Barrymore's body lay. Walsh told the caretaker that Barrymore's crippled aunt desperately wanted to say good-bye to her beloved nephew, but couldn't make it to the mortuary, and so he hoped to bring the body to her. After Walsh sweetened the deal with a few hundred bucks, the caretaker agreed. The group smuggled Barrymore's body into a box and then into Walsh's waiting station wagon.

Finding Flynn's house dark and the servants asleep, the men made their way inside and rested Barrymore's corpse on Flynn's favorite chair, which they placed in front of the door. Flynn says he was "drunk—sad drunk" when he got home from the bar. As he tells the story:

> As I opened the door I pressed the button. The lights went on and my God—I stared into the face of Barrymore! His eyes were closed. He looked puffed, white, bloodless. They hadn't embalmed him yet. I let out a delirious scream.

Flynn raced out of his house, intending to jump into his car and drive far away, but as he reached his porch he heard peals of laughter. Walsh emerged out of the shadows and explained that the whole thing had been a joke. Joke or not, Flynn couldn't sleep for the rest of the night.

Walsh repeated the tale in his own memoir, *Each Man in His Time,* as well as in interviews with film historian Richard Schickel for the television series and book *The Men Who Made the Movies.* Walsh's story aligns with Flynn's on the major points, although he names a different mortuary and says that Flynn returned from visiting his lawyer, not the bar. And in Walsh's tale, the mortuary caretaker was a moonlighting actor who had worked on Walsh's movies. When the caretaker found out where the body had really gone, he supposedly said, "Why the hell didn't you tell me? I'd have put a better suit on him."

Another variant of the story names Peter Lorre as the perpetrator. The source for this version is actor Paul Henreid's 1984 autobiography, *Ladies' Man.* Henreid writes that he was shooting scenes for *Casablanca* alongside Lorre and Humphrey Bogart when the group learned of Barrymore's passing. Lorre hatched the plan, and convinced the other two men to contribute a few hundred dollars for the bribe. According to Henreid, this is what happened when Flynn came home:

> He opened the door and flicked on the lights and came in, threw his hat and coat on a chair and walked across the room, past Barrymore's chair to the bar. He nodded at Barrymore and took about three steps, then froze. That moment was fantastic! There was a terrible silence, then he said, "Oh my God" . . .

But the orthodox version of the story says it never happened. In fact, some of Barrymore's friends say that the only unusual thing to occur the night after the actor's death was a visit from an extremely large prostitute, who knelt in front of the body and prayed. They say Barrymore was a great fan of the oldest profession, and that he would have appreciated the gesture.

LAST
WISHES

Life is a great surprise.
I do not see why death should not be an even greater one.
—VLADIMIR NABOKOV (1899–1977)

L ast wishes are our final way of making a mark in the world. While many deal with money or possessions, the ones in this chapter concern the fate of bodily remains. Though we begin with the trailblazing philosopher Jeremy Bentham, the other stories here come from the past few decades; the idea of using your corpse to express your individuality is relatively recent. Today, everyone wants to go out in style, and the famous are no different.

JEREMY BENTHAM

BORN: FEBRUARY 15, 1748,
LONDON, ENGLAND
DIED: JUNE 6, 1832 (AGE 84),
LONDON, ENGLAND

Jeremy Bentham was the founder of utilitarianism, a school of philosophy that says the best way to make decisions is to figure out what will cause the most happiness for the greatest number of people. That may not sound exciting now, but it was a pretty groundbreaking idea when Bentham began writing in the eighteenth century. He was an iconoclast, a campaigner for legal and social reform who believed in animal rights, women's rights, science, and progress. He also believed in the right to dissect dead bodies—including his own.

At the time of Bentham's death, scientists were often forced to use grave robbers to collect corpses for study. One of the many things that Bentham wanted to change about England was the legal prohibition against human dissection, which is what encouraged the grave-robbing in the first place. To make a point, Bentham's will asked for a public dissection of his own corpse, led by his best friend and protégé, Dr. Southwood Smith.

Two days after Bentham's death, Smith led the dissection at the Webb Street School of Anatomy in South London. He even delivered a speech over Bentham's corpse, praising the practicality and benevolence of the deceased. A thunderstorm broke over the city during the proceedings, and as Smith carved into Bentham's corpse between flashes of lightning, his face turned as pale as his dead friend's skin.

But Bentham's posthumous plans didn't end there. The year before he died, Bentham wrote a treatise entitled *Auto-Icon: or, Farther uses of the dead to the living,* which argued that corpses should be preserved for the use and enjoyment of future generations. Why not use the dead to adorn the home and garden, Bentham wondered, or employ them as stage props? Why not arrange them in a posthumous hall of fame, or hold debates between notable (dead) intellectuals? Bentham went on to devise eleven categories for the uses of corpses: "moral, political, honorific, dehonorific, money-saving, money-getting, commemorative, genealogical, architectural, theatrical, and phrenological."

The philosopher called such preserved and displayed bodies "auto-icons," and he wanted to turn his own corpse into the premier example. Following Bentham's will, Smith removed all of his friend's organs, stripped his skeleton of flesh, and preserved his skull in the "style of the New Zealanders," which involved drying it out with an air pump and some sulfuric acid. Next, Smith fitted the skeleton inside one of Bentham's favorite suits, stuffed hay and straw around the bones, and seated Bentham on one of his favorite chairs. As a final touch, Smith propped his friend's beloved walking stick (which Bentham had nicknamed "Dapple" after Sancho Panza's mule in *Don Quixote*) in one of his hands.

Unfortunately, all that sulfuric acid had left Bentham's

head looking something like a cheap Halloween mask. Smith knew that Bentham wasn't actually trying to terrify people, so he hired a sculptor to create a wax head instead. The resulting product is eerily lifelike, and even features some of Bentham's own hair, if not the glass eyes the philosopher used to carry in his pocket and told friends were destined for his corpse.

Thus stuffed, Bentham enjoyed pride of place in Smith's office for a number of years. He even served as a very special guest during periodic parties in his honor (Dickens may have attended one or two). But in 1850 Smith moved offices, and decided to donate Bentham's auto-icon to the Anatomy Museum of the University College London. While not a founder of the school, as is often reported, the philosopher had long been one of its supporters, and believed strongly in its motto of education for all.

Bentham is still there today, encased in a mahogany and glass cabinet in the south end of the school's cloisters. A wonderful—though entirely false—rumor has it that he is brought out to attend school meetings, where his vote is used to break a tie (supposedly he always votes yes). Unfortunately his real head, which once rested inside the cabinet, is no longer on display. It was moved into storage after World War II, when the auto-icon spent some time in the countryside to protect it from German bombs. Another rumor says students at a rival school stole the head in the 1960s and used it as a football, but that too is an urban legend.

The stories might be making Bentham angry. For decades, students at the university have sworn that at night they can hear Bentham tap-tap-tapping Dapple as he walks down the halls. He should be resting in peace—a month after he died, legislation he helped to shape finally made it legal in Britain to donate your body to science.

LAST ACTS

According to legend, the Renaissance artist and architect Michelangelo wanted to be buried in Florence so that he'd be able to see his favorite piece of architecture, the cupola of Florence Cathedral, when resurrected on Judgment Day. After he died in Rome in 1564, a nephew fulfilled his wishes by smuggling his remains through the country disguised as merchandise (probably to protect them from bandits). After months of squabbling over the building of his tomb, Michelangelo was finally buried at the Basilica of Santa Croce, where he's still waiting.

TIMOTHY LEARY

BORN: OCTOBER 22, 1920,
SPRINGFIELD, MASSACHUSETTS
DIED: MAY 31, 1996 (AGE 75),
BEVERLY HILLS, CALIFORNIA

"Personally, I've been looking forward to dying all my life," Timothy Leary once wrote. Ever since his first experiments with psychedelic drugs while teaching at Harvard in the 1960s, Leary considered his hallucinogenic trips a dry run for his journey into the afterlife. According to him, one of the best ways to prepare for death was to consume lots and lots of illicit substances, the better to rehearse the road into the unknown. For Leary, death would be the ultimate trip—although things didn't quite work out the way he originally planned.

As the psychologist-turned-psychonaut who urged the 1960s to "turn on, tune in, and drop out," Leary wanted everything about his death to reflect his values: autonomy, personal growth, creativity, and wild experimentation. In this approach, he mirrored Jeremy Bentham, whose auto-icon Leary definitely would have appreciated. He was also living out the fantasies of Voltaire (see pages 15–19), who rued the Church's control over dying in France and wanted to be able to perish however he pleased. For Leary, dying was a perfect opportunity to push the iconoclasm of the 1960s into new frontiers and to smash what he considered life's final taboo.

Rather than surrender to "factory death" in a hospital, when Leary knew he was dying he threw a months-long house party where friends, family, acolytes, and fellow celebrities could pay their final respects. As an early champion of digital technology, he allowed a tribe of young web enthusiasts to live with him, record his final moments, and construct his cyberspace estate, a website where he broadcast his thoughts, messages, and daily drug intake. (One average day in April 1996, he self-medicated with fifty cigarettes, two marijuana cookies, one joint, a fentanyl patch, two Dilaudid pills, two lines of cocaine, twelve balloons of nitrous oxide, forty-five cc's of ketamine, an undisclosed amount of DMT, and two Ritz crackers topped with butter and marijuana buds, which he called "Leary biscuits.") He also flirted with the idea of dying live online, by his own hand, a rumor that kept the traffic flowing to leary.com for months.

At the same time, Leary was also making plans for his body after death. When he went public with the news that he had inoperable prostate cancer, in an August 1995 interview with the *Los Angeles Times,* he was wearing two bracelets with the names and numbers of rival cryonics firms. A few months later a company called CryoCare installed preservation equipment in his Beverly Hills house, so the freezing process could begin immediately after his death. (Leary elected to have only his head preserved, because it was cheaper, and even more disturbing than putting his whole body on ice.) The tribe of devotees who lived with him decorated the equipment with beads and flowers, and stocked the gurney with everything he would need in the afterlife: wine, marijuana, a bong, junk food, and books by Allen Ginsberg and William S. Burroughs.

But Leary's emphasis on going his own way made things complicated. A few weeks before his death, CryoCare representatives removed the preservation equipment from his home. Officials said they were concerned by Leary's suggestions that he planned to kill himself, arguing that legal and medical issues after a suicide often made things tricky for them. The issue had been a delicate one since 1988, when allegations surfaced that the Alcor Life Extension Foundation had murdered a woman with barbiturates before freezing her head (the company insisted that the barbiturates had only been administered after her death and no charges were ever filed). However, friends said the truth was that Leary had gotten angry after a CryoCare representative showed up with a photographer for *Wired*. Leary himself said he'd decided the cryonics people had "no sense of humor," and worried he'd "wake up in fifty years surrounded by people with clipboards."

With the cryonics option killed off, Leary decided to embrace more conventional ways to go. He chose cremation, but didn't want his ashes to languish forever on someone's mantelpiece. Days before his death, he asked his friend Carol Rosin, an aerospace executive and former spokesperson for German rocket scientist Wernher von Braun, to get his ashes into space. She agreed, even though at the time she had no idea how she was going to fulfill Leary's last wish.

Leary ended up dying naturally, in bed, surrounded by friends. According to the writer and media theorist Douglas Rushkoff, just before losing consciousness Leary asked "Why?" When no one in the room answered, he responded by saying "Why not?" over and over in different intonations. His last performance was reminiscent of Gertrude Stein's final words almost exactly fifty years earlier. Before dying, Stein asked, "What is the answer?" When there was no response, she said, "In that case, what is the question?"

Ten months later, seven grams of Leary's ashes were flown into space on a Pegasus rocket, which was released from its carrier airplane over the Canary Islands. It was the world's first "space burial," arranged by the Houston-based company Celestis. (The remains orbited Earth for years before burning up in the atmosphere in May 2002.) Leary's ashes were joined by the remains of twenty-three other people, including Gene Roddenberry (creator of *Star Trek*), scientists, pilots, and a five-year-old boy. Leary would have appreciated the company. "You've got to approach dying the way you live your life," he said. "With curiosity, hope, experimentation, and with the help of your friends."

GRAM PARSONS

BORN: NOVEMBER 5, 1946,
WINTER HAVEN, FLORIDA
DIED: SEPTEMBER 19, 1973 (AGE 26),
JOSHUA TREE, CALIFORNIA

Gram Parsons is a man better known for what he started than what he finished. As a solo performer and a musician with the Byrds, among other bands, Parsons is credited with rescuing country music from its redneck associations and fusing it with the energy of rock and roll. Though he never had a hit, his music laid the foundations for the genres we now call country rock and alternative country (Parsons himself preferred the label "Cosmic American"). In some circles, he's practically a deity.

Make that a deity with a death wish. Though raised as a gentleman (he was heir to a Florida citrus fortune), in later years Parsons became progressively more Byronic—mad, bad, and dangerous to know. In between his haphazard recording sessions and chaotic performances, he consumed almost as many illicit substances as his pal Keith Richards, but without the latter's Kevlar constitution. Dysfunction ran in his blood: he was descended from a southern-gothic family in the most haunted tradition, littered with addictions and institutionalizations. His father, known as Coon Dog, killed himself when Gram was twelve.

When it all got to be too much, there was one place Parsons could go to get away: the Joshua Tree National Monument in California's Mojave Desert. Amid the stark beauty of the desert, he found the spiritual space to dream and write songs. He visited regularly, staying in the modest cinderblock rooms of the Joshua Tree Inn. But soon after completing the recording of his second solo album, *Grievous Angel*, he took a trip there from which he never returned.

Parsons spent his last vacation with his girlfriend, Margaret Fisher, and another couple, the heiress Dale McElroy and her boyfriend, Michael Martin. The group mostly hung out in dusty local bars, but on the second evening, Parsons decided he wanted something stronger than alcohol. He wanted heroin. The drug dealer he found could only supply morphine stolen from a nearby Marine base, and Parsons insisted on a double injection—his fatal mistake. He overdosed, and the dealer vanished.

His friends tried CPR and several junkie home remedies (a cold shower, ice cubes up his behind) before summoning an ambulance. By the time it arrived, Parsons was unconscious. He was pronounced dead not long after his arrival at the High Desert Memorial Hospital.

Two months earlier, Byrds guitarist Clarence White had been killed by a drunk driver. At his funeral (a formal and stuffy Catholic affair) Parsons had made a pact with his road manager, Phil Kaufman. According to Kaufman, the pact said that whoever died first would "take the other guy's body out to Joshua Tree, have a few drinks, and burn it."

Bob Parsons, Gram's stepfather, had other ideas. Bob, who had adopted Gram in childhood and gave him his surname, shared a tempestuous relationship with his stepson: earlier the same year, he had kicked Gram and his wife, Gretchen, off a boating trip because of their drug-addled antics. At the time of Gram's death, Bob was in the hospital, but checked himself out and arranged for Gram's body to be flown to New Orleans (Bob's hometown) for a private funeral. He did not consult any of Gram's friends about the arrangements, and he made it clear they would not be welcome at the funeral.

That's when Kaufman decided to take over. Kaufman was, and is, an unusual character: he calls himself the "Road Mangler," once lived with the Manson family, and lists "in-house confidant for Mick Jagger/Rolling Stones" as the first item in his online résumé. Kaufman says he felt guilty about failing to protect Gram from himself, and made up his mind to carry out his friend's last wishes. As he tells it, "I was sitting around the house playing 'shudda.' You know, 'I shudda done this, I shudda stayed with him' . . . and Kaphy, my old lady, said, 'Well, you know, shut your fucking mouth. Do it or shut up.' I said, 'You're right, toots.'"

After making some calls, Kaufman learned that Gram's body was being flown by a mortuary air service to Los Angeles International Airport. From there, it would travel on to New Orleans. Kaufman called up Dale McElroy and asked to borrow her car, a 1960 cherry-red hearse the heiress often used for camping trips. He also asked her boyfriend, Michael Martin, to come along for the ride.

When Kaufman and Martin arrived at the mortuary air service's hangar, well fortified with whiskey, they told the employees that Parsons's family had changed their minds and decided to fly the body via private plane from a different airport. Though the employees must have been at least a little suspicious, given the pair's long hair, cowboy boots, and obviously inebriated appearance, they bought the story. No one interfered even after Kaufman scrawled his name on the release form as "Jeremy Nobody," or when Martin accidentally dented the hangar with the hearse.

The two men drove off toward the desert, stopping along the way for hamburgers, beer, and a jerry can full of high-octane gasoline. Finally they realized they were too drunk to continue driving, and stopped at a parking area near a boulder formation known as Cap Rock. As they pulled the heavy coffin out of the hearse, its back end thudded onto the ground. "Sorry, Gram," they both said.

But if Kaufman still considered the body inside to be his friend Gram, he wasn't terribly respectful. By his own account, Kaufman opened the coffin and made a joke about the size of Parsons's penis. Then he played "gotcha" with the corpse, pointing down at its chest (wounded from the autopsy) and flicking his finger back up at its nose. Finally, car lights in the distance startled him, and he doused the body with gasoline. He threw in a lit match, and saw a fireball whoosh up into the night sky.

The pair watched as the corpse bubbled and burned, but when the car lights grew closer they fled, abandoning Parsons's burning body by the side of the road. The occupants of the other car—whoever they were—didn't notice the fire, and Parsons's body wasn't discovered until the next morning. Park rangers found it charred and barely recognizable.

A few days later, Kaufman was arrested at his house. (As he tells it, one of the police officers joked that he was being charged with "Gram Theft Parsons.") In court, both Kaufman and Martin pleaded guilty to misdemeanor theft, and were fined three hundred dollars each, plus the cost of the casket ($708), which was paid to the funeral home. McElroy paid the bills, but that provided little comfort to Parsons's family, who were shocked and horrified by Kaufman's actions.

(Kaufman's moves in the next few weeks did little to assuage their pain: with his funds low and employment chances slim, he threw a benefit concert for himself, called "Kaufman's Koffin Kaper Konsert." As guests listened to DJ Dr. Demento and other acts, they sipped from beer cans labeled "Gram Pilsner: a stiff drink for what ales you.")

Bob Parsons claimed what was left of Gram, about thirty-five pounds' worth, and brought the remains to New Orleans for a small family funeral. The ashes were interred at the Garden of Memories Cemetery in Metairie, Louisiana, beneath a modest circular plaque that reads "God's own singer" (the name of a Flying Burrito Brothers song). A larger bronze memorial was added in 2005, but for many fans, Parsons's true resting place is in Joshua Tree.

For decades, fans and friends have left graffiti and makeshift shrines near a particular boulder at the park, at a spot where some say the musician's cremation took place. Park personnel frequently remove the mementos and graffiti, but over the years, one concrete slab has escaped destruction and been moved to the Joshua Tree Inn. Surrounded by candles and offerings, the slab functions as Parsons's cenotaph. It is painted with the name of his first album: *Safe at Home.*

HUNTER S. THOMPSON

BORN: JULY 18, 1937,
LOUISVILLE, KENTUCKY
DIED: FEBRUARY 20, 2005 (AGE 67),
WOODY CREEK, COLORADO

When Hunter S. Thompson died, there was a note tacked up on his refrigerator. Scrawled in large black letters, it read: "Never call 9–1–1. Never. This means you. HST."

This was just one of Thompson's house rules, strictly enforced even though he kept loaded guns around the house the way some people stock Kleenex. As the nation's premier outlaw journalist, a role he practically invented, Thompson's disdain for authority was well established. It had started early: when he was nine, the FBI threatened him with a felony charge after he pushed a mailbox into the path of a bus. As an adult, he managed to channel his antiauthoritarian instincts into the creation of a new literary form, his unrepentantly first-person "Gonzo journalism."

But on February 20, 2005, his family was forced to disobey the note on the refrigerator and call in the authorities. They discovered the writer's lifeless body in his kitchen, slumped in front of his typewriter. There was just one word typed on the paper in front of him: "Counselor." Blood oozed from his face. He'd taken one of his beloved shotguns to his mouth.

Friends emphasized that this was no sudden act of desperation. Ralph Steadman, an illustrator and Thompson's frequent collaborator, said the writer had been talking about suicide for twenty-five years. Other friends pointed out that as a man who idolized youth, Thompson had little desire to confront the steady decay of aging. After a recent hip replacement surgery, he decided he just wasn't having fun anymore. In a statement, his wife, Anita, and son, Juan, said: "It is entirely fitting that Hunter, as a master of politics and control, chose to take his life on his own schedule by his own hand, rather than submitting to fate, genetics or chance."

Thompson took similar control over his own funeral, at least as best he could. Plans for his final send-off had been in the works since at least 1978, when a BBC documentary crew captured him and Steadman consulting with a Hollywood mortuary. Although years away from death, he was already thinking about how to go out in style. Wearing his usual sunglasses and Panama hat and speaking in his trademark whiskey-soaked murmur, Thompson described how he wanted to build a towering monument in the shape of his "Gonzo fist"—a red hand clutching a peyote button, his personal symbol since the early 1970s. He explained that he wanted the fist to conceal a cannon, which would shoot his cremated remains five hundred feet into the air over the valley near his home. "Mr. Tambourine Man" would be playing in the background when the cannon fired.

As the years went on, Thompson clung to what he called his "one true wish," even though it was never clear who was going to pay for it. Luckily for Thompson, in the late 1990s he befriended Johnny Depp, after the actor played the lead role in *Fear and Loathing in Las Vegas*. The two became fast friends, especially after they spent an evening shooting guns at Thompson's house in the Rockies. After the writer's suicide, Depp declared that he wanted to make sure his friend's wishes became a reality. For him, the estimated $2 million price tag was pocket change.

On August 20, 2005, six months to the day after Thompson's death, hundreds of his friends gathered for a private ceremony at the writer's Woody Creek home. Actors, musicians, and politicians mingled in a huge pavilion that one witness said was decorated like a "frontier bordello." After two hours of tributes, the guests turned their attention to a towering structure across the road that was wreathed in red fabric. As the fabric slithered off, Thompson's Gonzo fist stood shining in the sky, a multicolored peyote button glowing in the center. Just as Thompson requested, inside the fist was a cannon, packed with mortar shells that contained his remains mixed with fireworks.

After a reading of the Tibetan heart sutra and some Japanese drumming, the shells shot into the sky to the tune of "Mr. Tambourine Man." Thompson's ashes exploded into red, silver, blue, and green starbursts as Dylan sang, "I'm ready to go anywhere, I'm ready for to fade . . ." Then the real party began, and it lasted until dawn, the way Thompson would have wanted it.

ACKNOWLEDGMENTS

Tomás Eloy Martínez has written that "the art of the embalmer resembles that of the biographer: both try to immobilize a body or a life in the pose in which eternity is to remember it." This immobilization is a tricky business, and there are a number of people who helped me along the way. I owe a huge debt to the writers and researchers listed in the sources: my work would not have been possible without theirs. I also thank my agent, Jill Grinberg, and my editor, Michael Szczerban, for making the dream a reality; John Bemelmans Marciano, for convincing me the dream was worth pursuing; Ben Schott, for his years of tutelage; Mike Dash, for clearing up some of the finer points concerning Lord Byron, and for other research help; Colin Dickey, for his "skullblazing" work in *Cranioklepty*; Peter Manseau, whose work was essential to helping this Jewish girl understand Catholic relics; Caitlin Doughty, everyone's favorite mortician, for help with the gory details in the appendix; Kevin Chong, for suggesting Gram Parsons; Carol Barton, for her research and feedback on Milton; and Shira Zucker, for help with legal research. All the mistakes, of course, are my fault.

APPENDIX

THE WAY

OF

ALL FLESH:

WHAT HAPPENS

TO BODIES

AFTER DEATH

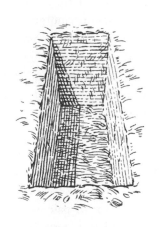

There are endless ways to die, and nearly endless ways for dead bodies to be treated. In some cultures, you might be placed in a tree, left for vultures to devour, preserved in honey, mummified with resin, or ritually eaten. But in North America, chances are you'll either be buried or cremated. What does this mean for your remains?

For decades, most Americans died in hospitals, but increasing numbers are spending their final days in nursing homes, hospices, or at home. Wherever you pass away, the process your body undergoes is the same. Minutes after death, your body goes slack. Your muscles relax, your jaw drops, your pupils dilate, and your eyes open slightly. Your limbs droop toward the floor, and the contents of your bladder and bowels are released. (If you have any respect for those who will be handling your body, try to die with an empty stomach.)

If you die in a hospital, a nurse will draw the curtains, close your eyes and mouth, take out any invasive devices, and wash your corpse. Then he or she will label your body and, if your family is coming, lay it out for viewing. After that, it's time for the hospital morgue. Your body will be wheeled down—morgues are usually in the basement—on a stretcher, perhaps one with a false cover so no one can tell you're a stiff. The morgue will be chilly (about forty degrees Fahrenheit) and the decor utilitarian; think lots of stainless steel and tile halfway up the walls. Most likely, you'll be slid into a refrigerated cabinet with a tag tied to your toe, just like in the movies.

By this time your body will have started to change color. Since your heart no longer works, your blood will be seduced by gravity, just like your limbs. The top of your body will start to turn pale as your blood settles, and a purple stain will begin spreading along your back, neck, and the bottom of your limbs. The stain is called *livor mortis*—literally, "the blueness of death." Consider it your final tattoo.

You'll also be cooling down. This is known as *algor mortis,* or the coldness of death. Your body heat will drop about one degree Fahrenheit per hour, until your skin is the same temperature as the air surrounding you. After two to six hours, *rigor mortis* (the stiffness of death) will set in. Thanks to chemical changes in your muscle tissue, your eyelids will start to stiffen, followed by your neck, your jaws, and the rest of your body. If you're in the cool of the morgue, rigor mortis will set in sooner than it would if you were in a warm room. A few days (between one and four) later, your muscles will relax again, this time for good.

By then someone from the funeral home will have picked you up. Embalming awaits, unless your family or religion prohibits it. During the embalming, you'll be cleaned and disinfected, and your orifices will be plugged up with cotton. Your blood will be drained into the sewers as embalming fluid is pumped through your veins. A hollow instrument called a trocar will puncture your abdomen and chest, suck out your blood, bacteria, and bodily fluids, and then inject more preservatives. (In some cases, the embalming fluid is tinted pink, in an effort to make you look more alive.)

If your family will be seeing you, the mortician will fix you up with putty, creams, sprays, and mortuary makeup. Then he or she will dress you in your last outfit, which is sometimes split up the back to make things easier. You haven't been this hard to clothe since you were a baby.

Most embalmings are designed to last just long enough for the funeral—a couple of days or weeks at most. Then the decay begins. No matter what kind of casket your family buys, air, insects, and water will eventually get in. The rate of decay depends on a variety of factors: the type of soil, how deep you're buried, what you're wearing, the temperature and humidity, the skill of the embalmer, and the strength of the chemicals used. Kenneth Iserson, author of *Death to Dust: What Happens to Dead Bodies?*, says that an embalmed adult corpse buried without a coffin six feet underground will become a skeleton in ten to twelve years. Children take about half that time. However, your bones and teeth are the most durable parts of your body, and if fossilized by the environment, they can last just about forever.

But what if you aren't embalmed? It's not a pretty sight. Two or three days after your last heartbeat, the bacteria in your body will start to take over. The first sign of putrefaction is a green stain that spreads from your right lower abdomen across your stomach, chest, and thighs. After the green, your body will turn purple, then black. You'll start to smell and bloat, your eyes and tongue will bulge, and your intestines will ooze out. A week after your death, blood-colored blisters will form, and your skin will start to peel off in sheets. Three to four weeks after death, your hair, nails, and teeth come loose, and your internal organs turn to liquid. If you're on land, maggots, flies, and wild animals may also feast on your body, and if you're in the water, you'll be food for the fishes.

Of course, if you're cremated, no one will be nibbling on your flesh. Cremation is an increasingly popular option in America: as of 2010, 41 percent of America's dead bodies were cremated, compared to 15 percent in 1985. Some states cremate more than others; Nevada leads the nation at 74 percent, while South Dakota torches only 29 percent of its dead.

If you are cremated, you'll be placed in a cardboard container (sometimes a wooden coffin) for easy burning. Any pacemakers you might have will be removed—they can explode when exposed to high heat, and then the crematorium might have more corpses than they were bargaining for. You and the cardboard will be slid into a furnace that will heat up to between 1,600 and 1,800 degrees Fahrenheit—higher if you're obese. The cardboard is the first part to go, followed by your skin and hair, then the rest of you. In the last stage—the whole process takes between one and four hours—your bones will glow red, then fall apart.

Afterward, all that's left is your tooth fillings, any metal plates or posts that were inside your body, and chunks from your larger bones, such as your vertebrae and pelvis. These are pulverized in a machine before being given to your family or friends. The average male becomes 7.6 pounds of cremains, the average female 6.1 pounds—about the weight of a large raw chicken.

In the end, all our bodies will turn to dust. But our spirit, our work, and the memories we leave behind can outlast us. That's true whether you're famous or not. Perhaps it's part of the beauty of being human: living with the inevitability of our demise, but striving to create something that survives.

SOURCES

Note: The material below is arranged in alphabetical order by corpse, including the bodies mentioned in sidebars. Sources for the appendix are located at the end.

ALEXANDER THE GREAT

Bianchi, Robert S. "Hunting Alexander's Tomb." *Archaeology* 46 (July/August 1993). http://www.archaeology.org/online/features /alexander/tomb.html.

Cummings, Lewis V. *Alexander the Great*. New York: Grove Press, 2004.

Curtius, Quintus. *History of Alexander*. Book X. Translated by John C. Rolfe. Cambridge, MA: Harvard University Press, 1946.

Doherty, Paul. *The Death of Alexander the Great: What—or Who— Really Killed the Young Conqueror of the Known World?* New York: Carroll & Graf, 2004.

Empereur, Jean-Yves. *Alexandria Rediscovered*. Translated by Margaret Maehler. New York: George Braziller, 1998.

Erskine, Andrew. "Life After Death: Alexandria and the Body of Alexander." *Greece & Rome* 49, no. 2 (October 2002): 163–79.

Fox, Robin Lane. *Alexander the Great*. New York: Penguin Books, 2004.

Gialoúris, Nikólaos. *The Search for Alexander: An Exhibition*. New York: Little, Brown, 1980.

Saunders, Nicholas J. *Alexander's Tomb: The Two Thousand Year Obsession to Find the Lost Conqueror*. New York: Basic Books, 2006.

Stoneman, Richard. *Alexander the Great: A Life in Legend*. New Haven, CT: Yale University Press, 2008.

JOHN BARRYMORE

Flynn, Errol. *My Wicked, Wicked Ways: The Autobiography of Errol Flynn*. New York: Cooper Square Press, 2003.

Kobler, John. *Damned in Paradise: The Life of John Barrymore*. New York: Atheneum, 1977.

Mank, Gregory William, Charles Heard, and Bill Nelson. *Hollywood's Hellfire Club: The Misadventures of John Barrymore, W. C. Fields, Errol Flynn and "the Bundy Drive Boys."* Los Angeles: Feral House, 2007.

Murphy, Edwin. *After the Funeral: The Posthumous Adventures of Famous Corpses*. New York: Carol Publishing Group, 1995.

Peters, Margot. *The House of Barrymore*. New York: Alfred A. Knopf, 1990.

Schickel, Richard. *The Men Who Made the Movies*. New York: Atheneum, 1975.

Wallace, David. *Lost Hollywood*. New York: St. Martin's Press, 2001.

THOMAS BECKET

Butler, John. *The Quest for Becket's Bones: The Mystery of the Relics of St. Thomas Becket of Canterbury*. New Haven, CT: Yale University Press, 1995.

Koopmans, Rachel. *Wonderful to Relate: Miracle Stories and Miracle Collecting in High Medieval England*. Philadelphia: University of Pennsylvania Press, 2010.

Morgan, Christopher and Andrew Alderson. "Becket's Bones 'Kept Secretly at Canterbury for 460 Years.'" *Sunday Times* (UK), June 22, 1997.

Thornton, W. Pugin. "Surgical Report on a Skeleton Found in the Crypt of Canterbury Cathedral (1888)." *Archaeologia Cantiana* XVII (1889): 257–60.

Walsham, Alexandra. "Skeletons in the Cupboard: Relics after the English Reformation." *Past and Present* 206, supplement 5 (2010): 121–43.

LUDWIG VAN BEETHOVEN

Bankl, Hans and Hans Jesserer. "The Discovery and Examination of Bone Fragments from Beethoven's Skull." Edited by William Meredith. Translated by Hannah Leibmann. *Beethoven Journal* 20, nos. 1 & 2 (Summer/Winter 2005): 66–73.

Breuning, Gerhard von. *Memories of Beethoven: From the House of the Black-Robed Spaniards*. Cambridge, UK: Cambridge University Press, 1992.

———. "The Skulls of Beethoven and Schubert." Edited by William Meredith. Translated by Hannah Leibmann. *Beethoven Journal* 20, nos. 1 & 2 (Summer/Winter 2005): 58–60.

Davies, Peter J. *Beethoven in Person: His Deafness, Illnesses, and Death*. Westport, CT: Greenwood Press, 2001.

Mai, François Martin. *Diagnosing Genius: The Life and Death of Beethoven*. Montreal, Canada: McGill-Queen's University Press, 2007.

Martin, Russell. *Beethoven's Hair*. New York: Broadway Books, 2000.

Meredith, William. "The History of Beethoven's Skull Fragments: Part One." *Beethoven Journal* 20, nos. 1 & 2 (Summer/Winter 2005): 1–25.

———. "Essential Facts and Principles Concerning the Beethoven Skull Fragments." *Beethoven Journal* 20, nos. 1 & 2 (Summer/Winter 2005): 94–95.

Murphy, Dave. "Beethoven Skull Fragments Resurface." *San Francisco Chronicle,* November 18, 2005. http://www.sfgate.com/bayarea/article/SAN-JOSE-Beethoven-skull-fragments-resurface-2560272.php.

Steen, Margaret. "Unravelling a 19th Century Mystery." *Stanford Business,* May 2006.

JEREMY BENTHAM

Harte, Negley. "Radical Pants and the Pursuit of Happiness." *Times Higher Education Supplement* (UK), September 9, 2005. http://www.timeshighereducation.co.uk/story.asp?storyCode=198332&sectioncode=26.

Marmoy, C. F. A. "The 'Auto-Icon' of Jeremy Bentham at University College, London." *Medical History* 2, no. 2 (April 1958): 77–86.

Rachlin, Harvey. "Jeremy Bentham: A Philosopher for the Ages." In *Lucy's Bones, Sacred Stones, and Einstein's Brain: The Remarkable Stories Behind the Great Objects and Artifacts of History, from Antiquity to the Modern Era,* 203–7. New York: Henry Holt, 1996.

Richardson, Ruth. "Bentham and 'Bodies for Dissection.'" *Bentham Newsletter* 10 (June 1986): 22–33.

Richardson, Ruth and Brian Hurwitz. "Jeremy Bentham's Self-Image: An Exemplary Bequest for Dissection." *British Medical Journal* 295 (1987): 195–98. doi: 10.1136/bmj.295.6591.195.

University College London Bentham Project. "Auto-Icon." http://www.ucl.ac.uk/Bentham-Project/who/autoicon.

BILLY THE KID

Billy the Kid Museum. "About Billy the Kid." http://billythekidmuseum.com/aboutbillythekid.htm.

Slatta, Richard W. *The Mythical West: An Encyclopedia of Legend, Lore, and Popular Culture.* Santa Barbara, CA: ABC-CLIO, 2001.

BIN LADEN, OSAMA

Harris, Paul. "Osama bin Laden Death: What to Do with Body Poses Dilemma for US." *Guardian* (UK), May 2, 2011. http://www.guardian.co.uk/world/2011/may/02/osama-bin-laden-body-burial.

Kakutani, Michiko. "Bin Laden's End, from the Beginning." Review of *Manhunt,* by Peter L. Bergen. *New York Times,* May 3, 2012. http://www.nytimes.com/2012/05/04/books/manhunt-by-peter-l-bergen-about-the-bin-laden-killing.html.

Lawrence, Chris. "'No Land Alternative' Prompts bin Laden Sea Burial." *CNN.com,* May 2, 2011. http://www.cnn.com/2011 /WORLD/aslapcf/05/02/bin.laden.burial.at.sea/index .html?iref=allsearch.

Leland, John and Elisabeth Bumiller. "Islamic Scholars Split Over Sea Burial for bin Laden." *New York Times,* May 2, 2011. http://www.nytimes.com/2011/05/03/world/asia/03burial .html.

Lithwick, Dahlia. "Habeas Corpses: What Are the Rights of Dead People?" *Slate,* March 14, 2002. http://www.slate.com/articles /news_and_politics/jurisprudence/2002/03/habeas_corpses.single .html.

"The 'Manhunt' to Capture Osama bin Laden." Review of *Manhunt,* by Peter L. Bergen. *NPR.com,* May 1, 2012. http://www .npr.org/2012/05/01/151766454/the-manhunt-to-capture-osama -bin-laden.

Matus, Victor. "On the Disposal of Dictators." *Policy Review,* no. 134 (December 1, 2005). http://www.hoover.org/publications/policy -review/article/6528.

Schmidle, Nicholas. "Getting bin Laden: What Happened That Night in Abbottabad." *New Yorker,* August 8, 2011. http:// www.newyorker.com/reporting/2011/08/08/110808fa_fact_ schmidle#ixzz1wWPAdSVY.

US Department of Defense. "DOD Background Briefing with Senior Defense Officials from the Pentagon and Senior Intelligence Officials by Telephone on US Operations Involving Osama bin Laden." Transcript. May 2, 2011. http://www.defense.gov/Transcripts /Transcript.aspx?TranscriptID=4818.

Van Woerkom, Barbara. "Timeline: The Raid on Osama bin Laden's Hideout." *NPR.org,* May 3, 2011. http://www.npr .org/2011/05/03/135951504/timeline-the-raid-on-osama-bin -ladens-hideout.

Weitz, Yechiam. "'We Have to Carry Out the Sentence.'" *Haaretz,* July 26, 2007. http://www.haaretz.com/weekend/week-s-end/we -have-to-carry-out-the-sentence-1.226299.

BLACK HAWK

King, Melanie. *The Dying Game: A Curious History of Death.* Oxford, UK: Oneworld Publications, 2008.

Trask, Kerry A. *Black Hawk: The Battle for the Heart of America.* New York: Henry Holt, 2006.

Wesson, Sarah, ed. "Makataimeshekiakiak: Black Hawk and His War." Davenport (Iowa) Public Library. http://www.qcmemory .org/genealogy-and-history/local-history-info/the-people/black -hawk/.

WILLIAM BLAKE

Bentley, G. E. Jr. *The Stranger From Paradise: A Biography of William Blake*. New Haven, CT: Yale University Press, 2001.

City of London. "Bunhill Fields Burial Ground." http://www.cityof london.gov.uk/Corporation/LGNL_Services/Environment_and_ planning/Parks_and_open_spaces/City_Gardens/bunhill.htm.

Friends of William Blake. "Blake Society's Proposed Design." http:// www.friendsofblake.org/blake_proposed_design.htm.

Garrido, Luis and Carol Garrido. *William Blake's Final Resting Place*. Self-published, 2005. Available at http://www.friendsofblake.org.

LORD BYRON

Barber, Thomas Gerrard. *Byron—And Where He Is Buried*. Hucknall, UK: H. Morley & Sons, 1939.

Crane, David. *The Kindness of Sisters: Annabella Milbanke and the Destruction of the Byrons*. New York: Alfred A. Knopf, 2002.

Dash, Mike. "Erotic Secrets of Lord Byron's Tomb." *Dry as Dust: A Fortean in the Archives* (blog). http://blogs.forteana.org/node/147.

Eisler, Benita. *Byron: Child of Passion, Fool of Fame*. New York: Alfred A. Knopf, 1999.

Houldsworth, Arnold E. "Opening of Lord Byron's Vault, 15 June 1938." In *The Life of Byron*, by Elizabeth Longford, 223–26. Boston: Little, Brown, 1976.

Lewis, Anthony. "At Last Lord Byron Gets Place in Poets' Corner in Westminster." *New York Times*, May 7, 1968.

MacCarthy, Fiona. *Byron: Life and Legend*. New York: Farrar, Straus & Giroux, 2002.

Minta, Stephen. *On a Voiceless Shore: Byron in Greece*. New York: Henry Holt, 1998.

Rogers, Byron. *Me: The Authorised Biography*. London: Aurum, 2009.

Whipple, A. B. C. *The Fatal Gift of Beauty: The Final Years of Byron and Shelley*. New York: Harper & Row, 1964.

BUDDHA

Herath, Dharmaratna. *The Tooth Relic and the Crown*. Colombo, Sri Lanka: s.n., 1994.

Manseau, Peter. *Rag and Bone: A Journey Among the World's Holy Dead*. New York: Henry Holt, 2009.

BURNHAM, LINDON FORBES

Zbarksy, Ilya and Samuel Hutchinson. *Lenin's Embalmers*. Translated by Barbara Bray. London: Harvill Press, 1999.

BUTCH CASSIDY

Meadows, Anne. *Digging up Butch and Sundance*. Lincoln: University of Nebraska Press, 2003.

Slatta, Richard W. *The Mythical West: An Encyclopedia of Legend, Lore, and Popular Culture*. Santa Barbara, CA: ABC-CLIO, 2001.

Walker, Dale L. *Legends and Lies: Great Mysteries of the American West*. New York: Forge, 1997.

CHARLIE CHAPLIN

"Archive: On This Day." *Birmingham (UK) Post,* March 2, 2002.

Associated Press. "Body Steal Suspect Sentenced." *Prescott (AZ) Courier,* December 13, 1978.

"Chaplin Body Stolen from Swiss Grave." *New York Times,* March 3, 1978.

"Chaplin's Body Found Near His Swiss Home." *New York Times,* May 18, 1978.

Fleischman, Sid. *Sir Charlie Chaplin: The Funniest Man in the World*. New York: Greenwillow Books, 2010.

Kannard, Brian. *Skullduggery: 45 True Tales of Disturbing the Dead*. Nashville, TN: Grave Distractions Press, 2009.

Molotsky, Irvin. "F.B.I.; The Chaplin Files: Can It Happen Again?" *New York Times,* January 22, 1986.

Robinson, David. *Chaplin: His Life and Art*. New York: Da Capo Press, 1994.

Scovell, Jane. *Oona: Living in the Shadows*. New York: Warner Books, 1998.

Vinocur, John. "Chaplin's Village Has Difficulty in Discussing Theft of His Coffin; He Wasn't Known Well." *New York Times,* March 4, 1978.

CICERO

Critchley, Simon. *The Book of Dead Philosophers*. New York: Vintage Books, 2009.

Edwards, Catharine. *Death in Ancient Rome*. New Haven, CT: Yale University Press, 2007.

CHRISTOPHER COLUMBUS

Associated Press. "DNA Verifies Columbus' Remains in Spain." NBCNews.com, May 19, 2006. http://www.msnbc.msn.com /id/12871458/ns/technology_and_science-science/t/dna-verifies -columbus-remains-spain/#.UCQqQo5xLpQ.

"Columbus Mystery Unravels." *BBC News,* September 19, 2002. http://news.bbc.co.uk/2/hi/europe/2268571.stm.

"'Columbus Remains' Taken for Tests." *BBC News,* June 3, 2003. http://news.bbc.co.uk/2/hi/europe/2958034.stm.

"Dominican Republic: Where Lies Columbus?" *Time,* January 13, 1961.

Granzotto, Gianni. *Christopher Columbus: The Dream and the Obsession.* Translated by Stephen Sartarelli. Garden City, NY: Doubleday, 1985.

Harney, Lisa. *Columbus: Secrets from the Grave.* DVD. Directed by Lisa Harney and Tom Pollock. Silver Spring, MD: Discovery Communications, 2004.

Hayden, Deborah. "Alas, Poor Yorick: Digging Up the Dead to Make Medical Diagnoses." *PLoS Medicine* 2, no. 3 (2005): 184–86. doi: 10.1371/journal.pmed.0020060.

Kraus, Hans P. *Sir Francis Drake: A Pictorial Biography.* Amsterdam: N. Israel, 1970.

Lorenzi, Rossella. "DNA Suggests Columbus Remains in Spain." *Discovery News,* October 6, 2004. http://dsc.discovery.com/news /briefs/20041004/columbus.html.

Nader, Helen. "Burial Places of Columbus." In *The Christopher Columbus Encyclopedia.* Vol. 1. Edited by Silvio A. Bedini. New York: Simon & Schuster, 1992.

———. "Last Will and Testament." In *The Christopher Columbus Encyclopedia.* Vol. 2. Edited by Silvio A. Bedini. New York: Simon & Schuster, 1992.

Schmidt-Nowara, Christopher. *The Conquest of History: Spanish Colonialism and National Histories in the Nineteenth Century.* Pittsburgh: University of Pittsburgh Press, 2006.

Sharrock, David. "DNA may reveal the last voyage of Columbus's bones." *Times* (UK), June 3, 2003.

Shea, John Gilmary. "Where Are the Remains of Christopher Columbus?" *Magazine of American History* IX (January 1883).

Thacher, John Boyd. *Christopher Columbus, His Life, His Work, His Remains as Revealed by Original Printed and Manuscript Records, Together with an Essay on Peter Martyr of Anghera and Bartolomé de las Casas, the First Historians of America.* New York: G. P. Putnam's Sons, 1903–4.

Twiss, Sir Travers. *Christopher Columbus: A Monograph on His True Burial Place.* London: Trübner, 1879.

Woolls, Daniel. "Who Is Really Buried in Columbus's Tombs? Teacher Pushes for DNA Tests on Remains." *Washington Post,* June 30, 2002.

ALISTAIR COOKE

"Alistair Cooke's Bones 'Stolen.'" *BBC News,* December 22, 2005.

Borenstein, Seth and Marilynn Marchione, Associated Press. "US Steps Up Inspections of Human Tissue Industry." *Boston Globe,*

June 13, 2007. http://www.boston.com/news/nation/articles/2007/06/13/us_steps_up_inspections_of_human_tissue_industry/.

Brick, Michael. "Alistair Cooke's Bones Were Stolen for Implantation, His Family Says." *New York Times,* December 23, 2005. http://www.nytimes.com/2005/12/23/nyregion/23cooke.html.

———. "4 Men Charged in What Officials Call a $4.6 Million Trade in Human Body Parts." *New York Times,* February 24, 2006. http://www.nytimes.com/2006/02/24/nyregion/24corpses.html.

Brick, Michael and Andy Newman. "Dentist's Surrender Sought in Inquiry Into Plot to Loot Corpses." *New York Times,* February 23, 2006. http://www.nytimes.com/2006/02/23/nyregion/23parts.html.

Cantor, Norman L. *After We Die: The Life and Times of the Human Cadaver.* Washington, DC: Georgetown University Press, 2010.

Chan, Sewell. "Man Sentenced for Plundering Body Parts." *New York Times,* June 27, 2008. http://cityroom.blogs.nytimes.com/2008/06/27/man-sentenced-for-plundering-body-parts/.

Feuer, Alan. "Dentist Pleads Guilty to Stealing and Selling Body Parts." *New York Times,* March 19, 2008. http://www.nytimes.com/2008/03/19/nyregion/thecity/19bones.html.

Howard, Kate. "Alistair Cooke's Ashes Scattered in Central Park." *Telegraph* (UK), May 30, 2004. http://www.telegraph.co.uk/news/1463173/Alistair-Cookes-ashes-scattered-in-Central-Park.html.

Kings County District Attorney. "Kings County District Attorney Charles J. Hynes, Police Commissioner Raymond W. Kelly, Department of Investigation Commissioner Rose Gill Hearn, and Rochester District Attorney Michael C. Green Announce Expanded Indictment in Illegal Tissue Harvesting Scheme." Press release. Brooklyn, NY: October 18, 2006. http://www.brooklynda.org/News/press_releases_2006.htm#054.

McCarty, Mark. "FDA Gathers New Task Force Focused on Tissue Bank Issues." *Medical Device Daily,* September 1, 2006.

"Plea Deal in US Body Parts Case." *BBC News,* January 16, 2008.

Wells, Martha. "Current Good Tissue Practice (CGTP) Draft Guidance." US Food and Drug Administration. http://www.fda.gov/downloads/BiologicsBloodVaccines/ . . . /UCM191675.pp.

Witten, Celia and David Elder. "Report of the Human Tissue Task Force." US Food and Drug Administration. http://www.fda.gov/downloads/ . . . /TissueSafety/UCM114829.pdf.

US Food and Drug Administration. "FDA Forms Task Force on Human Tissue Safety." Press release. http://www.fda.gov/NewsEvents/Newsroom/PressAnnouncements/2006/ucm108721.htm.

Zahn, Paula. "West Virginia Says Good-bye to Killed Miners." Transcript. *Paula Zahn Now,* CNN, January 9, 2006. http://transcripts.cnn.com/TRANSCRIPTS/0601/09/pzn.01.html.

OLIVER CROMWELL

Altick, Richard D. *The Shows of London*. Cambridge, MA: Belknap Press, 1978.

Arnold, Catharine. *Necropolis: London and Its Dead*. London: Simon & Schuster UK, 2006.

Fitzgibbons, Jonathan. *Cromwell's Head*. Kew, UK: National Archives, 2008.

"Religion: Roundhead on the Pike." *Time,* May 6, 1957.

DANTE ALIGHIERI

Barbi, Michele. *Life of Dante*. Edited and translated by Paul G. Ruggiers. Berkeley: University of California Press, 1954.

"Discovery of Dante's Remains." *New York Times,* July 2, 1865.

Lindskoog, Kathryn Ann. *Dante's Divine Comedy*. Macon, GA: Mercer University Press, 1997–98.

Moore, Edward. *Studies in Dante: Textual Criticism of the "Convivio" and Miscellaneous Essays*. Oxford, UK: Clarendon Press, 1917.

Moore, Malcolm. "Dante's Infernal Crimes Forgiven." *Telegraph,* June 17, 2008. http://www.telegraph.co.uk/news/newstopics /howaboutthat/2145378/Dantes-infernal-crimes-forgiven.html.

"Perpetual Lamps for Dante's Tombs." *New York Times,* October 20, 1907.

Reynolds, Barbara. *Dante: The Poet, the Political Thinker, the Man*. Emeryville, CA: Shoemaker & Hoard, 2006.

Roush, Sherry. "Dante Ravennate and Boccaccio Ferrarese? Post-Mortem Residency and the Attack on Florentine Literary Hegemony, 1480–1520." *Viator* 35 (2004): 543–62.

Toynbee, Paget. *Dante Alighieri: His Life and Works*. New York: Macmillan, 1910.

RENÉ DESCARTES

Critchley, Simon. *The Book of Dead Philosophers*. New York: Vintage Books, 2009.

Hughes, Stella. "Skull's Odyssey Tracked." *Times Higher Education Supplement* (UK), August 30, 1996. http://www.timeshigher education.co.uk/story.asp?storyCode=99414&sectioncode=26.

Shorto, Russell. *Descartes' Bones: A Skeletal History of the Conflict Between Faith and Reason*. New York: Doubleday, 2008.

JOHN DILLINGER

Gorn, Elliott J. "Is It True What They Said About John Dillinger?" *OUPblog* (blog). http://blog.oup.com/2009/07/dillinger_dick/.

Perrottet, Tony. *Napoleon's Privates: 2,500 Years of History Unzipped*. New York: HarperCollins, 2008.

GEORGI DIMITROV

Carvalho, Joaquim, ed. *Religion and Power in Europe: Conflict and Convergence.* Pisa, Italy: Edizione Plus, Pisa University Press, 2007.

King, Melanie. *The Dying Game: A Curious History of Death.* Oxford, UK: Oneworld Publications, 2008.

ALBERT EINSTEIN

Abraham, Carolyn. *Possessing Genius: The Bizarre Odyssey of Einstein's Brain.* New York: St. Martin's Press, 2002.

Anderson, Britt and Thomas Harvey. "Alterations in Cortical Thickness and Neuronal Density in the Frontal Cortex of Albert Einstein." *Neuroscience Letters* 210, no. 3 (June 1996): 161–64.

Avril, Tom. "Samples of Einstein's Brain on Display at the Mütter Museum." *Philadelphia Inquirer,* November 18, 2011. http://articles.philly.com/2011–11–18/news/30414935_1_slides-brain-samples.

Bunn, Geoff. "Einstein's Brain." *A History of the Brain,* BBC Radio 4, November 18, 2011.

Burrell, Brian. *Postcards from the Brain Museum: The Improbable Search for Meaning in the Matter of Famous Minds.* New York: Broadway Books, 2004.

Hamilton, Jon. "Einstein's Brain Unlocks Some Mysteries of the Mind." *Morning Edition,* NPR, June 2, 2010. http://www.npr.org/templates/story/story.php?storyId=126229305.

Inskeep, Steve. "The Long, Strange Journey of Einstein's Brain." *Morning Edition,* NPR, April 18, 2005. http://www.npr.org/templates/story/story.php?storyId=4602913.

Isaacson, Walter. *Einstein: His Life and Universe.* New York: Simon & Schuster, 2007.

Kong, Dolores. "Einstein's Brain Was Different, Study Finds; Greater Parietal Lobe Width Cited." *Boston Globe,* June 18, 1999.

Roberts, Siobhan. "A Hands-on Approach to Studying the Brain, Even Einstein's." *New York Times,* November 14, 2006. http://www.nytimes.com/2006/11/14/science/14prof.html.

FREDERICK THE GREAT

Alford, Kenneth D. *Nazi Plunder: Great Treasure Stories of World War II.* Cambridge, MA: Da Capo Press, 2001.

Edsel, Robert M. and Bret Witter. *The Monuments Men: Allied Heroes, Nazi Thieves, and the Greatest Treasure Hunt in History.* New York: Center Street, 2009.

Fisher, Marc. "Frederick the Grave; Germany Split over Prussian's Reburial." *Washington Post,* August 17, 1991.

James, Barry. "200 Years Later, Frederick the Great Still Makes Trouble." *New York Times,* August 15, 1991. http://www.nytimes.com/1991/08/15/news/15iht-grea.html?pagewanted=all.

MacDonogh, Giles. *Frederick the Great: A Life in Deed and Letters.* New York: St. Martin's Press, 2000.

Palmer, Alan W. *Frederick the Great.* London: Weidenfeld & Nicolson, 1974.

GALILEO GALILEI

Bronowski, Jacob. *The Ascent of Man.* Boston: Little, Brown, 1973.

Donadio, Rachel. "A Museum Display of Galileo Has a Saintly Feel." *New York Times,* July 22, 2010. http://www.nytimes.com/2010/07/23/world/europe/23galileo.html?pagewanted=all.

Finocchiaro, Maurice A. "That Galileo Was Imprisoned and Tortured for Advocating Copernicanism." In *Galileo Goes to Jail: And Other Myths About Science and Religion.* Edited by Ronald L. Numbers, 69–78. Cambridge, MA: Harvard University Press, 2009.

"Galileo's Tooth, Thumb and Finger Go on Display." *Telegraph* (UK), June 8, 2010.

Galluzzi, Paolo. "The Sepulchers of Galileo: The 'Living' Remains of a Hero of Science." In *The Cambridge Companion to Galileo.* Edited by Peter Machamer. 417–47. Cambridge, UK: Cambridge University Press, 1998.

Hooper, John. "Scientists to Test DNA to Find Out if Galileo Could Really See Stars." *Guardian* (UK), January 22, 2009. http://www.guardian.co.uk/world/2009/jan/23/galileo-dna-test.

Shea, William and Mariano Artigas. "The Galileo Affair." Universidad de Navarra. http://www.unav.es/cryf/galileoaffair.html.

Sobel, Dava. "Galileo's Universe." *New York Times,* November 21, 1999. http://www.nytimes.com/1999/11/21/magazine/galileo-s-universe.html.

———. *Galileo's Daughter: A Historical Memoir of Science, Faith, and Love.* New York: Walker & Co., 1999.

GERONIMO

Bass, Carole. "The Story behind the Geronimo Lawsuit." *Yale Alumni Magazine,* February 19, 2009.

Giago, Tim. "Where Are They Hiding Geronimo's Skull?" Knight Ridder/Tribune News Service, August 28, 2000.

Lassila, Kathrin Day and Mark Alden Branch. "Whose Skull and Bones?" *Yale Alumni Magazine,* May/June 2006. http://www.yalealumnimagazine.com/issues/2006_05/notebook.html.

McKinley, James C. Jr. "Geronimo's Heirs Sue Secret Yale Society over His Skull." *New York Times,* February 19, 2009. http://www.nytimes.com/2009/02/20/us/20geronimo.html.

Pember, Mary Annette. "'Tomb raiders': Yale's Ultra-Secret Skull

and Bones Society Is Believed to Possess the Skull of Legendary Apache Chief Geronimo." *Diverse Issues in Higher Education,* July 12, 2007.

Robbins, Alexandra. *Secrets of the Tomb: Skull and Bones, the Ivy League, and the Hidden Paths of Power.* Boston: Little, Brown, 2002.

Rosenbaum, Ron. "I Stole the Head of Prescott Bush! More Scary Skull and Bones Tales." *New York Observer,* July 17, 2000. http://www.observer.com/2000/07/i-stole-the-head-of-prescott-bush-more-scary-skull-and-bones-tales.

Tomsho, Robert. "Dig Through Archives Reopens the Issue of Geronimo's Skull." *Wall Street Journal,* May 8, 2006. http://online.wsj.com/article/SB114705004282246274.html.

Wortman, Marc. "The Skull—and the Bones." *Vanity Fair,* September 15, 2011. http://www.vanityfair.com/culture/features/2011/10/geronimo-201110.

KLEMENT GOTTWALD

Zbarksy, Ilya and Samuel Hutchinson. *Lenin's Embalmers.* Translated by Barbara Bray. London: Harvill Press, 1999.

FRANCISCO GOYA

Dickey, Colin. *Cranioklepty: Grave Robbing and the Search for Genius.* Denver: Unbridled Books, 2009.

Fuentes, Carlos. *The Buried Mirror: Reflections on Spain and the New World.* Boston: Houghton Mifflin, 1992.

GRIP THE RAVEN

Capuzzo, Mike. "The Raven of Poe's Famous Poem Is a Feather in Free Library's Cap." *Philadelphia Inquirer,* June 13, 1993. http://articles.philly.com/1993–06–13/living/25974023_1_grip-barnaby-rudge-raven.

"Grip." Free Library of Philadelphia. http://libwww.freelibrary.org/dickens/CharlesDickens_Grip.pdf.

Johnson, Celia Blue. *Dancing with Mrs. Dalloway: Stories of the Inspiration Behind Great Works of Literature.* New York: Perigee, 2011.

CHE GUEVARA

Anderson, Jon Lee. *Che Guevara: A Revolutionary Life.* New York: Grove Press, 1997.

Castañeda, Jorge G. *Compañero: The Life and Death of Che Guevara.* Translated by Maria Castañeda. New York: Vintage Books, 1998.

Harris, Richard. *Death of a Revolutionary: Che Guevara's Last Mission.* New York: W. W. Norton, 2000.

Rohter, Larry. "Cuba Buries Che, the Man, but Keeps the Myth Alive." *New York Times,* October 18, 1997. http://www.nytimes .com/1997/10/18/world/cuba-buries-che-the-man-but-keeps-the -myth-alive.html?pagewanted=all&src=pm.

THOMAS HARDY

Millgate, Michael. *Thomas Hardy: A Biography.* New York: Random House, 1982.

Murphy, Edwin. *After the Funeral: The Posthumous Adventures of Famous Corpses.* New York: Carol Publishing Group, 1995.

JOSEPH HAYDN

Butterworth, Neil. *Haydn: His Life and Times.* Neptune City, NJ: Paganiniana Publications, 1980.

Calvert, George H., ed. *Illustrations of Phrenology: Being a Selection of Articles from the Edinburgh Phrenological Society.* Baltimore: W. & J. Neal, 1832.

Dickey, Colin. *Cranioklepty: Grave Robbing and the Search for Genius.* Denver: Unbridled Books, 2009.

Gall, Franz Josef. *On the Functions of the Brain and of Each of Its Parts: With Observations on the Possibility of Determining the Instincts, Propensities, and Talents, or the Moral and Intellectual Dispositions of Men and Animals, by the Configuration of the Brain and Head.* Boston: Marsh, Capen & Lyon, 1835.

Hadden, James Cuthbert. *Haydn.* London: J. M. Dent, 1902.

"Haydn's Skull Is Returned: After Theft 145 Years Ago, Body Is Complete." *Life,* June 28, 1954.

R. "The Skull of Joseph Haydn." *Musical Times* 73, no. 1076 (October 1, 1932): 942–43.

"Skull Is Restored to Haydn's Grave." *New York Times,* June 6, 1954.

Townley, Simon. "Hunting Haydn's Head." BBC Radio 4, May 30, 2009. http://www.bbc.co.uk/programmes/b00kmgrx.

ADOLF HITLER

Ainsztein, Reuben. Review of *The Death of Adolf Hitler: Unknown Documents from Soviet Archives,* by Lev Bezymenski. *International Affairs* 45, no. 2 (April 1969): 294–95.

———. "How Hitler Died: The Soviet Version." *International Affairs* 43, no. 2 (April 1967): 307–18.

Beevor, Antony. "Hitler's Jaws of Death." *New York Times,* October 10, 2009. http://www.nytimes.com/2009/10/11/opinion/11beevor .html.

Bezymenski, Lev. *The Death of Adolf Hitler: Unknown Documents from Soviet Archives.* New York: Harcourt, Brace & World, 1968.

Bullock, Alan. *Hitler and Stalin: Parallel Lives.* New York: Alfred A. Knopf, 1992.

Fest, Joachim C. *Inside Hitler's Bunker: The Last Days of the Third Reich.* New York: Farrar, Straus & Giroux, 2004.

Fuchs, Thomas. *A Concise Biography of Adolf Hitler.* New York: Berkley Books, 2000.

Goñi, Uki. "Tests on Skull Fragment Cast Doubt on Adolf Hitler Suicide Story." *Guardian* (UK), September 26, 2009. http://www.guardian.co.uk/world/2009/sep/27/adolf-hitler-suicide-skull-fragment.

Halpin, Tony and Roger Boyes. "Russia fights back in battle of Hitler's skull—DNA tests have got it all wrong, says Moscow archive." *Times* (UK), December 9, 2009.

Kershaw, Ian. *Hitler: 1936–1945: Nemesis.* New York: W. W. Norton, 2000.

———. *Hitler: A Biography.* New York: W. W. Norton, 2008.

Parparov, Fyodor. *The Hitler Book: The Secret Dossier Prepared for Stalin from the Interrogations of Hitler's Personal Aides.* Edited by Hank Eberle and Matthias Uhl. Translated by Giles MacDonogh. New York: Public Affairs, 2005.

Petrova, Ada and Peter Watson. *The Death of Hitler: The Final Words from Russia's Secret Archives.* London: Richard Cohen Books, 1995.

Rosenbaum, Ron. *Explaining Hitler: The Search for the Origins of His Evil.* New York: Random House, 1998.

Sognnaes, Reidar F. "Dental Evidence in the Postmortem Identification of Adolf Hitler, Eva Braun, and Martin Bormann." *Legal Medicine Annual* 1977: 173–235.

———. "Talking Teeth: The Developing Field of Forensic Dentistry Can Increasingly Aid the Legal and Medical Professions in Problems of Identification." *American Scientist* 64, no. 4 (July–August 1976): 369–73.

Tkachenko, Maxim. "Official: KGB Chief Ordered Hitler's Remains Destroyed." *CNN.com,* December 11, 2009. http://articles.cnn.com/2009-12-11/world/russia.hitler.remains_1_soviet-army-soviet-military-facility-soviet-communist-party-leadership?_s=PM:WORLD.

Toland, John. *Adolf Hitler.* Vol 2. Garden City, NY: Doubleday, 1976.

Trevor-Roper, Hugh. *The Last Days of Hitler.* Chicago: University of Chicago Press, 1992.

Vinogradov, V. K., J. F. Pogonyi, and N. V. Teptzov. *Hitler's Death: Russia's Last Great Secret from the Files of the KGB.* London: Chaucer Press, 2005.

HO CHI MINH

Zbarksy, Ilya and Samuel Hutchinson. *Lenin's Embalmers*. Translated by Barbara Bray. London: Harvill Press, 1999.

ZORA NEALE HURSTON

Plant, Deborah G. *Zora Neale Hurston: A Biography of the Spirit*. Westport, CT: Praeger Publishers, 2007.

Walker, Alice. *In Search of Our Mothers' Gardens: Womanist Prose*. San Diego: Harcourt Brace Jovanovich, 1983.

JESSE JAMES

"Exhumation Is Approved for Jesse James's Remains." *New York Times,* July 9, 1995.

Hanna, Bill. "In Search of Jesse James: Second Disinterment Debated." Knight Ridder/Tribune News Service, January 18, 2001.

"Jesse James's Remains Disinterred and Moved." *New York Times,* June 30, 1902.

Kammen, Michael G. *Digging Up the Dead: A History of Notable American Reburials*. Chicago: University of Chicago Press, 2010.

Ripley, Amanda. "Bone Hunter." *Washington City Paper,* March 13, 1998. http://www.washingtoncitypaper.com/articles/14597/bone-hunter.

Settle, William A. Jr. *Jesse James Was His Name: Or, Fact and Fiction Concerning the Careers of the Notorious James Brothers of Missouri*. Columbia: University of Missouri Press, 1966.

Stiles, T. J. *Jesse James: Last Rebel of the Civil War*. New York: Alfred A. Knopf, 2002.

Stone, Anne C., James E. Starrs, and Mark Stoneking. "Mitochondrial DNA Analysis of the Presumptive Remains of Jesse James." *Journal of Forensic Sciences* 46, no. 1 (2001): 173–76.

"The True Story of Jesse James." Jesse James Wax Museum. http://www.jessejameswaxmuseum.com/true_story.php.

Walker, Dale L. *Legends and Lies: Great Mysteries of the American West*. New York: Forge, 1997.

Yeatman, Ted P. *Frank and Jesse James: The Story Behind the Legend*. Nashville, TN: Cumberland House, 2000.

JESUS

Farley, David. "Fore Shame: Did the Vatican Steal Jesus' Foreskin So People Would Shut Up About the Savior's Penis?" *Slate.com,* December 19, 2006. http://www.slate.com/articles/life/faithbased/2006/12/fore_shame.single.html.

Manseau, Peter. *Rag and Bone: A Journey Among the World's Holy Dead*. New York: Henry Holt, 2009.

Perrottet, Tony. *Napoleon's Privates: 2,500 Years of History Unzipped*. New York: HarperCollins, 2008.

JOAN OF ARC

Butler, Declan. "Joan of Arc's Relics Exposed as Forgery." *Nature* 446, no. 593 (April 5, 2007). doi: 10.1038=446593a.

Taylor, Larissa Juliet. *The Virgin Warrior: The Life and Death of Joan of Arc*. New Haven, CT: Yale University Press, 2009.

Viegas, Jennifer. "Joan of Arc 'Relics' Confirmed to Be Fake." *Discovery News,* January 20, 2010. http://news.discovery.com/history/religious-relics-joan-of-arc-forgery.html.

JOHN PAUL JONES

Farquhar, Michael. *A Treasury of Great American Scandals: Tantalizing True Tales of Historic Misbehavior by the Founding Fathers and Others Who Let Freedom Swing*. New York: Penguin Books, 2003.

"Finding the Body of Admiral Paul Jones in Paris." *Scientific American,* May 6, 1905.

"John Paul Jones." US Naval Academy Public Affairs Office. http://www.usna.edu/PAO/facts/faqjpj.htm.

Kammen, Michael G. *Digging Up the Dead: A History of Notable American Reburials*. Chicago: University of Chicago Press, 2010.

Murphy, Edwin. *After the Funeral: The Posthumous Adventures of Famous Corpses*. New York: Carol Publishing Group, 1995.

Porter, Horace. "The Recovery of the Body of John Paul Jones." In *Paul Jones, Founder of the American Navy: A History,* by Augustus C. Buell, 335–92. New York: Charles Scribner's Sons, 1906.

Rachlin, Harvey. "The Crypt of John Paul Jones." In *Lucy's Bones, Sacred Stones, and Einstein's Brain: The Remarkable Stories Behind the Great Objects and Artifacts of History, from Antiquity to the Modern Era,* 157–172. New York: Henry Holt, 1996.

NED KELLY

"Anatomy and Ned Kelly." *Adelaide Advertiser* (Australia), August 4, 1945.

Australian Associated Press. "Public's Help Sought to Identify Ned Kelly's Skull." *Sydney Morning Herald* (Australia), June 21, 2010. http://www.smh.com.au/national/publics-help-sought-to-identify-ned-kellys-skull-20100620-ypce.html.

———. "Scientists Identify Ned Kelly's Remains." *Sydney Morning Herald* (Australia), September 1, 2011.

Ballantine, Derek. "I've Got Ned's Head." *Melbourne Herald Sun* (Australia), December 6, 1998.

Castles, Alex C. and Jennifer Castles. *Ned Kelly's Last Days: Setting the Record Straight on the Death of an Outlaw*. Crows Nest, New South Wales, Australia: Allen & Unwin, 2005.

Ciallella, Rebecca. *Ned's Head*. Special Broadcasting Service (Australia), 2011.

Crossland, Zoe. "Of Clues and Signs: The Dead Body and Its Evidential Traces." *American Anthropologist* 111, no. 1: 69–80. doi: 10.1111/j.1548–1433.2009.01078.x.

Heinrichs, Paul. "Skullduggery Denied in the Story of How Ned Kelly's Head Was Lost and Found Again." *Age* (Australia), April 17, 1998.

Kenneally, Christine. "A Hero's Legend and a Stolen Skull Rustle Up a DNA Drama." *New York Times*, August 31, 2011. http://www.nytimes.com/2011/09/06/science/06kelly.html.

Levy, Megan. "Ned Kelly's Remains Found." *Age* (Australia), September 1, 2011.

McDermott, Alex, ed. "The Apocalyptic Chant of Edward Kelly." In *The Jerilderie Letter*, by Ned Kelly, v–xxxiv. London: Faber & Faber, 2001.

The Ned Kelly Project. "Scientists at the Victorian Institute of Forensic Medicine Have Identified the Body of Ned Kelly." Victorian Institute of Forensic Medicine. http://www.vifm.org/forensics/the-ned-kelly-project.

"Ned Kelly's Bones." *Launceston (Tasmania) Examiner*, April 16, 1929.

"Ned Kelly's Bones Must Be Returned." *Sydney Morning Herald* (Australia), April 16, 1929.

"Ned Kelly's Grave." *Melbourne Argus* (Australia), April 13, 1929.

"Ned's Head." Transcript. *Rewind*, ABC (Australia), 2004. http://www.abc.net.au/tv/rewind/txt/s1168553.htm.

O'Brien, Kerry. "Ned Kelly's Skull." Transcript. *7:30 Report*, ABC (Australia), January 25, 2000. http://www.abc.net.au/7.30/stories/s95433.htm.

O'Loughlin, Toni. "Australian Farmer Claims Skull Is Ned Kelly's." *Guardian* (UK), November 13, 2009. http://www.guardian.co.uk/world/2009/nov/13/farmer-ned-kelly-skull-claim.

SØREN KIERKEGAARD

Lowrie, Walter. *A Short Life of Kierkegaard*. Princeton, NJ: Princeton University Press, 1970.

Taylor, Mark C. and Dietrich Christian Lammerts. *Grave Matters*. London: Reaktion Books, 2002.

KIM IL SUNG

McCurry, Justin. "North Korea Announces Kim Jong-il Will Be Embalmed and Put on Display." *Guardian* (UK), January 12,

2012. http://www.guardian.co.uk/world/2012/jan/12/kim-jong-il
-embalmed-display.

Zbarksy, Ilya and Samuel Hutchinson. *Lenin's Embalmers*. Translated by Barbara Bray. London: Harvill Press, 1999.

KIM JONG IL

McCurry, Justin. "North Korea Announces Kim Jong-il Will Be Embalmed and Put on Display." *Guardian* (UK), January 12, 2012. http://www.guardian.co.uk/world/2012/jan/12/kim-jong -il-embalmed-display.

Yoon, Sangwon. "Kim Jong Un Mourns Father in Pyongyang." *Bloomberg,* December 28, 2011. http://www.bloomberg.com/news /2011–12–27/north-korea-may-fete-touching-drama-for-kim -funeral-ushering-power-shift.html.

D. H. LAWRENCE

Bachrach, Arthur J. *D. H. Lawrence in New Mexico: "The Time Is Different There."* Albuquerque: University of New Mexico Press, 2006.

Ellis, David. *D. H. Lawrence: Dying Game, 1922–1930*. Cambridge, UK: Cambridge University Press, 1998.

————. *Death and the Author: How D. H. Lawrence Died, and Was Remembered*. Oxford, UK: Oxford University Press, 2008.

Ferris, Tina and Virginia Hyde. "National Register Nomination for the D. H. Lawrence Ranch, Section 8: Narrative Statement of Significance, Continued; Pt. 6: Frieda's Ranch Years." D. H. Lawrence Society of North America, 2004. http://dhlsna.com /Frieda.htm.

Maddox, Brenda. *D. H. Lawrence: The Story of a Marriage*. New York: Simon & Schuster, 1994.

Maurer, Rachel. "The D. H. Lawrence Ranch." Taos Summer Writers' Conference. http://www.unm.edu/~taosconf/Taos/DHlawrence .htm.

Murphy, Edwin. *After the Funeral: The Posthumous Adventures of Famous Corpses*. New York: Carol Publishing Group, 1995.

Sagar, Keith Milson. *The Life of D. H. Lawrence: An Illustrated Biography*. London: Methuen, 1982.

Thackray, Rachelle. "D. H. Lawrence Must Stay in US, Say Family." *Independent* (UK), June 14, 1998. http://www.independent.co.uk /news/d-h-lawrence-must-stay-in-us-say-family-1164854.html.

Worthen, John. *D. H. Lawrence: The Life of an Outsider*. New York: Counterpoint, 2005.

TIMOTHY LEARY

Ahrens, Frank. "Up in Smoke: For 24 Dearly Departed, a Rocket Trip Around the World." *Washington Post*, March 3, 1997.

Colker, David. "Leary Severs Ties to Cryonics Advocates." *Los Angeles Times,* May 9, 1996. http://articles.latimes.com/1996–05–09/local /me-7623_1_cryonic-suspension.

Greenfield, Robert. *Timothy Leary: A Biography.* Orlando, FL: Harcourt, 2006.

Leary, Timothy and R. U. Sirius. *Design for Dying.* New York: HarperEdge, 1997.

Mansnerus, Laura. "Timothy Leary, Pied Piper of Psychedelic 60's, Dies at 75." *New York Times,* June 1, 1996.

Rushkoff, Douglas. "Leary's Last Trip." *Esquire,* August 1996.

Simons, Marlise. "A Final Turn-On Lifts Timothy Leary Off." *New York Times,* April 22, 1997. http://www.nytimes.com/1997/04/22 /world/a-final-turn-on-lifts-timothy-leary-off.html.

Wertheimer, Linda. "Counterculture Icon Timothy Leary Tunes Out for Good." *All Things Considered,* NPR, May 31, 1996.

VLADIMIR LENIN

Ayres, Sabra. "Lenin Still a Draw—Bleach Fixes and All." *Seattle Post-Intelligencer,* February 18, 2005. http://www.seattlepi.com /national/212722_lenin19.html.

Brooke, Caroline. *Moscow: A Cultural History.* New York: Oxford University Press, 2006.

Carvalho, Joaquim, ed. *Religion and Power in Europe: Conflict and Convergence.* Pisa, Italy: Edizione Plus, Pisa University Press, 2007.

Chivers, C. J. "Russia Weighs What to Do with Lenin's Body." *New York Times,* October 5, 2005. http://www.nytimes.com/2005/10/05 /international/europe/05lenin.html.

Harrigan, Steve. "Yeltsin Vows to Bury Lenin Once and for All." *CNN.com,* July 13, 1999. http://www.cnn.com/WORLD/europe /9907/13/lenin.burial.

Kaplan, Fred. "He's Had Work: Preserving the Face of a Revolution." *New York Times,* February 28, 2010. http://www.nytimes .com/2010/02/28/theater/28embalmer.html.

"Lenin's Brain." Max Planck Institute for Brain Research. http:// www.brain.mpg.de/institute/history/lenins-brain/.

Tumarkin, Nina. *Lenin Lives! The Lenin Cult in Soviet Russia.* Cambridge, MA: Harvard University Press, 1997.

Verdery, Katherine. *The Political Lives of Dead Bodies: Reburial and Postsocialist Change.* New York: Columbia University Press, 1999.

Weir, Fred. "Goodbye Lenin? Russians Consider Burying Former Soviet Leader's Corpse (Finally)." *Christian Science Monitor,* January 28, 2011. http://www.csmonitor.com/World/Europe/2011/0128 /Goodbye-Lenin-Russians-consider-burying-former-Soviet-leader -s-corpse-finally.

Zbarksy, Ilya and Samuel Hutchinson. *Lenin's Embalmers.* Translated by Barbara Bray. London: Harvill Press, 1999.

ABRAHAM LINCOLN

Craughwell, Thomas J. *Stealing Lincoln's Body*. Cambridge, MA: Harvard University Press, 2007.

"Gleanings from the Mails: A Remarkable Counterfeit." *New York Times,* October 1, 1877.

Hickey, James T. "Robert Todd Lincoln and His Father's Grave Robbers: Or, Left in the Lurch by the Secret Service." *Illinois Historical Journal* 77, no. 4 (Winter 1984): 295–300.

Hill, Nancy. "The Transformation of the Lincoln Tomb." *Journal of the Abraham Lincoln Association* 27, no. 1 (Winter 2006). http://hdl.handle.net/2027/spo.2629860.0027.105.

Power, John Carroll. *History of an Attempt to Steal the Body of Abraham Lincoln*. Springfield, IL: H. W. Rokker, 1890.

"Rare Photos of Lincoln's Exhumation: Strange History Brought to Light." *Life,* February 15, 1963.

DAVID LIVINGSTONE

Jeal, Tim. *Livingstone*. New York: G. P. Putnam's Sons, 1973.

Livingstone, David. *The Life and African Explorations of Dr. David Livingstone*. New York: Cooper Square Press, 2002.

Murphy, Edwin. *After the Funeral: The Posthumous Adventures of Famous Corpses*. New York: Carol Publishing Group, 1995.

Pettitt, Clare. *Dr. Livingstone, I Presume?: Missionaries, Journalists, Explorers, and Empire*. Cambridge, MA: Harvard University Press, 2007.

Ransford, Oliver. *David Livingstone: The Dark Interior*. New York: St. Martin's Press, 1978.

Seaver, George. *David Livingstone: His Life and Letters*. New York: Harper & Brothers, 1957.

Watson, Jeremy. "Heroes of Livingstone's Last Trek Revealed." *Scotland on Sunday* (UK), May 20, 2007.

MAO ZEDONG

Gay, Kathlyn. *Mao Zedong's China*. Minneapolis: Twenty-first Century Books, 2008.

GROUCHO MARX

Associated Press. "Groucho Marx's Ashes Taken." *New York Times,* May 19, 1982. http://www.nytimes.com/1982/05/19/us/groucho-marx-s-ashes-taken.html.

MICHELANGELO

Giunta, Jacopo. *The Divine Michelangelo: The Florentine Academy's Homage on His Death in 1564.* Introduced, translated, and annotated by Rudolf and Margot Wittkower. London: Phaidon, 1964.

Walker, Paul Robert. *The Feud That Sparked the Renaissance: How Brunelleschi and Ghiberti Changed the Art World.* New York: HarperCollins, 2002.

JOHN MILTON

Barton, Carol. "'Ill Fare the Hands That Heaved the Stones': John Milton, a Preliminary Thanatography." *Milton Studies* 43 (2004): 198–260.

Howell, A. C. "Milton's Mortal Remains and Their Literary Echoes." *Forum* 4, no. 2 (Autumn 1963): 17–30.

"John Milton's Bones." *Notes and Queries,* no. 228 (May 10, 1890).

"The Opening of Famous Tombs." *New York Times,* June 12, 1897.

Read, Allen Walker. "The Disinterment of Milton's Remains." *PMLA* 45, no. 4 (December 1930): 1050–68.

Sitwell, Edith. *English Eccentrics.* New York: Vanguard Press, 1957.

MOLIÈRE

Brown, Frederick. *Père Lachaise: Elysium as Real Estate.* New York: Viking Press, 1973.

Crowley, Martin, ed. *Dying Words: The Last Moments of Writers and Philosophers.* Amsterdam: Rodopi, 2000.

Gaines, James F. "Le Malade Imaginaire." In *The Molière Encyclopedia,* edited by James F. Gaines. Westport, CT: Greenwood Press, 2002.

Murphy, Edwin. *After the Funeral: The Posthumous Adventures of Famous Corpses.* New York: Carol Publishing Group, 1995.

Palmer, John. *Molière.* New York: Brewer & Warren, 1930.

Scott, Virginia. *Molière: A Theatrical Life.* Cambridge, UK: Cambridge University Press, 2000.

THOMAS MORE

Aubrey, John and Richard Barber. "Sir Thomas More." In *Brief Lives,* edited by Oliver Lawson Dick. Suffolk, UK: Boydell Press, 1982.

Chambers, Robert, ed. "July 6." In *The Book of Days: A Miscellany of Popular Antiquities in Connection with the Calendar.* Vol. 2, 25–26. London: W. & R. Chambers, 1832.

Guy, John. *A Daughter's Love: Thomas More and His Dearest Meg.* Boston: Houghton Mifflin, 2009.

Hall, S. C. "Pilgrimage to the Home of Sir Thomas More." *Harper's New Monthly Magazine* 1, no. 3 (August 1850): 289–96.

Knight, Charles. "Canterbury." In *The Land We Live In: A Pictorial, Historical, and Literary Sketch-Book of the British Isles*. London: W. S. Orr, 1853.

Marshall, Peter. "The Last Years." In *The Cambridge Companion to Thomas More*, edited by George M. Logan, 116–38. Cambridge, UK: Cambridge University Press, 2011.

Simpson, W. Sparrow. "On the Head of Simon of Sudbury, Archbishop of Canterbury." *Journal of the British Archaeological Association* 1 (1895): 126–47.

WOLFGANG AMADEUS MOZART

Abert, Hermann. *W. A. Mozart*. Edited by Cliff Eisen. Translated by Stewart Spencer. New Haven, CT: Yale University Press, 2007.

Dickey, Colin. *Cranioklepty: Grave Robbing and the Search for Genius*. Denver: Unbridled Books, 2009.

Karhausen, L. R. "The Mozarteum's Skull: A Historical Saga." *Journal of Medical Biography* 9, no. 2 (May 2001): 109–17.

Landon, H. C. Robbins. *1791, Mozart's Last Year*. New York: Schirmer Books, 1988.

Stadlbauer, Christina, Christian Reiter, Beatrix Patzak, Gerhard Stingeder, and Thomas Prohaska. "History of Individuals of the 18th/19th Centuries Stored in Bones, Teeth, and Hair Analyzed by LA–ICP–MS—A Step in Attempts to Confirm the Authenticity of Mozart's Skull." *Analytical & Bioanalytical Chemistry* 388, no. 3 (2007): 593–602.

Wakin, Daniel J. "After Mozart's Death, An Endless Coda." *New York Times*, August 25, 2010. http://www.nytimes.com/2010/08/25/arts/music/25death.html?adxnnl=1&adxnnlx=1344812637-3i6PWFN2Ys+7gWO6BkF5ag.

MUHAMMAD

Manseau, Peter. *Rag and Bone: A Journey Among the World's Holy Dead*. New York: Henry Holt, 2009.

BENITO MUSSOLINI

Associated Press. "Mussolini's Body Stolen in Milan; 'Democratic Fascists' Claim Deed." *New York Times*, April 24, 1946.

Bosworth, R. J. B. *Mussolini*. London: Arnold, 2002.

Bracker, Milton. "Slain by Partisans: The Inglorious End of a Dictator." *New York Times*, April 30, 1945.

Calvino, Italo. "Il Duce's Portraits." *New Yorker*, January 6, 2003. http://www.newyorker.com/archive/2003/01/06/030106fa_fact_calvino.

Falasca-Zamponi, Simonetta. *Fascist Spectacle: The Aesthetics of Power in Mussolini's Italy.* Berkeley: University of California Press, 1997.

Foot, John. "The Dead Duce." *History Today* 49, no. 8 (1999). http:// www.historytoday.com/john-foot/dead-duce.

Hamburger, Philip. "Letter from Rome." *New Yorker,* May 19, 1945.

Hevesi, Dennis. "Domenico Leccisi, Italian Political Figure, Dies at 88." *New York Times,* November 5, 2008. http://www.nytimes .com/2008/11/06/world/europe/06leccisi.html?ref=benitomuss.

Moseley, Ray. *Mussolini: The Last 600 Days of Il Duce.* Dallas: Taylor Trade, 2004.

"Mussolini's Brain." *Science Digest* 19 (August 1946): 50–51.

"On This Day: April 28, 1945: Italian Partisans Kill Mussolini." BBC News. http://news.bbc.co.uk/onthisday/hi/dates/stories/april/28 /newsid_3564000/3564529.stm.

Povoledo, Elisabetta. "A Dead Dictator Who Draws Tens of Thousands in Italy." *New York Times,* November 2, 2011. http://www .nytimes.com/2011/11/03/world/Europe/tourists-still-drawn-to -tomb-of-mussolini-il-duce-in-italy.html.

NAPOLEON BONAPARTE

Dale, Philip Marshall. "Napoleon Bonaparte." In *Medical Biographies: The Ailments of Thirty-three Famous Persons,* 151–70. Norman: University of Oklahoma Press, 1987.

Perrottet, Tony. *Napoleon's Privates: 2,500 Years of History Unzipped.* New York: HarperCollins, 2008.

Proger, L. W. "A Napoleonic Relic." *Annals of the Royal College of Surgeons of England* 26, no. 1 (January 1960): 57–62.

Rachlin, Harvey. "Napoleon's Penis." In *Lucy's Bones, Sacred Stones, and Einstein's Brain: The Remarkable Stories Behind the Great Objects and Artifacts of History, from Antiquity to the Modern Era,* 190–96. New York: Henry Holt, 1996.

St. Denis, Louis-Étienne. *Napoleon From the Tuileries to St. Helena: Personal Recollections of the Emperor's Second Mameluke and Valet.* New York: Harper & Brothers, 1922.

Weider, Ben and Sten Forshufvud. *Assassination at St. Helena Revisited.* New York: John Wiley & Sons, 1995.

LORD NELSON

King, Melanie. *The Dying Game: A Curious History of Death.* Oxford, UK: Oneworld, 2008.

Quinion, Michael. "Tapping the Admiral." World Wide Words. http://www.worldwidewords.org/qa/qa-tap1.htm.

AGOSTINHO NETO

Zbarksy, Ilya and Samuel Hutchinson. *Lenin's Embalmers*. Translated by Barbara Bray. London: Harvill Press, 1999.

LEE HARVEY OSWALD

Bugliosi, Vincent. *Reclaiming History: The Assassination of President John F. Kennedy*. New York: W. W. Norton, 2007.

Eddowes, Michael. *The Oswald File*. New York: Clarkson N. Potter, 1977.

Norton, Linda E., I. M. Sopher, and V. J. M. DiMaio. "The Exhumation and Identification of Lee Harvey Oswald." *Journal of Forensic Sciences* 29, no. 1 (January 1984): 19–38.

"Officials Seek to Examine Body in Oswald's Grave." *New York Times,* October 19, 1979.

THOMAS PAINE

Associated Press. "Thomas Paine's Remains Are Still a Bone of Contention." *Los Angeles Times,* April 1, 2001.

Bressler, Leo A. "Peter Porcupine and the Bones of Thomas Paine." *Pennsylvania Magazine of History and Biography* 82, no. 2 (April 1958): 176–85.

Chen, David W. "Rehabilitating Thomas Paine, Bit by Bony Bit." *New York Times,* March 30, 2001. http://www.nytimes.com/2001/03/30/nyregion/rehabilitating-thomas-paine-bit-by-bony-bit.html.

Collins, Paul. *The Trouble with Tom: The Strange Afterlife and Times of Thomas Paine*. New York: Bloomsbury, 2009.

Conway, Moncure. "The Adventures of Thomas Paine's Bones." *Journal of the Thomas Paine National Historical Association,* March 2002.

Nelson, Craig. *Thomas Paine: Enlightenment, Revolution, and the Birth of Modern Nations*. New York: Viking, 2006.

"The Paine Monument at Last Finds a Home." *New York Times,* October 15, 1905.

van der Weyde, William M. "Paine's Long Lost Remains Home by Parcel Post." *New York Times,* May 31, 1914.

DOROTHY PARKER

Acocella, Joan Ross. *Twenty-eight Artists and Two Saints: Essays*. New York: Pantheon Books, 2007.

Adams, Franklin Pierce, Robert Benchley, Heywood Broun, Edna Ferber, Ruth Hale, Dorothy Parker, and Donald Ogden Stewart. *Bon Bons, Bourbon, and Bon Mots: Stories from the Algonquin Round Table*. El Paso, TX: Traveling Press, 2011.

"Dorothy Parker Memorial Garden, NAACP Headquarters, Baltimore." *Dot City.* http://www.dorothyparker.com/dot33.htm.

Fitzpatrick, Kevin C. *A Journey into Dorothy Parker's New York.* Berkeley, CA: Roaring Forties Press, 2005.

Meade, Marion. *Dorothy Parker: What Fresh Hell Is This?* New York: Villard Books, 1988.

———. "Estate of Mind: Dorothy Parker Willed Her Copyright to the NAACP—An Organization Her Executor, Lillian Hellman, Detested." *Bookforum,* April/May 2006. http://www.bookforum.com/archive/apr_06/meade.html.

GRAM PARSONS

Fong-Torres, Ben. *Hickory Wind: The Life and Times of Gram Parsons.* New York: Pocket Books, 1991.

"Gram Parsons Dies; Rock Star Was 27." *New York Times,* September 21, 1973.

Hennig, Gandulf and Sid Griffin. *Fallen Angel: Gram Parsons.* DVD. Directed by Gandulf Hennig. Burbank, CA: Rhino Entertainment, 2004.

Kaufman, Phil and Colin White. *Road Mangler Deluxe.* Glendale, CA: White Boucke, 1993.

Meyer, David N. *Twenty Thousand Roads: The Ballad of Gram Parsons and His Cosmic American Music.* New York: Villard, 2007.

Wasserzieher, Bill. "Gram Parsons Dies in Desert." *Village Voice,* September 27, 1973.

EVA PERÓN

Fraser, Nicholas and Marysa Navarro. *Eva Perón.* New York: W. W. Norton, 1981.

Martínez, Tomás Eloy. *Santa Evita.* Translated by Helen Lane. New York: Alfred A. Knopf, 1996.

Ortiz, Alicia Dujovne. *Eva Perón: A Biography.* Translated by Shawn Fields. New York: St. Martin's Press, 1996.

Perón, Eva. *Evita: In My Own Words.* Translated by Laura Dail. New York: New Press, 2005.

JUAN PERÓN

Christian, Shirley. "Perón Hands: Police Find Trail Elusive." *New York Times,* September 6, 1987. http://www.nytimes.com/1987/09/06/world/peron-hands-police-find-trail-elusive.html.

Johnson, Lyman L., ed. *Death, Dismemberment, and Memory: Body Politics in Latin America.* Albuquerque: University of New Mexico Press, 2004.

Brumfield, Sarah. "Poe Fans Call an End to 'Toaster' Tradition." Associated Press, January 19, 2012.

Miller, John C. "The Exhumations and Reburials of Edgar and Virginia Poe and Mrs. Clemm." *Poe Studies* 7, no. 2 (December 1974): 46–47. http://www.eapoe.org/pstudies/ps1970/p1974204 .htm.

"Poe's Memorial Grave." The Edgar Allan Poe Society of Baltimore, March 6, 2012. http://www.eapoe.org/balt/poegrave.htm.

Smith, Gary. "Once Upon a Midnight Dreary." *Life* 13, no. 9 (July 1990).

Tucker, Abigail. "Who Knows Who Started Poe Toast?" *Baltimore Sun,* August 15, 2007. http://articles.baltimoresun.com/2007–08– 15/features/0708150222_1_porpora.

Walsh, John Evangelist. *Midnight Dreary: The Mysterious Death of Edgar Allan Poe.* New Brunswick, NJ: Rutgers University Press, 1998.

Wan, William. "Never More Doubt." *Washington Post,* August 18, 2007. http://www.washingtonpost.com/wp-dyn/content/ article/2007/08/17/AR2007081702145.html.

ELVIS PRESLEY

Associated Press. "4 Accused of a Plot to Take Presley Body." *New York Times,* August 30, 1977.

———. "Four Arrested in Plot to Steal Elvis' Body." *Sonora (CA) Daily Union Democrat,* August 29, 1977.

———. "Police Seize Three Men Fleeing Elvis' Tomb." *Miami News,* August 30, 1977.

Brown, Peter Harry and Pat H. Broeske. *Down at the End of Lonely Street: The Life and Death of Elvis Presley.* New York: Dutton, 1997.

Brown, Scott. "Elvis Presley: It's a Hound Dig." *Entertainment Weekly,* October 6, 2000. http://www.ew.com/ew/article /0,,277847,00.html.

Comfort, David. *The Rock & Roll Book of the Dead: The Fatal Journeys of Rock's Seven Immortals.* New York: Citadel Press, 2009.

Denenberg, Barry. *All Shook Up!: The Life and Death of Elvis Presley.* New York: Scholastic Press, 2001.

Doss, Erika. *Elvis Culture: Fans, Faith & Image.* Lawrence: University Press of Kansas, 1999.

Eicher, Peter. *The Elvis Sightings.* New York: Avon Books, 1993.

Gregory, Neal and Janice Gregory. *When Elvis Died.* Washington, DC: Communications Press, 1980.

Hayslett, Chandra M. "Elvis's empty crypt an $800,000 steal?" *Memphis (TN) Commercial Appeal,* August 9, 1997. http://www .commercialappeal.com/news/1997/aug/09/elviss-empty-crypt -an-800000-steal/.

Lacy, Patrick. *Elvis Decoded: A Fan's Guide to Deciphering the Myths and Misinformation.* Bloomington, IN: AuthorHouse, 2006.

Marcus, Greil. *Dead Elvis: A Chronicle of a Cultural Obsession.* Garden City, NY: Doubleday, 1991.

"Notes on People." *New York Times,* September 30, 1977.

Ponce de Leon, Charles L. *Fortunate Son: The Life of Elvis Presley.* New York: Hill & Wang, 2006.

Rawls, Wendell Jr. "Presley Associates Say Torment and Drugs Marked Final Months." *New York Times,* September 23, 1979.

Reed, J. D. and Maddy Miller. *Stairway to Heaven: The Final Resting Places of Rock's Legends.* New York: Wenner Books, 2005.

Rosenbaum, Ron. "Among the Believers." *New York Times Magazine,* September 24, 1995.

Smith, I. C. *Inside: A Top G-Man Exposes Spies, Lies, and Bureaucratic Bungling in the FBI.* Nashville, TN: Nelson Current, 2004.

Sperry, Paul. "FBI Witness: Presley Clan Staged Elvis Grave-robbing." *WorldNet Daily,* August 13, 2002. http://rc-dfw-wnd-app1.ha-hosting.com/index.php?fa=PAGE.printable&pageId=14898.

Strausbaugh, John. *E: Reflections on the Birth of the Elvis Faith.* New York: Blast Books, 1995.

United Press International. "Police Doubt Informant's Tip: Presley Body Case Charges Dropped." *Los Angeles Times,* October 5, 1977.

————. "Presley Body Snatch Plot a Hoax?" *Ellensburg (WA) Daily Record,* August 31, 1977.

SIR WALTER RALEIGH

Adamson, J. H. and H. F. Holland. *The Shepherd of the Ocean: An Account of Sir Walter Ralegh and His Times.* Boston: Gambit, 1969.

Trevelyan, Raleigh. *Sir Walter Raleigh: Being a True and Vivid Account of the Life and Times of the Explorer, Soldier, Scholar, Poet, and Courtier—The Controversial Hero of the Elizabethan Age.* New York: Henry Holt, 2004.

GRIGORI RASPUTIN

Cook, Andrew. *To Kill Rasputin: The Life and Death of Grigori Rasputin.* Stroud, UK: Tempus, 2005.

"Erotic Museum 'Remembers' Rasputin." *St. Petersburg Times* (Russia), August 6, 2004. http://www.sptimes.ru/index.php?action_id=2&story_id=1234.

King, Greg. *The Man Who Killed Rasputin: Prince Youssoupov and the Murder That Helped Bring Down the Russian Empire.* Secaucus, NJ: Carol Publishing Group, 1995.

Page, Jeremy. "Museum Claims Rasputin Has Returned to St. Petersburg as an Old Member." *Times* (UK), May 7, 2004.

Radzinsky, Edvard. *The Rasputin File*. Translated by Judson Rosengrant. New York: Nan A. Talese, 2000.

Rasputin, Maria and Patte Barham. *Rasputin: The Man Behind the Myth: A Personal Memoir*. Englewood Cliffs, NJ: Prentice-Hall, 1977.

MARQUIS DE SADE

Gray, Francine du Plessix. *At Home with the Marquis de Sade: A Life*. New York: Simon & Schuster, 1998.

Schaeffer, Neil. *The Marquis de Sade: A Life*. New York: Alfred A. Knopf, 1999.

Thomas, Donald. *The Marquis de Sade*. London: Weidenfeld & Nicolson, 1976.

SAINT ANTHONY OF PADUA

Manseau, Peter. *Rag and Bone: A Journey Among the World's Holy Dead*. New York: Henry Holt, 2009.

Rufus, Anneli. *Magnificent Corpses: Searching Through Europe for St. Peter's Head, St. Chiara's Heart, St. Stephen's Hand, and Other Saints' Relics*. New York: Marlowe, 1999.

SAINT NICHOLAS

"Anatomical Examination of the Bari Relics." St. Nicholas Center. http://www.stnicholascenter.org/pages/anatomical-examination.

Bennett, William J. *The True Saint Nicholas: Why He Matters to Christmas*. New York: Howard Books, 2009.

Craughwell, Thomas J. *Saints Preserved: An Encyclopedia of Relics*. New York: Image Books, 2011.

Davidson, Linda Kay and David M. Gitlitz. "Bari (Apulia, Italy)." In *Pilgrimage: From the Ganges to Graceland: An Encyclopedia*. Vol. 1. Santa Barbara, CA: ABC-CLIO, 2002.

"Devotion and Use of the Manna of Saint Nicholas." St. Nicholas Center. http://www.stnicholascenter.org/pages/manna.

Farmer, David Hugh. *The Oxford Dictionary of Saints*. Oxford, UK: Oxford University Press, 2004.

Geary, Patrick J. *Furta Sacra: Thefts of Relics in the Central Middle Ages*. Princeton, NJ: Princeton University Press, 1990.

Head, Jonathan. "Turkey Seeks Return of Santa Claus' Bones." *BBC News,* December 28, 2009. http://news.bbc.co.uk/2/hi/europe/8432314.stm.

"Is St. Nicholas in Venice, Too?" St. Nicholas Center. http://www.stnicholascenter.org/pages/relics-in-the-lido-of-venice.

Jones, Charles W. *Saint Nicholas of Myra, Bari, and Manhattan: Biography of a Legend*. Chicago: University of Chicago Press, 1978.

McBrien, Richard P. *Lives of the Saints: From Mary and St. Francis of*

Assisi to John XXIII and Mother Teresa. San Francisco: HarperSan-Francisco, 2001.

Papirowski, Martin. *In Search of Santa Claus.* Smithsonian Channel, 2009. http://www.smithsonianchannel.com/site/sn/show.do?show=131259.

"Push to Bring Santa's Bones Home." ABC News (Australia), December 29, 2009. http://www.abc.net.au/news/2009-12-29/push-to-bring-santas-bones-home/1191714.

Quigley, Christine. *Skulls and Skeletons: Human Bone Collections and Accumulations.* Jefferson, NC: McFarland, 2001.

"Relics of St. Nicholas—Where Are They?" St. Nicholas Center. http://www.stnicholascenter.org/pages/relics.

"Santa Claus's Bones Must Be Brought Back to Turkey from Italy." *Today's Zaman* (Turkey), December 28, 2009. http://www.todayszaman.com/news-196814-100-santa-clauss-bones-must-be-brought-back-to-turkey-from-italy.html.

Seal, Jeremy. *Nicholas: The Epic Journey from Saint to Santa Claus.* New York: Bloomsbury, 2005.

Sora, Steven. *Treasures from Heaven: Relics from Noah's Ark to the Shroud of Turin.* Hoboken, NJ: John Wiley & Sons, 2005.

PERCY BYSSHE SHELLEY

Bieri, James. *Percy Bysshe Shelley: A Biography.* Baltimore: Johns Hopkins University Press, 2008.

Crofton, Ian. *The Totally Useless History of the World.* London: Quercus, 2007.

Holmes, Richard. "Death and Destiny." *Guardian* (UK), January 23, 2004. http://www.guardian.co.uk/books/2004/jan/24/featuresreviews.guardianreview1.

Lee, Hermione. "Shelley's Heart and Pepys's Lobsters." In *Virginia Woolf's Nose: Essays on Biography.* Princeton, NJ: Princeton University Press, 2005.

Norman, Arthur M. Z. "Shelley's Heart." *Journal of the History of Medicine and Allied Sciences* X, no. 1 (1955): 114–16. doi:10.1093/jhmas/X.1.114-a

SHI HUANGDI

Sima, Qian. *The First Emperor: Selections from the Historical Records.* Translated by Raymond Dawson. Oxford, UK: Oxford University Press, 2007.

JOSEPH STALIN

Carvalho, Joaquim, ed. *Religion and Power in Europe: Conflict and Convergence.* Pisa, Italy: Edizione Plus, Pisa University Press, 2007.

Kammen, Michael G. *Digging Up the Dead: A History of Notable American Reburials.* Chicago: University of Chicago Press, 2010.

Tumarkin, Nina. *Lenin Lives! The Lenin Cult in Soviet Russia.* Cambridge, MA: Harvard University Press, 1997.

LAURENCE STERNE

Howard, Philip. "Is This the Skull of Sterne?" *Times* (UK), June 5, 1969.

Hughes, J. Trevor. "'Alas, Poor Yorick!': The Death of Laurence Sterne." In *Essays in Medical Biography,* 135–47. Oxford, UK: Rimes House, 2008.

Hughes, J. T. "The Good Is Oft Interred with Their Bones." *Brain* 130, no. 4 (2007): 1167–71. doi:10.1093/brain/awm015.

King, Melanie. *The Dying Game: A Curious History of Death.* Oxford, UK: Oneworld, 2008.

Monkman, Kenneth and W. G. Day. "The Skull." *Shandean* 10 (1998): 45–79.

Richardson, Ruth. *Death, Dissection, and the Destitute.* London: Routledge & Kegan Paul, 1987.

ALEXANDER T. STEWART

Fanebust, Wayne. *The Missing Corpse: Grave Robbing a Gilded Age Tycoon.* Westport, CT: Praeger, 2005.

SUNDANCE KID

Meadows, Anne. *Digging Up Butch and Sundance.* Lincoln: University of Nebraska Press, 2003.

Slatta, Richard W. *The Mythical West: An Encyclopedia of Legend, Lore, and Popular Culture.* Santa Barbara, CA: ABC-CLIO, 2001.

Walker, Dale L. *Legends and Lies: Great Mysteries of the American West.* New York: Forge, 1997.

EMANUEL SWEDENBORG

Benz, Ernst. *Emanuel Swedenborg: Visionary Savant in the Age of Reason.* West Chester, PA: Swedenborg Foundation, 2002.

Dickey, Colin. *Cranioklepty: Grave Robbing and the Search for Genius.* Denver: Unbridled Books, 2009.

"Emanuel Swedenborg." *British Medical Journal* 1, no. 2788 (Jun. 6, 1914): 1261–62.

"Emanuel Swedenborg." *Times* (UK), March 31, 1823.

Henschen, Folke. *Emanuel Swedenborg's Cranium: A Critical Analysis.* Uppsala, Sweden: Almqvist & Wiksells, 1960.

————. *The Human Skull: A Cultural History*. Translated by Stanley Thomas. New York: Praeger, 1966.

Hultkrantz, Johan Vilhelm. *The Mortal Remains of Emanuel Swedenborg; An Account of the Historical and Anatomical Investigations Executed by a Committee, Appointed on May 27th, 1908*. Uppsala, Sweden: University Press, 1910.

Lenhammar, Harry and Jane Williams-Hogan. "Swedenborg in Uppsala's Cathedral." *The New Philosophy Online*, January–July 2003. http://swedenborg-philosophy.org/journal/article.php?page=1007&issue=106a.

Rutherford, W. "A Swedenborg Mystery: The Rival Skulls." *Journal of Anatomy and Physiology* 48 (1913): 86–88.

Thompson, Ian J. "Swedenborg and Modern Science." *Theistic Science*. http://www.theisticscience.org/papers/smn3b.html.

Trobridge, George. *Swedenborg: Life and Teaching*. New York: Swedenborg Foundation, 1962.

HUNTER S. THOMPSON

Brinkley, Douglas. "Football Season Is Over." *Rolling Stone*, September 21, 2005.

"Cannon Fire Send-off for Thompson." *BBC News*, April 6, 2005. http://news.bbc.co.uk/2/hi/entertainment/4417897.stm.

"Citizen Thompson." *Smoking Gun*, March 7, 2005. http://www.thesmokinggun.com/documents/crime/citizen-thompson.

Fear and Loathing on the Road to Hollywood. Directed by Nigel Finch. *Omnibus*, BBC, 1978.

"Hunter Thompson Blown Sky High." *Billboard*. http://www.billboard.com/news/hot-product-1001018730.story#/news/hot-product-1001018730.story.

Seelye, Katharine Q. "Ashes-to-Fireworks Send-off for an 'Outlaw' Writer." *New York Times*, August 22, 2005. http://www.nytimes.com/2005/08/22/national/22hunter.html?scp=60&sq=Hunter+S.+Thompson&st=nyt&gwh=ED4F1E2C0BC97A1EB50AF3544925240A.

"Thompson 'Shot Himself on Phone.'" *BBC News*, February 25, 2005. http://news.bbc.co.uk/go/pr/fr/-/2/hi/entertainment/4298095.stm.

"Thompson's Ashes Fired into Sky." *BBC News*, August 21, 2005. http://news.bbc.co.uk/2/hi/entertainment/4168266.stm.

Thompson, Hunter S. "Fear and Loathing at the Watergate: Mr. Nixon Has Cashed His Check." *Rolling Stone*, September 27, 1973.

JIM THORPE

Associated Press. "Lawsuit to Reclaim Oklahoma Athlete Jim Thorpe's Body Proceeds." November 26, 2011.

Black, Joan. "Jim Thorpe Remembered as One-of-a-Kind Athlete." *Wind Speaker* (Alberta, Canada), March 1, 2000.

"A Brief History of Mauch Chunk." Mauch Chunk Historical Society. http://mauchchunkhistory.com/historical.html.

Bruchac, Joseph. *Jim Thorpe: Original All-American.* New York: Dial Books, 2006.

Buford, Kate. *Native American Son: The Life and Sporting Legend of Jim Thorpe.* New York: Alfred A. Knopf, 2010.

Carpenter, Mackenzie. "Jim Thorpe's Son Sues for Father's Body." *Pittsburgh (PA) Post-Gazette,* June 26, 2010. http://old.post-gazette.com/pg/10177/1068434–139.stm#ixzz1qdzMZvq0.

Newman, Bruce, ed. "Scorecard." *Sports Illustrated,* November 20, 1978. http://sportsillustrated.cnn.com/vault/article/magazine/MAG1094312/index.htm.

Norris, Michele. "Son Sues Pennsylvania Town for Jim Thorpe's Remains." *All Things Considered,* NPR, June 25, 2010. http://www.npr.org/2010/06/25/128112746/son-sues-pa-town-for-jim-thorpes-remains.

Wang, Hansi Lo. "A Fight for Jim Thorpe's Body." *Morning Edition,* NPR, August 3, 2011. http://www.npr.org/2011/08/03/138524619/a-fight-for-jim-thorpes-body.

TUTANKHAMEN

Marchant, Jo. "On the Trail of Tutankhamen's Penis." *CultureLab,* June 25, 2010. http://www.newscientist.com/blogs/culturelab/2010/06/on-the-trail-of-tutankhamens-penis.html.

Townsend, Allie. "Is King Tut's Penis Missing?" *Time NewsFeed,* June 29, 2010. http://newsfeed.time.com/2010/06/29/is-king-tuts-penis-missing/#ixzz1k20VBIiB.

VALERIAN

Crofton, Ian. *The Totally Useless History of the World.* London: Quercus, 2007.

Gibbon, Edward. *The History of the Decline and Fall of the Roman Empire.* Volume 1. Philadelphia: J. B. Lippincott, 1871.

VOLTAIRE

Davidson, Ian. *Voltaire in Exile: The Last Years.* New York: Grove Press, 2004.

Kammen, Michael G. *Digging Up the Dead: A History of Notable American Reburials.* Chicago: University of Chicago Press, 2010.

Mason, Haydn. *Voltaire: A Biography.* Baltimore: Johns Hopkins University Press, 1981.

Pearson, Roger. *Voltaire Almighty: A Life in Pursuit of Freedom.* New York: Bloomsbury, 2005.

"The Remains of Voltaire." *New York Times,* July 18, 1881.

"Voltaire and Rousseau; Their Tombs in the Pantheon Opened and Their Bones Exposed." *New York Times,* January 8, 1898.

GEORGE WASHINGTON

Craughwell, Thomas J. *Stealing Lincoln's Body.* Cambridge, MA: Harvard University Press, 2007.

Power, John Carroll. *History of an Attempt to Steal the Body of Abraham Lincoln.* Springfield, IL: H. W. Rokker, 1890.

Washington, George. "The Will of George Washington." *The Papers of George Washington.* http://gwpapers.virginia.edu/documents/will/text.html.

WALT WHITMAN

Burrell, Brian. *Postcards from the Brain Museum: The Improbable Search for Meaning in the Matter of Famous Minds.* New York: Broadway Books, 2004.

———. "The Strange Fate of Whitman's Brain." *Walt Whitman Quarterly Review* 20, no. 3 (Winter 2003): 107–33.

TED WILLIAMS

Cantor, Norman L. *After We Die: The Life and Times of the Human Cadaver.* Washington, DC: Georgetown University Press, 2010.

Johnson, Carrie. "Williams' Shift from Will Must Be Proved." *St. Petersburg (FL) Times,* July 20, 2002. http://www.sptimes.com/2002/07/20/news_pf/Citrus/Williams__shift_from_.shtml.

Johnson, Larry and Scott Baldyga. *Frozen: My Journey into the World of Cryonics, Deception, and Death.* New York: Vanguard Press, 2009.

"Response to Larry Johnson Allegations." Alcor Life Extension Foundation, February 10, 2012. http://www.alcor.org/press/response.html.

Sandomir, Richard. "Please Don't Call the Customers Dead." *New York Times,* February 13, 2005.

———. "Report Says Facility Beheaded Williams." *New York Times,* August 13, 2003.

———. "Williams Children Agree to Keep Their Father Frozen." *New York Times,* December 21, 2002.

Verducci, Tom. "Tip of the Iceberg? Questions and Allegations About the Alcor Life Extension Foundation Extend Beyond the Williams Case." *Sports Illustrated,* August 18, 2003.

———. "What Really Happened to Ted Williams." *Sports Illustrated,* August 18, 2003.

APPENDIX: THE WAY OF ALL FLESH: WHAT HAPPENS TO BODIES AFTER DEATH

Cantor, Norman L. *After We Die: The Life and Times of the Human Cadaver*. Washington, DC: Georgetown University Press, 2010.

Iserson, Kenneth V. *Death to Dust: What Happens to Dead Bodies?* Tucson, AZ: Galen Press, 1994.

"Statistics." National Funeral Directors Association. http://www.nfda.org/index.php/media-center/statisticsreports.html.

INDEX

About the Author

BESS LOVEJOY is a writer, editor, and researcher based in Seattle. Her writing has appeared in *The New York Times*, *The Believer*, *The Boston Globe*, *The Stranger*, and various publications around the Pacific Northwest. She worked on the *Schott's Almanac* series of reference books for five years, and is the former editor of the Vancouver, BC, newspaper *Terminal City*. This is her first book.